About the Author

SELENA ROBERTS, formerly a columnist for the *New York Times*, is a senior writer for *Sports Illustrated*. She lives in Connecticut.

A-ROD

ALSO BY SELENA ROBERTS

A Necessary Spectacle: Billie Jean King, Bobby Riggs, and the Tennis Match That Leveled the Game

A-ROD

THE MANY LIVES OF ALEX RODRIGUEZ

SELENA ROBERTS

HARPER

NEW YORK • LONDON • TORONTO • SYDNEY

HARPER

A hardcover edition of this book was published in 2009 by HarperCollins Publishers.

A-ROD. Copyright © 2009 by Selena Roberts. All rights reserved. Printed in the United States of America. No part of this book may be used or reproduced in any manner whatsoever without written permission except in the case of brief quotations embodied in critical articles and reviews. For information address HarperCollins Publishers, 10 East 53rd Street, New York, NY 10022.

HarperCollins books may be purchased for educational, business, or sales promotional use. For information please write: Special Markets Department, HarperCollins Publishers, 10 East 53rd Street, New York, NY 10022.

FIRST HARPER PAPERBACK PUBLISHED 2010.

Library of Congress Cataloging-in-Publication Data is available upon request.

ISBN 978-0-06-179165-9 (pbk.)

10 11 12 13 14   DIX/RRD   10 9 8 7 6 5 4 3 2 1

For Laura and David

Contents

A-ROD

Prologue

ON SEPTEMBER 3, 2008, Alex Rodriguez lounged on a leather couch in the visiting clubhouse at Tropicana Field, the domed stadium of the Tampa Bay Rays. From a distance, the massive structure's roofline looks tilted, as if it's an optical illusion.

Which is appropriate, because weird things happen at The Trop. High fly balls ricochet off catwalks; some go up but never come down. And on this night The Trop was the site of something especially bizarre: baseball's version of an upended world order. The coupon-clipping Rays, with the second-lowest payroll in the major leagues, held the top spot in the American League East, and the Yankees, all $200 million of them, had dropped to third, 11 games out of first.

August had been dreadful yet exhilarating for Alex. He was reveling in his summer-long status as the Tabloid Prince of New York. On newsstands, the snarky details of his breakup with his wife of six years, Cynthia, were split-screened with images of his new E! life as Madonna's boy toy. The game's greatest, richest player had hit .337 in July and .243 in August for the Yankees but seemed unmoved by the parallels of his swoon: the bigger his celebrity, the worse his stats.

He couldn't have been more pleased with his new label as Bachelor Number One of Gotham. He said as much as he stood up from the couch in the clubhouse when I approached as a writer for *Sports Illustrated*. No, he didn't want to be quoted for a profile in the magazine that my colleague and I had been working on because he was certain it would be negative. (He didn't particularly like me or any other of the half-dozen media members he spoke of dismissively.) So, no, he didn't care to explain himself at all. Except that he did.

The tenderhearted pleaser in Alex had not gone completely dormant during his transformation from the wholesome family man to the swingin' single guy. He still wanted to be understood and embraced and loved. In his new form, in any form.

For several minutes, he rubbed the handle of a bat as if a genie could be coaxed from its barrel. In his Yankee uniform, Alex looked his interviewer in the eye as much as possible and spoke of feeling liberated—as if he'd just peeled off a mask. This was a new Alex. He was emphatic as he detailed three self-revelations: He was the happiest he'd ever been; he had learned to embrace his flaws; he didn't care what anyone else thought of him.

"In Seattle, when I played there, I acted perfect and everyone loved me," he said of his late 1990s career with the Mariners. "Now I'm not perfect, and I love it."

His defiance sounded at times forced, as if he were trying on toughness with a press-on tattoo. *Am I convincing this reporter? Am I convincing myself? How do I look saying this?*

In this moment he was taking rebellion for a spin, having spent his spring and summer in the midst of a confetti shower of headlines dousing his once-pristine image with tawdry tales of club crawling, Madonna squiring and stripper dalliances. I mentioned how complicated he seemed now.

"I am complicated," he said. "Isn't that better than being simple?"

Alex liked thinking of himself as an enigma. It made him feel more dramatic and alluring and worthy of attention. He lived like an A-lister. He had "people"—one agent, one manager, three publicists, a Hollywood talent broker and an entourage—so he felt he'd arrived.

In a less-is-more philosophy, he was starting to think like a celebrity: He was not as available to the baseball media, sometimes skipping out of the clubhouse without talking after games.

"He'd still ask someone, 'Did the [beat writers] come to my locker last night?'" a friend says. "He wanted to know they had wanted him."

Alex had, in effect, adopted a Lindsay Lohan mantra about the media. Although she was besieged by the press, she once said, "I wouldn't ever want them to *not* take my picture. I'd be worried. I'd be like 'Do people not care about me?'"

Alex needed to be needed. He liked to be at the heart of the public's fascination. He staged paparazzi moments—sunbathing himself on a rock in Central Park, wiping his mouth with a hundred-dollar bill at an outdoor café with the lens on him, slowing down his car to let the entertainment press catch him—because he enjoyed the pop-culture fishbowl.

He indulged the TMZ camera crews that followed him on the New York streets with polite "no comments." He courted the gamesmanship, resisting their questions while at the same time craving the attention. "I thrive on the negative," he said to me in the clubhouse that evening. "Bring it on."

Okay, then. The topic of conversation changed. Suddenly the subject wasn't about the adrenaline kick of freedom but about doping—as in his. Most of the beat writers had left the clubhouse to attend Manager Joe Girardi's daily pregame press conference in the dugout on the field. It was a good time to pose a sensitive question. I asked him about information I had dating to 2004, his first season as a Yankee: Alex, did you ever share human growth hormone with Kevin Brown?

His jaw jutted forward, his mouth fell open. An exaggerated response. Almost cartoonish. It was always difficult to read the flash of surprise on Alex's face because he acted surprised so often. Growth, as players have called HGH, is illegal to consume without a prescription—AIDS patients with wasting disease are its most common users—but it provides benefits that are considered performance-enhancing, such as the expedited recovery from the injuries and fatigue that bedevil players through a 162-game season.

By 2005, HGH was listed as a banned substance even though the urine-sample testing in baseball could not detect it. Brown's interest in HGH was well known. In the 2007 Mitchell Report—an investigation into baseball's steroid era—Brown was noted in the documents for his knowledge of HGH. He received a shipment in June 2004 from convicted steroid distributor Kirk Radomski. On the return receipt of Brown's package was the address of his agent. That was Scott Boras, the agent for Alex, too.

I went to Alex because a player told me he had witnessed a strange scene: Brown and Alex had had ampoules of HGH in their possession at Yankee Stadium. "I don't know what they were doing with it," he said. The player was very clear that he hadn't seen either Brown or Alex inject it and reminded me that the "stuff wasn't banned then." That was true. What was going on, if anything? Brown declined to comment when asked about the scenario face-to-face, but later, through his lawyer, he denied it had happened. Alex wasn't interested in providing any clarification from his end except to say that he hardly knew Brown and wouldn't speak about his former teammate because he didn't want to "throw him under the bus."

He had to go. Conversation over.

He'd spoken his mind, unveiled what he wanted to, leaning on the vague whenever asked for specifics. What did "I don't want to throw him under the bus" mean? As always, he presented a certain charm in his quest to project an unflustered veneer. He never cursed. He didn't raise his voice. He even threw out a compliment despite the fact that he disagreed with some of the columns I'd written about him when I worked for the *New York Times*. He didn't even seem that upset about the HGH issue.

"At least you asked me," he said.

But now he had to take batting practice. Back to work. His devotion to the game was unquestionable, with a diligence that bordered on OCD: He was meticulous about his diet; he brought his own food to the ballpark. He rarely indulged in fattening training-table grub after the game. He was vigilant about his routine, sparking eye rolls from teammates because he danced through fancy agility drills in front of crowds during batting practice. He was fixated on his body. Teammates would catch him gazing at himself in the clubhouse bathroom mirror.

Self-absorption focused him.

Alex trotted down the tunnel. A moment later he stretched out his arms and walked toward the place where the Yankees' All-Star third baseman had created his most life-sustaining identity: the batter's box. Alone in this chalk-lined rectangle, Alex was the greatest ever to play the game.

What August slump? In the ninth inning against the Rays that September night, Alex made history. He drove a 2–2 pitch off reliever Troy Percival deep to left field, arching higher and higher, until it disappeared over the foul pole. It appeared to glance off the "D-Ring" catwalk in the eyes of third-base umpire Brian Runge, who signaled it a fair ball. Home run. The Rays were livid. Manager Joe Maddon joined his catcher, Dioner Navarro, on the field to argue the call, believing the ball had drifted foul.

Only a week earlier, after a series of botched home run decisions during the 2008 season, Major League Baseball had taken an HD leap of technology and instituted instant replay. This was its first tryout. The umpires shuffled into a dugout tunnel, reviewed the play, and just 2 minutes and 15 seconds later reconfirmed the call. Alex's 31st homer of the season and his 549th of his career was in the books. Not only had he moved past Mike Schmidt for sole possession of 12th place among all-time home run leaders, he became a trivia question: What player was part of MLB's first ever use of instant replay?

After the game, an 8–4 victory by the Yankees, reporters gathered around Alex for his thoughts on the review. He was in great humor, which is always when he's the best, most likable Alex.

"There are probably eight hundred players in the big leagues. And the odds of me being in some controversy are probably two to one," Alex said, drawing a chuckle from reporters. "It's funny, somehow I find myself in these situations all the time."

Yes. As shortstop Derek Jeter would one day admit, "It's always something."

For five seasons in New York, Alex had tried to puncture the Plexiglas resistance of the Yankee faithful. They could see him, even admire him, but he never touched them. There was no tactile connection there. Many fans celebrated his obvious talent but were alienated by three hardened perceptions: He was disingenuous; he failed in the clutch; and, most of all, he wasn't a leader like Derek Jeter.

"Jeter doesn't put up close to the stats Alex puts up, but Jeter is a tremendous team captain and has won four championships," explains Bill Haselman, who was a teammate of Alex's in the minor and major leagues. "You have personalities that are more team-oriented in a Derek Jeter, and then more self-driven in statistics with Alex Rodriguez. And it's pretty clear-cut. I think people see that. I think Alex tries to be a good team player; it just doesn't come as natural as it does for Jeter."

The issue of the inauthentic Alex was at least publicly confined to persona, not the veracity of his performance in January 2009, when former Yankee manager Joe Torre and *SI* senior writer Tom Verducci combined to write *The Yankee Years*. It was a thoughtful narrative about Torre's dozen years in pinstripes, filled with emotion and joy, four World Series championships, and, ultimately, a painful parting in 2007.

What the spring-loaded New York press pounced on most, however, was chapter 8, "The Issues of Alex." As his manager for four seasons, Torre said, "Alex monopolized all the attention. I don't think that's important. We never really had anybody who craved the attention. I think when Alex came over he certainly changed just the feel of the club, whether or not that was because of certain assumptions people had just made by Alex being there, that he was this kind of player."

That disclosure didn't titillate like the rest of the chapter. Verducci expanded on Alex's high-maintenance ways and also detailed his case of Jeter envy, writing, "The inside joke in the clubhouse was that Rodriguez's preoccupation with Jeter recalled the 1992 film *Single White Female*, in which a woman becomes obsessed with her roommate to the point of dressing like her." Alex, Verducci wrote, was also given a nickname by teammates: A-Fraud.

This was catnip to the tabloids. On the back page of the New York *Daily News* dated January 27, there was a photo of Alex in a wide-mouth laugh with the headline "Joe Who? Friends: A-Rod Laughs Off Criticism Because He Was Never Close to Torre."

It sounded good: Alex, impervious to negativity. Just beaded up and rolled off. This coating was not so much a function of a man growing callous after repeated media hits, often self-induced, as much as it was Alex's devotion to Kabbalah. In September before the Rays game, he had mentioned feeling more at ease with imperfection. Did he really believe that, or was he simply parroting his new celebrity peer group?

In 2008, he had become a dedicated follower of Kabbalah, a mystical teaching of Judaism that has, by some accounts, been larded with self-help guidance for insecure celebrities. Alex visited the Kabbalah Centre in New York on occasion and once, in the fall of 2008, was seen by parishioners lifting the Torah during Yom Kippur.

"I don't think anyone in his family was happy about it," one associate of the Rodriguez family says. "He drifted away. Even when he was there, he wasn't there. Know what I mean?"

He started to isolate himself. He didn't call relatives and friends as much. He dropped trainers and associates. It was a jarring religious transformation to those close to him.

Alex was raised a devout Christian but was introduced to Kabbalah in the winter of 2007 after meeting Guy Oseary, a publicity specialist and manager for Madonna. To some experts, classical Kabbalists are a very separate variety from the postmodern, Hollywood-esque Kabbalah followers consisting of movie stars and pop icons like Madonna and Britney Spears.

"All kinds of people find their way in the door of the Kabbalah Centre," says Allan Nadler, the director of Jewish studies at Drew University. "All kinds of lost souls with all kinds of problems . . .

dumb, good-looking people who don't know what the meaning of life is."

Alex searched for meaning constantly as if the right catchphrase from a self-help book could ground him in a normalcy he at once longed for and feared. Normal people aren't famous. A normal life isn't big enough. Normal isn't eye-catching or exciting or seductive or dangerous.

"The classical Kabbalists were people who fasted two days a week at least, engaged in all kinds of self-mortification and self-denial, almost a monastic set," Nadler says. "The Kabbalah Centre seems to have turned that on its head. What they tell people is that it's good to indulge yourself, to fill yourself with the pleasures of the world in a very directed way. They kind of replace the asceticism of classic Kabbalists with a certain hedonistic element. It's all about feeling great about yourself."

Alex's pleasure pursuits were notable by 2008—marked by indulgence in a fast life with fast company—and worry began to set in for those who cared about him. *How could he be so careless? How could he be so soulless? Who was he now?*

"I think that he's just gotten caught up in all the media hype, and I guess you start believing your own press, and believe you are almost godlike," Alex's longtime trainer Dodd Romero said in the summer of 2008. "That's a dangerous thing to be acting and living. You're going to cause yourself to fall. I think that's where he's at. I think Mike Tyson was on his way to being the greatest boxer of all time. He self-destructed. There's a strong possibility Alex could go through with that."

Alex self-destructive? He had an answer for that. He used Kabbalah as a shield from scrutiny (what he would call negativity) that enabled him to withstand anything—even the winter of 2009.

No one could penetrate Alex's armor. He was inoculated against evil forces by a piece of red string. In 2008 and 2009, he was often photographed wearing the accessory—actually white wool dyed red—tied around his left wrist. For Kabbalists, it is a tool that provides protection from influences that might cause harm. It had steeled him against the thorns of Torre's book in January. He would rely on the red string's strength again in February and March.

In the summer of 2008, Alex's profile in the New York tabloids had taken an exponential leap. At *Sports Illustrated,* we wanted to know why. Our main interest was why this self-described family man with a newborn daughter was running around town with Madonna. But in the course of reporting that story, I (and my colleague David Epstein) found a more complicated tale of a multilayered life that went far beyond the headlines. This book is the result of our investigation.

A palm-lined parking lot stretched the distance between the University of Miami's Hecht Athletic Center and its baseball complex, which was still bathed in construction dust on February 5, 2009, at the end of renovations that were, in large part, underwritten by Alex's generous $3.9 million donation to the Hurricanes' program. He hadn't attended UM, but his DNA was ribboned with Hurricane orange and green. He was a proud product of the Miami suburbs, and, as a fervent Hurricanes fan as a child, he used to climb the fences to watch baseball games. He signed a baseball letter of intent with the University of Miami, which would have made him an official Hurricane if he had not chosen to sign a contract with the Mariners after he was drafted number one in 1993.

The UM staff and fans delighted in their A-Rod ties. He was part of the heart and soul of the campus and a ubiquitous fixture around the athletes' center in the off-season. Alex was easy to find on a chilly morning. Not far from where workers were polishing off a new marquee, ALEX RODRIGUEZ PARK AT MARK LIGHT FIELD, there was a conspicuous sign of Alex's whereabouts: a hulking black Maybach worth around $400,000 bore a silver license plate frame engraved ALEX RODRIGUEZ on the bottom.

It was freezing by Miami standards, about 39 degrees, prompting citrus growers to fret over the damage to their crops. "What's colder," one athlete asked another as they walked by, "Miami or Santa's ass?" They were convinced Miami would win.

The icy dew made a workout in the Hecht facility far preferable to fielding short hops on a field. Alex must be inside. For years, Alex spent the better part of his off-season workouts pumping iron next to varsity athletes. He once allowed a newspaper photographer to snap an essay of his sweat ethic to underscore his work ethos for all to see.

His presence at UM wasn't a secret. I certainly knew of it as I walked into the lobby of the athletes' center, identified myself and asked the college student working the front desk if she knew whether Alex Rodriguez was around.

She checked the office of Andreu Swasey, the strength and conditioning coach at UM, who often guided Alex's regimen.

"He's not there," the receptionist said. "Let me try someone else."

She made another call or two and verified the obvious: "He's in the varsity weight room."

An athletic department official offered up the winding directions to reach the other side of the Hecht complex. A few minutes later, after a couple of wrong turns, I walked into a sprawling but nearly empty varsity weight room that smelled of rubber mats and cleanser. I showed my business card at the door to a gentleman in a glassed-in office.

"Is Alex Rodriguez around?" I asked.

"In the back," said a man in a Hurricanes jacket.

I walked past two athletes churning pedals on stationary bikes, but hardly anyone else was around. Alex cut a tall figure near the back wall at 6-foot-3, 225 pounds. He was dressed in a white T-shirt and sweat pants, working out with a trainer and a friend as lyricless music vibrated in the background. A good beat was sometimes all that was needed to push the last pound. In rhythm with the thumping, Alex stretched out his arms behind him, a flex that made his triceps look as if they were stuffed with coils.

He caught someone walking toward him out of the corner of his eye. He turned, looked over his shoulder and pursed his lips. He was not pleased to see me inside a place he had trusted was his sanctuary.

"You're not supposed to be here," he said more than once.

"I have a couple of questions for you, important questions," I said.

He relented reluctantly but was not unpleasant about it. He didn't know why I was there, and that seemed unfair. What I knew would be devastating to him. All he knew was that I was bugging him. Blind question. Hated it. But my job was to ask.

He rested his forearm on a parallel bar used for triceps dips and leaned in to listen with a bored sigh. He mentally flipped through possible topics, all annoying to him, but not unexpected. *Was this about Joe Torre and the book? Or maybe it was about Madonna? Could be another Derek Jeter question?*

It could have been any supermarket tabloid topic du jour. But it wasn't.

This was about steroids. This was about lies. In December 2007, Katie Couric had interviewed Alex about several topics, including steroids, because the Mitchell Report had just been revealed. She had specifically asked Alex if he had ever been tempted to use steroids or growth hormone.

Alex had been completely composed. Hours earlier, anticipating the Mitchell Report question, he had practiced his response with his concentric circle of handlers prior to the interview. He had looked straight at Couric and said, "I've never felt overmatched on a baseball field. . . . So, no." Experts at facial expression would later point out the slight twitch in Alex's left cheek as he spoke, indicating a possible lie. But he was very convincing to the home audience, who applauded his purity amid a bunch of 'roided-up stinkers in the news.

Whatever Alex was—postseason choker or phony teammate—he didn't seem like a typical steroid user. His stats were fairly consistent. His hat size hadn't grown. His body hadn't expanded overnight. In fact, I'd written an article with a colleague clearing Alex of the steroid allegations made by Jose Canseco in the spring of 2008. But in the process of a follow-up personality profile on Alex, we began hearing other rumblings. "He's not so squeaky clean," one source said. The rumors eventually gained traction in reality after I checked and double-checked the credibility of the sources. Finally, the information that Alex had used steroids reached the point where it became irrefutable.

All that was left was to confront Alex face-to-face.

The question I posed to Alex in the UM gym was direct and specific: "I have information that in 2003 you tested positive for anabolic steroids—Primobolan and testosterone—while you were with the Rangers. Is there an explanation?"

His mouth dropped slightly. His green eyes widened. But this was not the prepared reflex of surprise he had used so often. This wasn't feigned. This was different. He stepped back and stared into the distance, processing the question. In his gaze there was confusion. *What do I say? What can I say?*

In his fixed stance there was vulnerability. A steroid revelation would undermine the credibility of Alex's precious body of work as a Hall of Famer in progress. A steroid revelation would render his

2003 MVP as a performance gained with an asterisk. It would also transform Alex into the one thing most crushing to his core: He would be like everyone else. Not uniquely gifted. Not singularly spectacular. Not one of a kind. Only tainted—like the others.

All Alex had ever wanted was to stand out. Baseball made him special. He loved the game, and it loved him right back. Baseball gave and gave to Alex. It supplied the attention he craved. It soothed the insecurities he battled. It filled holes opened by childhood abandonment. Baseball wasn't like his father. Baseball never left him.

Baseball had created a cocoon for Alex at the start, from a mother and siblings who supported him and the youth coaches who fathered him. But then came the agent who enabled him and the opportunists who preyed on him and the handlers who misguided him and the pals who lived off him.

He'd had so many various protectors—pieces of red string throughout his whole life—to stand between him and accountability. But now it was just Alex in a weight room searching for an answer that hadn't been scripted.

Could a single question destroy baseball as his one truth if it revealed a lie? Could a query betray the secrets of an entire career shaped into legend by the steroid era? Could he confront this or would his narcissistic resistance allow him to play only the position of victim?

He prayed he'd never have to find out.

Chapter One

THE GOOD SON

THE BACK PORCH OF the Emerald Park Retirement Center opens onto a large green lawn with a stone walkway that loops through the neatly trimmed grass and curls by a half-dozen benches. It's not an entirely bucolic scene, though. Over a stucco wall, there is a sprawling strip mall where a pub boasts that it opens "daily at 7 a.m."

Across the road out front there is a trailer park where residents live in single-wides on cinder blocks and aged RVs with broken headlights. A six-lane highway borders the center on the left, which makes this one of the noisier parts of Hollywood, Florida, with sedans, vans and 18-wheelers blasting past the corporate parks and the multiple storefronts for psychics.

Inside Emerald, where Muzak bathes a vast community room of white tile, Victor Rodriguez feels fortunate.

"It's a nice place," Victor says. "I'm taken care of."

He looks sturdier than any of the other residents. Most appear to be at least 10 years older than Victor, who is 79. Behind him, a brittle-looking man in blue shorts, black socks and orthopedic shoes is slumped in a chair asleep, oxygen tubes plugged into his nostrils. A woman with a walker moves slowly across the lobby, asking why the room is so cold—again and again. Victor sits next to the glass elevator, upright in his chair, dressed in a crisp short-sleeved button-down shirt and brown slacks with a sharp crease. His jaw is still square. He still resembles the ballplayer he once was.

"My son, Alex, he is, let me tell you, a much better player than I was," Victor says. "He is the best, I think. But I am a father, so . . ."

His son is Alex Rodriguez, the 33-year-old third baseman for the New York Yankees. Alex is the richest player in baseball, set to make nearly $400 million before age 42, as he glides along a seemingly clear path to pass Barry Bonds as the all-time home-run king, the sexiest moniker in baseball.

Alex and his father share the same caramel-colored skin and charming disposition. They both listen thoughtfully, never interrupting. They are both obsessed with neatness and speak with a similar cadence. Victor, like Alex, talks deliberately, with occasional pauses as he searches for the right word. Both men have been through a divorce that involved small children.

Cynthia filed for divorce in July 2008. When it was finalized in September, ending two months of mud slinging, the iron-clad prenuptial agreement called for Alex to make generous child-support payments. He moved out of the couple's dream home, a Mediterranean-style estate on the water in Coral Gables, and put it on the market for $14 million. Cynthia also signed a confidentiality agreement; if Alex's secrets were going to come out, they would not be disclosed by his ex-wife.

By the spring of 2009, the asking price for their estate was reduced to $10 million. Cynthia expected to receive the proceeds from the sale of the home, which the couple had bought for $12 million in 2004 in a transaction that was mostly in cash, according to mortgage records. Meanwhile, Alex was living in a rental mansion on Star Island, where monthly leases were listed at $75,000 per month even in Florida's horrifically depressed real estate market.

This enclave for the superwealthy is an artificial landmass shaped like a pill afloat in Biscayne Bay. It's open to the public, but a guard at a gate takes the names of all who enter to protect the high-profile residents from autograph seekers and groupies. About 30 mansions of various pastel colors rise above the 15-foot hedges along the road. From the homes' deepwater docks, where 40-foot yachts rest, residents can see the cosmopolitan high-rises of Miami to the west and the sun rise over the Art Deco vibe of South Beach to the east.

The glitziest of Miamians live here. Alex liked the idea of being one of them. Over the years, sugar cane magnates, financial barons, and entertainers such as Madonna, Sylvester Stallone, Shaquille O'Neal and Gloria Estefan have maintained residences on Star Island.

The Emerald Park Retirement Center is about 20 miles—and at least several tax brackets—away. Victor lives in an apartment; they typically rent for about $2,200 a month, but he doesn't pay a nickel. "Alex is a very good son," he explains. "Of course, I never ask him for nothing, but he helps me. He doesn't want me to pay for where I live. But I never ask." (Victor won't live here for very long. In early 2009, he moved to another retirement enclave—with luxury upgrades.)

He hasn't spoken to Alex in several weeks. They were estranged for almost 20 years but reconciled in 2003—to a point. Part of Alex still can't fully embrace a father who left the family when he was 10. Victor reads about his son in the papers and hears about him through the entertainment news. "I worry about Alex and Cynthia," Victor says. "I hear about Madonna. I don't know. I talk to Cynthia and ask about my grandchildren, but the conversations are short."

It's before the holidays. He expects to see Alex but understands if he doesn't. He doesn't push Alex for fear of losing him again. "He's so busy," Victor says. "He has so many dealings. He is doing many big things at once."

Victor was always ambitious, too.

Victor Rodriguez was born in a verdant valley below the Cordillera Mountains of the Dominican Republic, in the village of San Juan de la Maguana. Shacks and small houses in hard-candy hues of yellow, pink and blue dotted the valley; most of them had walls made from palm trees and roofs made of dried branches and palm fronds. Victor remembers his town as an agrarian idyll—good land for rice fields and, farther into the plains, good grazing land for cattle. Donkeys pulled wagons loaded high with burlap sacks of grain, sugar and coffee beans over dirt roads toward San Juan de la Maguana. Men played dominoes in the park, while children piled up bananas to sell in the market. "No one was rich," he says. "We didn't know what rich was. Everyone was in the same situation."

Victor was born in 1929, one year before General Rafael Trujillo seized power in the Dominican Republic. Trujillo ruled for the next 31 years, regularly winning 95 percent of the vote through fraud and threats, bribes and violence. "He was all that I knew," Victor says. "Let me tell you, he was one terrible dictator. He controlled everything. He abused people. He was cruel in many opinions."

Trujillo was a diabolical despot who promulgated a cult of personality; he erected statues of himself throughout the country and renamed the capital Ciudad Trujillo (night and day, a large electric sign there blazed the words *Dios y Trujillo*—"God and Trujillo").

Trujillo was also a brazen and brutal racist who tried to purge the African strain of his people; he dreamed of "whitening" his island to make it more European and even used bleach to whiten his own brown skin.

Yet, despite his ironfisted persona, Trujillo fancied himself a refined gentleman with a sophisticated taste for fine art and race-horses. He loved equine pursuits, but he was savvy enough to understand how sport could play a role in perpetuating his stranglehold on his country. Baseball, he knew, would be an excellent distraction from his political manipulations. He encouraged the sport's popularity. His son ran a team in Santo Domingo.

"Everyone played baseball to escape and dream," Victor recalls. "We talked about it all the time. We breathed it. In every city, it was the sound of a bat and a ball that thrilled everyone. By the time I was seven, I played every day."

The children played even when they had no gloves, no bats, no balls. The gloves of poor children were sometimes made from milk cartons or old socks. A broomstick or even a large wooden spoon might be the bat. The balls were sometimes just beans wrapped in tape. "Everyone played without knowing what a glove really felt like," Victor says. "Your hands hurt, but we were crazy for baseball. For us, baseball was life. Boys and even the girls played. All the cities, no matter how small, had at least two teams. It was a small island, but it had so much talent."

The D.R.'s thrumming amateur leagues first caught the eye of American baseball scouts in the 1950s when the amazing Juan Marichal was signed. He was a different kind of pitcher, one never seen before, with a high leg kick that gave him the vertical look of an exclamation mark. He became the nation's first major-league superstar when he left the island to play for the San Francisco Giants in 1960 at age 23. "He was the beginning for us," Victor says. "He was a great, great hero. He brought so much good to the Dominican when he went to the major leagues. It was a proud moment for us."

Victor was a talented catcher who had a strong arm and a fine grasp of the game—calling pitches was his forte—but he never emerged as one of the country's top stars. "I never played professionally," he says. "I didn't play for money." He played organized ball for 18 years, though, from age 18 to 36, until injuries finally forced him to stop.

Victor poured his soul into baseball, but he didn't neglect his studies or restrict his dreams to sports. He was a well-read young man with a keen interest in current events, and his circle of friends included many polished professionals and businessmen. Politics was a close second to baseball as their favorite topic of discussion.

It is unclear how intensely active Victor was as a revolutionary. Former teammates of Victor's remember him as a good catcher and simple man. Others who lived through the Trujillo era believe that Victor was a freedom fighter and a member of the underground resistance in the late 1950s. A Spanish-language, online history guide of San Juan de la Maguana also portrays Victor as a rebel leader. Juan Rivas, who grew up in San Juan de la Maguana, says Victor was the editor of an anti-Trujillo newspaper near the end of the dictator's reign. "Victor was a very smart man," Rivas says. "He was a brave man."

On a Dominican history blog, one tale of Victor's past is told from 1959. He was 30 years old and targeted by Trujillo's military thugs at a bar. Victor was approached by several men who dragged him from a table and, in front of patrons, began beating him with brass knuckles.

In 1960, Victor, as the story continues, became a galvanizing force in the western part of the D.R. against Trujillo when the entire nation turned on its dictator after he tortured and killed the

Mirabal sisters, the heroines of the underground resistance. Turmoil erupted across the country. In 1961, Trujillo was assassinated.

"It was over," Victor says. "The end, I couldn't believe, had come."

But what about his role in the resistance? Was it fact, folklore or something in between? Victor laughs but does not answer. "So long ago," he says.

Victor married Pouppe Martinez in 1955. She gave birth to their first child, Victor Rodriguez, Jr., in 1960, but a year later, the couple divorced. Victor was getting restless. The country was in transition and there were new opportunities he was itching to explore, but he continued to play baseball a few years more. His son, Victor Jr., never saw him play.

"I didn't know him that well when I was a young boy," Victor Jr. says. "I remember him only the few times he came to see me. I always had good memories of him. All the encounters I had with him—up to the time when I actually saw him more often when I was a teenager—were always very positive. He was a tender person."

Victor was warm and attentive in the moments with his son, but then he was off, gone for stretches at a time. He had a wide-eyed sense of adventure. Victor decided the United States was where he had the best chance of realizing his dreams, so he moved to New York City.

He left behind a nation in turmoil, one that was about to become a very dangerous place to live. The U.S. military unilaterally invaded the D.R. on April 28, 1965, based on the fears of the LBJ White House that the political tumult there might foster a Communist regime and a second Cuba. As U.S. soldiers poured into the country, they were met with resistance from organized militants and snipers. Civilians fled from the fighting; five-year-old Victor

Jr. and his mother evacuated to the countryside, where they lived with relatives.

A year later, Victor Jr. and his mother returned to their home, now pockmarked by bullets. He grew up with only a fleeting interest in baseball. "I played," he says. "I was okay. I wasn't anything special." He was more fascinated by academics, believing books would open new worlds to him. By his teen years, he, too, lived in the United States. On occasion he saw his half brother, Alex, who was only five years old when Victor Jr. went off to see the globe as a U.S. Air Force officer. He was stationed overseas as Alex grew up, unaware that his half brother was developing into a baseball superstar.

Young Alex sits transfixed on his father's lap, a binkie on a string tied around his neck, as his father watches baseball's *Game of the Week* on their old black-and-white in a scene captured in family photos and described by relatives. His father's chin brushes Alex's soft, curly brown hair as he leans toward the convex screen no bigger than a hubcap, trying to see what is happening in the game.

From the TV's tiny, tinny speaker Joe Garagiola's excited midwestern voice rises as he announces, "Another hit for the Reds!" Victor quickly analyzes the trajectory of the skipping rock hit by Pete Rose into the hole between short and third. "Defense was in the wrong place," he says to no one except Alex, whose vocabulary is limited to "truck," "cat" and "ball." He is just two years old, after all, but he listens as his father peers into the screen through thick glasses with black square rims.

Victor is 48 but still has smooth skin and a toned body. He is active, trim and neatly groomed. His second wife, Lourdes Navarro, is an animated, beautiful woman with expressive eyes like those of Sophia Loren. Victor is on another lap with fatherhood with his second family. "Alex was a gift," Victor says. "Such a good boy."

In a whirl, Alex slides down his father's shin like a fireman twisting down a brass pole, picks up a balled sock and throws it to his father. They play catch until Victor, trying to keep his eye on the game, hurls the sock out the door. "Go run it down, Alex," he says. And off Alex waddles in his denim overalls, searching for a grounder sliced into the corner of the home. "He was always crazy for baseball," Victor says. "He could not get enough."

His parents say that Alex was always bouncing things off the walls—rattling the framed photos of family and the Catholic crosses hanging on picture hooks—in what was, in truth, half a home. The sand-colored brick apartment on 183rd Street in Manhattan—a two-lane road that divided a Yeshiva school from a Latin bodega in Washington Heights—was also a storefront.

"Victor's Shoes" filled the front room of the apartment. Shelves filled with wedge sandals, pumps and zip-up go-go boots lined the walls. Victor had a smooth patter for the ladies looking to buy shoes, a twinkle in his eyes, and a flirtatious lilt in his voice. He flattered his customers and diligently made note of every change in hairstyle or pound lost on a diet. He remembered their names, knew their stories and asked about their lives. Eloquent and charming, he would try out a sales pitch in his head before delivering it to one of his regulars. He was methodical about his work and meticulously—if not expensively—dressed. "Hardly anyone else wore a tie for their business on that street, but he did," recalls Doreen Ruiz, who lived on the same block as the Rodriguez family. "He was a very handsome, kind man."

Victor had always been good with numbers—baseball stats and profit margins—but he also knew people. "The women loved my shoes," he says with a chuckle. "I'm telling you, the ladies would wait for *my* shoes."

The store was a success, but the living accommodations were stifling for Victor's family—two bedrooms for two adults and three children. There were Susy and Joe, still in elementary school, from Lourdes's previous relationship, and the baby, Alex. He wedged his way into the flat after his birth on July 27, 1975. Since there was no living room—except when the children played in the store after hours, throwing boots into sale bins—open space for playing indoors was confined to one long hallway, where Alex would pedal his red, yellow and blue buggy while tugging on his diapers. When he got to the end of the hall, he'd pick the buggy up, spin it around and go speeding off the other way, wheels slipping and sliding on the floor.

At 4 a.m. each day, Lourdes would get out of bed, pull the curlers from her hair, pat on her makeup and slip into the pre-dawn darkness of 183rd Street for her shift on a GM assembly line. When it was time for Victor to open the store, he would leave Alex with an elderly lady in an upstairs apartment.

These were tense times in New York. The streets were dirty and dangerous, crack cocaine was decimating the ghettos, graffiti was as prevalent as rust and disco was blanketing the country with appalling clothes and worse music. Even the good news came with a black border—in 1977 an extraordinarily dysfunctional Yankees team overcame a toxic clubhouse to win the World Series, the subject of Jonathan Mahler's social history–cum–sports biography, *Ladies and Gentlemen, the Bronx Is Burning*. But the story that dominated the tabloid headlines in the summer of 1977 was the manhunt for the Son of Sam, a serial killer who had been on the loose for a year, targeting women. He used a .44-caliber handgun to terrorize New Yorkers, shooting victims as they walked a dog late at night or sat in a car in the early morning hours or strolled home from college.

In that atmosphere, there was no way Alex would be allowed to play outside or scurry about the streets of Washington Heights.

Indoors became his outdoors. "Alex started carrying a little red bat [in the house]," Susy says. "He would not let go of that. He'd hit us with the bat when he got out of the stroller. You'd turn around and he'd be, like, *pow!* Or, if he wanted something and didn't get it, he'd hit you. I had red marks on my back from that bat. He was a baby who would really throw fits. He'd throw a fit if you took his bat."

As a child, Alex seldom did without. "He was doted on," Susy says. He was excused when he wielded his bat wildly and coddled when he cried. "Once he was born, it seemed that everything in our house turned to plastic," Joe once said. "All he wanted to do was throw a baseball or swing a bat. So we couldn't have any china."

On hot summer days, the family would sometimes venture to the area beaches, where Alex liked to build sand castles. "You'll live in a castle just like this one day," Victor told him. "A castle big and great."

Years later, Alex would say, "I remember New York as my perfect world." He doesn't remember the danger, the constant scream of sirens, the bitterly cold winters or the busted heating pipes. He doesn't remember being cooped up in half an apartment or the New York City that was littered with burned-out car carcasses left beneath underpasses. As a child, he didn't see the suburban exodus of residents running from the crime and moral decay linked to the rise in crack cocaine. "New York City wasn't like it is now," Susy says. "It wasn't safe then. We didn't play outside. But my mom realized that being in New York was making a future for us to live better in the Dominican."

That was Victor's goal: to make enough money in New York City so that he could build a bridge back to the Dominican, where his children could live in a fine house with a beach within walking distance. "Monday through Friday we'd come home from school in New York and stay inside and do laundry, run errands, cook or clean," Susy says. "And it gets cold in September. In the Dominican, everything is open and you have housekeepers, so you go out-side and play with your neighbors. You play all year round."

Victor took his family back to the Dominican Republic in 1979. Their new stucco dream home outside Santo Domingo had a deco-rative four-foot-high wrought-iron fence that protected a modest patch of grass from the road. The warmth of the sun in the D.R. felt like a healing balm—no more slushy snow, no more frozen pipes, no more neighbors stomping on the floor above their heads. Breezes from the beach a block away cooled each of the four bed-rooms, and the neighborhood was safe. "We even had a live-in maid," Alex recalls. It was paradise in so many ways compared to 183rd Street. This is what Lourdes and Victor had worked so hard for, understanding that the peso-to-dollar exchange rate would buy them a comfortable existence in the D.R. It would also allow them to send Susy, Joe and Alex to good schools.

At age five, after putting on a pink button-down shirt and brown pants, after grabbing a blue lunchbox and kissing his par-ents good-bye, Alex left for his first day of classes—at an Ameri-canized school in Santo Domingo. Victor and Lourdes knew the world revolved around English and wanted him to have his educa-tion rooted in it.

His baseball education, though, was strictly Dominican. All around him was a love of the game, an obsession with it. Kids swung at dried kidney beans with sticks when there were no balls and bats available. They invented games that sharpened their base-ball skills. One was called platicka: In a park across the street from Alex's house, with grass that grew knee high in the sultry summers, children placed old license plates in the weeds. A pitcher aimed at the plates with a rubber ball while the hitter tried to protect the plate with a stick. "Whatever game I played, I couldn't handle los-ing," Alex once said.

He didn't often feel that sting. He was very good at baseball from the beginning and hardly ever lost at platicka. When he did, he was smothered in love by his parents, his siblings, his grandparents. Making sure Alex was happy was the family's mission, a project of utmost importance. Not that anyone considered it an onerous job—Alex was irresistible with his handsome features, soulful eyes and charming disposition. His satin cheeks were pinched early and often. He could get just about anything with the crook of his small finger—or an earnest "Please, oh, *please* . . ."

There was a basketball court in the park across the street from the Rodriguez's front yard where Joe played hoops with his buddies, but all Alex wanted to do was play catch and hit balls. "He wanted to play catch *every* day for a couple of hours," Joe once said. "I couldn't get rid of him."

When Joe couldn't stand another minute of catch, he would hit the ball as far as he could, forcing Alex to chase it down the road. While Alex ran one way, Joe would run the other way with his friends. There was always someone else there for Alex, though. Susy often became his battery mate.

Alex walked around the neighborhood with a toy bat in his hand, constantly honing his swing. He would set up bases to steal in the yard. He would swing his arm around and around as if hurling an imaginary ball.

He can remember his first home run, when he was six. It was a ball he ripped over the third baseman's head and down the line. As Alex rounded third, he recalls, "I was almost crying, I was so happy."

He started playing organized ball that year—he was small and the youngest player on his team, so the coaches decided that second base was the safest place to put him. There he wouldn't need a strong arm, just an accurate one.

Joe, Alex and Victor would talk about the mental part of the game, strategy, as well as the stats of the game and critique the umpire's calls. They bonded over the love of baseball, but Victor didn't pressure Alex to play. "You never saw his father out there running with him," Susy explains. "He'd pitch to him with a whiffle ball or beans, but he wasn't pushing him to play. He wasn't one of those parents."

Victor would have been proud of Alex no matter what path he'd chosen. It just happened to be a base path. Victor says he was amazed by Alex's speed and baseball acumen at such an early age: "When he was seven years old, I said to his mother, 'Someday you're going to see him be a superstar playing in the major leagues.'"

Young Alex lived a charmed, middle-class life in the Dominican, but in 1980 the family finances began to crumble and it was time to move on. The Washington Heights shoe store, which Victor had left in the care of relatives, went under. An investment he'd made in a pharmacy in the Dominican wasn't paying off, and Joe and Susy, about to graduate from high school, were eager to go back to the United States for their college education. Lourdes didn't want to remain in the D.R. without Joe and Susy, so by 1981, it was time for the family to find their way back to America.

This time they settled in Miami. Victor found a rental in suburban South Miami, a white cinder-block ranch home. The neighborhood had sidewalks and palm trees and plenty of grass. At night, Alex would listen to the breathing of his parents lying in the bedroom next to his. He would know by the sound of it—heavier, slower, getting heavier and slower—when he could sneak in, wiggle in between them and fall asleep in a human sandwich. "When we woke up, there was Alex," Victor recalls.

Even though they were scratching out a living, Alex's parents made sure their son went to a good school. "I always sent him to private schools," Victor says. "I think public schools didn't give enough attention to children."

One day, when Alex was eight, he watched a team practice on a field next to his elementary school. The coach, Juan Diego Arteaga, a warm man with a thick mustache, saw Alex sitting alone next to a tree.

"Hey, kid, do you want to play?"

"What do you want me to do?'

"Have you ever caught before?"

Although his father had been a catcher, Alex had never played behind the plate. But since it was Victor's position, Alex knew enough to fake it. "Sure," he said. "I'm a *good* catcher."

That day, Alex caught a beautiful game, even though he was playing with boys two years older than he was. Arteaga's son J.D. was on that team. They lived two blocks from Alex. The two boys became close friends and played in every youth league Mr. Arteaga could find for them.

A year went by. Alex was still skinny but now tall with angular facial features, his xylophone ribs showing through his skin and his elbows as sharp as arrowheads. He idolized Baltimore Orioles All-Star Cal Ripken, Jr., and wanted to be a shortstop, just like Cal. If one of his idols swung a black bat, Alex would use shoe polish and a felt-tip pen to blacken his own bat. In one boyhood photo, Alex is wearing red shorts and a dark cap, smiling at the camera but batting left-handed. His favorite player that week must have been a lefty. Alex liked imitating his idols.

His father felt joy at his son's passion for the game. "He knew more than I did," Victor says. "It made me feel good that he had something that always made him smile."

Victor himself was struggling with just what would make him happy. He was a searcher in need of something new, different and exciting. He was antsy again. He was having trouble finding a business venture that suited his ambitions. He was 59 now but not ready for the sedentary life of bingo parlors amid the swaying palms. He had business ties to a pharmacy, but he wanted something bigger, one more hit of adrenaline. He decided that New York City was the best place for him. Victor says Lourdes had no desire to return: "I told her, 'Let's move back to New York. I have my credit in New York. We know how to do business in New York.' And she said, 'I don't go back to New York. If you want, you can go.' I said to her, 'You want to go or you want to stay?' She said, 'I want to stay.' I said, 'Okay, bye-bye.' I went by myself to New York."

Victor took one suitcase when he left in 1985, when Alex was 10. Day after day, Alex waited for him to return. He would stop bouncing his ball on the pavement to look down the street whenever he heard a car. *How long can a man live out of one suitcase?* "He'd always say, 'Daddy's coming, Daddy's coming,'" Susy says.

It was a natural response of a boy who couldn't imagine any first in his life—first date, first driver's license, first stolen base—unfolding without his daddy.

"What did I know back then?" Alex once said. "I thought he was coming back. I thought he had gone to the store or something. But he never came back. He had been so good to me, actually spoiled me because I was the baby of the family. I couldn't understand what he had done. I still don't know how a man could do that to his family: turn his back."

At night, for a couple of years after Victor left, Alex would wait for his mother to drift off and then crawl into bed next to her, sleeping where his father had slept.

He was suddenly a kid of divorced parents. He wasn't the only one in the world. But to Alex, it certainly felt like it. Wasn't he worthy of a father? Wasn't he smart enough and talented enough to deserve a dad? Alex would go through his life always trying to overachieve and please to be forever good enough. Even great.

What Alex couldn't have known was that the grieving went both ways.

Victor was liberated but devastated by his distance from Alex. "You cannot imagine how much I suffered when I separated from him," Victor says. "I cannot describe it. Sometimes, when I woke up, my face was covered with tears. I was crying. I gave so much love to that small child."

Victor still left, though. He didn't turn back. There would be no father to shield a boy from the minefield of opportunists ahead, all of whom believed one thing: that Alex could be the best ball-player of all time.

Chapter Two

THE PHENOM OF WESTMINSTER

To watch Alex Rodriguez swing a bat in Yankee pinstripes is to witness a split-second gala of force and grace and confidence. The clumsiness comes after the game, when questions sometimes result in awkward answers and contradictions. "I don't think Alex is very good at communicating," says Yankees General Manager Brian Cashman. "This isn't something he does well."

He doesn't talk as reflexively as he hits. It's as if he's pulling the cord on a See 'n Say in search of the right phrase. Where does the arrow point? This scripted Alex reveals the frailty beneath the brawn, a layer not at all surprising considering the roots of his vulnerability.

In the spring of 1993, Alex was a teen pinup in the office of every major-league GM. The scouts practically had personalized parking spaces in Miami's Westminster Christian School lot as they tracked Alex's every throw, swing and slide during his senior year. They raved about his five tools—hitting for average, hitting for power, running speed, arm strength, and fielding ability— often crowding around, hoping for a little face time with the hottest prospect since Ken Griffey, Jr., had come out of high school in 1987. They held their clipboards close to their chests as they scribbled love notes about Alex's talent. They were almost unanimous in their belief that he would be the first or second player chosen in the upcoming amateur draft. The Seattle Mariners had the top pick, and they, too, were swooning.

Alex seemed to feed off the scrutiny; he hit an unworldly .606 through the first month of his senior season. He clearly liked the attention.

Throughout Westminster's 1993 season, a Mariners scout poked the lens of his video camera through the chain-link backstop to capture Alex's every twitch at the plate on film. "We wanted to make sure if he got injured, we'd know it," says Roger Jongewaard, the head of the Mariners scouting and development that year. "We had lots of video on him."

One spring afternoon, Alex ripped through his BP pitches in the Westminster cage, then leaned in close to the camera being held by a Mariners scout and said, "Hey, Chuck, this is Alex. And I can't wait to get to Seattle." (Chuck Armstrong was then and still is the president of the Mariners.) "He was the most confident high school kid I've ever seen," says Jongewaard. "How many kids would have the nerve to say that to the president of a major-league team? Chuck was impressed."

Alex, like any star, needed the camera, but in a way that went deeper than vanity. If people were looking, they cared—and Alex felt validated.

The attention tempered the insecurity that played tricks with his mind and even his sense of who he was. He would constantly ask friends if he was considered popular. On bus rides after away games, far from the scouts and media, he would ask teammates, even after going four for four, "How did I play today?" He needed to be told that he was good, that he was special. That he was loved.

When Victor Rodriguez left his family to return to New York City in 1985, Alex was devastated. Why had his father left? What had he done?

Everyone around Alex poured love into the space vacated by his father. "He was doted on," Susy says. That's what families do. They rally, even if they overcompensate. The family encircled the 10-year-old Alex as if he were the subject of a seance, as if it were their common mission to lift his spirits.

But still he cried, longing for his father and not understanding why he wasn't coming home. Until the last day Victor was in the house in Miami, he had hugged and held and kissed Alex, made him feel nurtured. Victor was very good at doing that for people—customers and sons alike. He would make them feel beautiful and wonderful and irreplaceable. And then he would leave.

It jarred Alex. At such a young age, his emotions ranged from guilt to anger and, ultimately, resentment. "I lied to myself," Alex explained in 1998. "I tried to tell myself it didn't matter. But when I was alone, I often cried. Where was my father? Finally, my hope dried up. Dad never came back. I have to let go of that anger to move forward. The problem is, I can't forget what he did."

For months, Alex would lean on the frame of his front door, watching the street. Neighbors could see the little boy craning his neck to scrutinize every man walking toward him. *Is that Daddy?* Alex would come home from school and sometimes check his parents' bedroom, hoping that his father would be there, napping.

His pain often distorted reality. Later in his life, Alex would speak of years going by without hearing from his father, even though Victor called and sent him gifts. "I tried all the time to talk to him," Victor insists. "I loved him. He was always with me, I thought. I sent as much home as I could."

Over the holidays, in the winter of 1985, a TV materialized in a bedroom Alex shared with his Cal Ripken, Jr., poster. The gift from Victor meant that Susy could watch *Charlie's Angels* reruns in the living room while her brothers Joe and Alex watched sports. "I loved that boy," Victor says. "I always made sure he was taken care of." But Alex craved more than presents. "I thirsted for Dad for so long," he once said.

Being an "abandoned" child gave Alex an identity. It enveloped him, and that gave him a small measure of comfort. At least he knew he was the kid without a dad, a fact that often elicited sympathy from adults. He had always been a sensitive boy; Victor's departure made him even more fragile emotionally. Neighbors recall seeing Alex's eyes brim with tears at the slightest criticism. "I remember telling him not to play near my flowerpots," a former neighbor, Sandra Gonzalez, says. "He must have said, 'Sorry,' a hundred times, until he was almost crying."

Alex cried when his team lost, when movies ended with sadness or with joy, when he sensed that his mother was worrying about something. *Was she lonely, too?*

There was a sweetness to Alex that must have made it easy to baby him. In old family photos, his striking eyes, a pearlescent green, are almost always wide and bright as he makes himself a willing subject for every picture. He wants to please. He never looks distant or disaffected like the grunge and Goth children of the 1980s and '90s.

"We were very protective of him," Susy recalls. "He was an only child, in a sense, because I was seventeen at the time and Joe was nineteen." The family revolved around his needs: Where would he go to school? How would Alex get to practice?

Victor sent the occasional check, but most of the burden of

raising Alex was on Lourdes. "Her perseverance and inner strength kept us together," Alex once recalled in a television interview. "She was willing to do whatever it took to make our lives better."

Each weekday morning, Lourdes would go to work as a secretary at an immigration office in Miami. At night, she slipped into her waitress uniform and then traveled 20 minutes away to a Latin restaurant where the regulars tipped in singles and quarters for meals that didn't cost much more than $5 a plate. "I would always count her tip money," Alex has said. "I always remember Monday through Wednesday it was a little dry, a little short. And it would probably be $18 to $24. But then Thursday, Friday and Saturday, I can remember counting that money and it would be $38, $39 or $42. If we ever got to $45, I knew it was one heck of a day."

Alex became the family's wishing well—Susy and Joe tossed him whatever spare change they had, hoping it would make him happy. "Every time I got paid, I would buy him a little something," Susy says.

Despite all the love, attention and generosity, Alex would later describe his childhood as a struggle against poverty and loneliness. He would talk wistfully of the many baseball games at which the other children had parents in attendance. He understood, of course, why his mother couldn't be there—she was working—but he longed to have someone clap for him when he got a hit. "I felt like an underdog," Alex once said of his childhood, "but I never let my situation keep me down."

Juan Diego Arteaga, his first youth baseball coach, became a sturdy stand-in for a father. Alex leaned on Arteaga, became best friends with his son J.D. and spent countless hours with both of them. The Arteaga house was his second home.

Arteaga saw instantly that Alex was blessed with abundant baseball talent. At age 10, he was flat-out gangly, with lug nuts for kneecaps and the oversized feet of a puppy, but he could move— he had great range and gobbled up grounders. As soon as his arm strength improved, he was moved from second base to shortstop. He had speed enough to beat out dribblers to the mound. He had an accurate arm, instinctually scooping and throwing.

Another quality set him apart: his baseball maturity. Alex played with kids who were two—and sometimes four—years older, yet he was often the most composed player on the field. In one team photo, the 12-year-old Alex kneels on the grass of a baseball field in the front row. There are two teenage boys with thick necks, who fill out their light blue uniforms with broad shoulders. The team's name—Corsairs—is stretched in an arc across another player's broad chest. Two other players have heavy eyebrows and full mustaches. Then there is Alex, a wisp who appears to be swallowed up by his uniform. He looks like a boy playing dress-up in his father's clothes. He is by far the smallest boy on the team.

He wasn't lost among the big boys on the field, though. "Never intimidated me," Alex once said about playing against older boys. His reflexes and focus were superior to theirs, but it was his baseball intellect that astounded his coaches. Alex didn't realize it, but his father was with him as an echo: "Play the ball, don't let the ball play you."

Victor's voice was in Alex's subconscious, but it was Arteaga who honed his talent. He watched over him and supplied him with essentials as any father would: a new glove, an entry fee for a league, a bag of popcorn after a game. He never dropped off Alex at an empty house.

Lourdes was grateful. Her son was growing up grounded and thoughtful, and she must have noticed that there was still some Victor in him. Alex was a sweet talker and meticulous about his appearance. "When you look like a slob, generally, you get treated like a slob," Alex wrote in a 1998 children's book. "As you get older, you'll find people will respect you more if you're well dressed. It can open all kinds of doors for you."

There is a picture of Alex with his mom as they stand in the

living room the night of his junior high prom. Alex is dressed in
black pants and a white linen jacket with the kind of skinny red tie
Rick Springfield and Michael Jackson were wearing in videos on a
cable network called MTV.

Alex's right hand is stashed in his pants pocket in the style of
a child model. His mother is lovely, smiling in a lightly colored
silk shirt and matching skirt, with her right arm around Alex's
shoulder. Lourdes's red-painted nails are a perfect match to her
son's tie.

At age 14, Alex is still slender but not ungainly, even though
he is sprouting toward five-foot-ten at a rapid rate, cutting a lean
figure in his party best.

His casual grin suggested that he was fully aware of his charms
and his abilities.

He was already a star. He was able to dunk as a freshman at
Christopher Columbus Catholic High School, where he played before transferring to Westminster his sophomore year. "Actually he
came to Columbus to play basketball," says Brother Herb Baker,
the Columbus varsity baseball coach. "He was a very good basketball player. He had the quick feet, all right. And when he came
over to play baseball he was just a little . . . well, the bats were too
heavy for him. He was a good hitter, but everything went to right.
He couldn't get the bat around."

Sometimes Alex wondered if basketball would be the better
sport for him to pursue. Once, just before his sophomore year, he
told his family he hated baseball. He was burned out. He wanted
to quit. "I'm tired," he said as he fidgeted in a dining table chair,
surprising his mother. "It's no fun anymore." No one in the family could believe it. "He had a great basketball coach, and all he
wanted to do was play basketball," Susy recalls. "He said his future
was in basketball. That was a family crisis for two days."

Mr. Arteaga knew better than anyone—more than a mother
who was working two jobs, more than a sister who was in college

and a brother who had a full-time job already—how critical it was for Alex to keep playing baseball.

Baseball was a proven escape route to a better life in Miami during the late 1980s and early 1990s. The Boys & Girls Club in South Miami was famous for the quality of talent in its youth league baseball teams. The Cuban-born Rafael Palmeiro and Jose Canseco, who were already big leaguers, had grown up on its dirt fields just a half generation ahead of Alex. Canseco, in particular, elicited rock-star worship from the teens who marveled at his muscle and fame as the Oakland A's All-Star slugger. They also knew Canseco as the pied piper of a steroid revolution at a time before steroids were a dirty word. "It was a completely different time," says one former youth ballplayer in Miami. "Everything was so competitive."

There were recruiting battles among the powerhouse baseball schools that grew ugly at times, with finger-pointing between coaches over alleged payments and charges of player stealing.

Arteaga understood the intensity of Miami baseball—and its promise. He believed Alex had baseball stardom in his blood. He was the one who placed Alex on club teams with older players to sharpen his skills. He was the one who had the connections to help Alex prosper.

"Mr. Arteaga knew the movers and shakers of the baseball world; and we were relatively new to Miami," Susy recalls. "Mr. Arteaga told us baseball is where Alex's future is. He saw something in Alex that maybe I didn't see in my little brother. He begged us not to let Alex have one off season."

Alex resisted. He dug in, with hoop dreams in his head. The family had a meeting in their apartment. Seated around a table, they kept imploring Alex to take a deep breath, to think his decision through. Lourdes didn't want to push him, but Arteaga kept saying to her, "Your son is special." He kept telling Alex, "Baseball is your path."

"But I'm bored," Alex said. "I want something different. I love basketball."

Basketball was the hot sport among teens then. Every weekend, it was Magic vs. Bird on the TV in Alex's room. That could be him one day, he'd think, defying a defense with the kind of serpentine dunks Dr. J was throwing down for the 76ers. NBA players were the new TV stars. It was a fast-paced game on a hardwood stage—no dead time as there was in baseball.

"I think he liked the noise and the atmosphere," Susy says. "When you like the attention, well . . . I think he was born that way, and he knows how to handle himself. Then, when you get a taste of it, there are some personalities that handle that so well. That attention is basically food for your soul or mind."

Alex Rodriguez was—and will always be—an adulation junkie. "Some people are their own worst enemy when they get better, but not him," says Susy.

Nothing was decided over the family table that night, and the discussions continued for two more days. Finally, a deal was struck at Mr. Arteaga's urging: One more season, they told Alex, and if he still felt baseball was boring, he could quit.

Says Susy, "He never turned back after that."

Westminster Christian School looks more like an insurance office than a school, with its low-slung concrete exterior behind a circular drive and palm trees. It is secluded, on the southern outskirts of suburban Miami.

The ride to school took Alex about 30 minutes. He rode past affluence, past hedges surrounding sprawling homes with tiled roofs and swimming pools, past the swaying palms lining Coral Reef Drive as it passed Westminster on its way toward the yachts anchored in the marina two miles farther along. It was a world away from Alex's working-class neighborhood, where homes had barred windows. Some of his classmates drove BMWs. He drove a battered Mazda. "He had to break into the back window just to get in," says a former teammate, Steve Butler. Westminster was a difficult transition for Alex, who went there to play for coach Rich Hofman, the John Wooden of Florida high school baseball. All he did was win at a small, elite school with only 100 students in its senior class.

Did Alex feel as if he belonged there? He didn't know, but he desperately wanted to. He liked his surroundings.

Tuition wasn't cheap. The $5,000 yearly fee was too much for the Rodriguez family. There would be allegations that recruiting rules had been broken when Alex attended Westminster. His family received some financial aid, but school board administrators were never clear about who was paying the rest. No improprieties were ever proved. Alex was on his way, set to play for a national powerhouse in 1991 under Hofman.

"At first blush, Alex didn't stand out because when he first started with us he was like six foot, 165 pounds," recalls Hofman. "He came into a program that was one of the best in the country, so there were other good players around him. He probably wasn't the best player on our team his sophomore year, but he certainly had all the indications that he was going to be a terrific ballplayer."

Baseball dominated Alex's life at Westminster. "I'd leave the house at six-thirty a.m. and wouldn't get home until eight p.m.," he recalled. He'd leave his house each morning with $20 in his pocket for breakfast, lunch and, sometimes, dinner. "I didn't realize until later how Mom sacrificed her needs to give me that money every day," Alex said.

Most of his friends at Westminster came from far wealthier families. Doug Mientkiewicz, who would become his teammate with the Yankees 15 years later, was one of them.

The Mientkiewiczs' home was just a mile from the campus. "It took twenty-two seconds to get from my house to school . . . if you caught the light," Mientkiewicz says. It wasn't the biggest house on the block, but it must have seemed like a palace to Alex. The ranch-style house in a peach shade of stucco was perched on a corner lot with a vast lawn, a circular drive, and the must-have for every fine Florida home: a sparkling swimming pool. But there was one more amenity that lit up Alex, lit up the whole baseball team for that matter: The Mientkiewicz family had built a batting cage off the back porch. "It was a clubhouse," Alex has joked. Doug's mother became very skilled at cooking for many mouths, because half the baseball team often ended up at her dining room table. "We killed everything," Alex said. "[His parents] probably had to get an extra job to support us."

Alex was growing into his body, shooting past six feet by age 15. He was sprouting out of his clothes, which made Doug's closet a good place to look for new ones. "I used take all of his clothes," Alex remembered. "[I wore] T-shirts and shorts. . . . He was rich, and I was poor."

He was growing into the identity of a kid struggling against the odds. It fueled him, and at a school with manicured grounds extending into the woods, where the baseball field was cut out of the groves of scrub oaks and palms, he was confronted with what he didn't have every day. Behind the left field wall, there was an Olympic-sized pool and two tennis courts—tantalizing targets for home-run hitters. The football field lay just beyond.

With his basketball jones behind him, Alex focused on base-ball, earning the starting shortstop position as a sophomore. But he also loved football. He was a quarterback with a limber arm, and football was big in Miami. This is where the Gino Torretta legend was born. Alex, J.D. and Doug often attended University of Miami games to watch Torretta play quarterback, checking out the Hurri-canes' potent offense in an era when the team was a perennial con-tender for the national championship, and Alex became immersed in Hurricanes lore. Alex was a great passer at Westminster—he set school records and made the papers as an All-State selection—but his most enduring memory of Westminster football was a tragic one.

The team was in the locker room at halftime his sophomore season when a parent flung open the door and said, "A man collapsed in the stands." There was confusion, and then someone said, "It's Mr. Arteaga." J.D. ran out the door to find his father, and Alex darted after him. Inside a patch of gathering people, they discovered paramedics standing over Mr. Arteaga, checking his vital signs. He was still breathing, but his chest was rising and falling erratically. He was laboring. His heart was failing. A few minutes later, a helicopter landed on the field and Mr. Arteaga was airlifted to a hospital with everyone else on their way by car to be by his side.

Alex didn't go. He couldn't bear to feel the pain, to see Mr. Arteaga in distress, to see J.D. agonizing over his father.

A day later, Mr. Arteaga died. "I felt someone had torn my heart out and smashed it," Alex recalled. "At the time, I couldn't say good-bye. I lost a father for the second time. I know Mr. Arteaga and his family have forgiven me for not showing up at the hospital. I'm not sure I've forgiven myself."

The Westminster baseball jersey was trimmed in the deep green of infield grass. It billowed on Alex's slender frame during his sophomore season. He had enough arm to start at shortstop but was a self-professed weakling at 15, once admitting that he could "barely bench-press a hundred pounds" in a season he finished with a .256 average. Shortly after the last game that season, Hofman challenged Alex to get stronger, to hit the weight room.

"Well, tenth grade you had an okay year," Hofman told him. "Next year everyone will get to know you, and in twelfth grade you'll be the number one pick in the country. Work hard this year."

The vote of confidence was exhilarating for Alex . . . and scary as hell. The number one pick in the country?

"He raised the stakes," Alex said of Hofman. "I felt I couldn't let him down."

The pressure of expectations may have tended to make Alex cut corners when no shortcuts were necessary. Former classmates say he asked them how to cheat on tests.

One former teacher of Alex's at Westminster points out, "He was a flat character, one-dimensional." Alex didn't join social clubs and he wasn't active in anything but sports. The teacher says it didn't seem as if Alex had grown up with storytelling in his life to enrich his imagination. In some ways, this explains why Alex would, as an adult, react to situations without understanding the arc of a story, how it has a beginning, middle and an end. He would often fabricate scenes and events without understanding that embellishment had repercussions.

Alex was an honor roll student at Westminster, but his insecurity got the best of him when he thought about the Plan B alternate to the MLB draft: a college scholarship. He didn't want just a good score on entry exams but a great score to open as many options as possible. A former Westminster student says Alex offered him $50 to take the SAT for him. The student believed he was serious and declined the payout.

Alex was smart enough and talented enough, but he didn't always trust himself.

To fall short would be to fail. No one clamored for failures. No one lined up to see failures play. And failing to reach number one might mean losing yet another father figure in Hofman.

At Westminster, Hofman was successful—with six state titles as proof—but he was also a polarizing figure. The faculty enjoyed the higher profile that baseball success brought the small private school. They were A Little Team That Could with only 300 students in the high school, one highlighted in *USA Today* as state champions and national champions. But some educators worried about the fiefdom Hofman had created in his 25 years as head coach. One year after a big victory for the team, he was seen in front of the school lowering the American flag and the school's Christian flag and then raising the team flag above all else. This was blasphemy to some faculty, who worked at a school where one slogan read, "Jesus is the reason for the season."

Westminster was holier than thou to some rivals and the object of envy to others. Opposing schools coveted its facilities, titles and national status. But some coaches wondered if Hofman was assembling his powerhouse in good faith. "He started talking to my players during the game, to bring them over [to Westminster]," says Brother Herb Baker.

Hofman filled his rosters with eye-catching size for a tiny school. His lineups looked more minor league than prep level to opponents. "We used to play them regularly, and his kids were always much bigger than our kids," Baker says. "And that's what I didn't understand."

In the early 1990s, few teams had the size advantage Westminster boasted. Soon enough, Alex would fit right in after undergoing a before-and-after-worthy body makeover.

Hofman would drift by the school's weight room and hear the barbells ringing like wind chimes. One single student was in there huffing and blowing out through lifts. It was Alex. "He had grown so much, the scouts didn't recognize him," Hofman says. "They were stunned."

The spindly Alex had morphed into a diamond-cut man-child. He had put on 25 pounds of muscle between his sophomore and junior year. He wasn't massive, but he was lean and strong. His shoulders were broad, his legs were thick and his biceps looked defined even when he wasn't flexing. His strength went off the charts. He benched 310 pounds and could hit a ball 400 feet. "Today, I probably bench-press 240 or 250," says Alex now. "I did it because

I played football, quarterback, and the big challenge was that if you could [bench press 300 pounds], you would get a letter jacket with white sleeves. I was poor. I thought, 'What a great way to get a free jacket.'"

Alex didn't explain *how* he had managed to gain entrée into the hulking "white-sleeves" crew. He didn't have a personal trainer. He didn't have a high-performance program to follow. How did he get so big and strong so fast over three to four months? In February 2009, he would call any allegations about his steroid use at Westminster "baloney."

"That's an automatic red flag," says Fernando Montes, a longtime strength and condition trainer on the college and major-league level who worked with Alex in the pros. "It's so out of the ordinary. It's not physically possible without some type of steroid enhancement."

Vitamin shops in the malls were stocked with steroid-tainted substances that would later be banned by MLB. Steroids were not the raging symbol of cheating in the early 1990s that they are today, but even in 1992 they were illegal. Drugs such as Dianabol and Winstrol were added to the list of controlled substances in 1990 with the Anabolic Steroid Control Act. They still remained easier to purchase than pot.

In the Miami area during the 1980s and '90s, there was a steroids source known by some in the baseball community: dog-kennel owner Steve Caruso. He raced greyhounds, coached baseball and was "kind of just always around," says Mike Lopez, a former youth player who knew Caruso in the 1990s. "I remember him being real competitive."

A former business associate, Steve Ludt, says Caruso used to buy steroids for his kennel operation through local animal hospitals. "He could buy it cheap," says Ludt, who worked with Caruso in the kennel business. "He could get a 1,000-count of testosterone tablets for around $70."

Caruso didn't always use his steroid supply for medical purposes with his dogs. He was known to juice his greyhounds at the racetrack, Ludt says, and was admonished for it by racing officials. Caruso's access to steroids made him popular with friends. He apparently didn't sell steroids, but he did allow his men's league softball teammates to dip into his stash.

Some players popped testosterone and Winstrol tablets, says a former teammate of Caruso's. "Everyone was using it back then," says the source. "I was."

Baseball sources in Miami believe Caruso also gave steroids to up-and-coming ballplayers—including Alex Rodriguez. "They knew each other, for sure," says Ludt. "I was at Caruso's house one night when Alex called. He offered to fly Caruso up to Seattle for his first pro game. Alex was going to pay for the plane ticket and everything."

(Caruso has since left the dog-kennel business but still lives in Florida. He remains silent about his ties to Alex. Caruso did not respond to repeated messages left for him at his home and through his lawyer.)

A former Westminster player says Alex used steroids in high school and that Coach Hofman knew about it. Another Westminster graduate says Hofman's son, David, who played on the football team with Alex, told him that he witnessed Alex's use of steroids.

Rich Hofman says he is surprised by these accounts and denies any knowledge of Alex's steroid use in high school. "Whatever he was doing, he was doing it somewhere else," he says. His son, David Hofman, did not respond to messages asking for his recollections.

"I know Rich real well," says Joe Arriola, a former public servant in Miami who coached youth baseball and advised Alex's family. "Rich was a good guy. He really cared about the kids. Did he go by the book? Probably not. He probably recruited or had people recruit, but that's a long way from [allowing] Alex drugs."

Alex wasn't the only teen ballplayer in South Miami said to be on performance enhancers. Dozens more just like him were becoming the first generation of ballplayers to begin their careers during baseball's steroid era. He was one of the firstborn of the Canseco program.

Chapter Three

THE NUMBER ONE HIT

THE EARLY 1990S—ALEX RODRIGUEZ'S high school years—
were a pop-cultural celebration of the outsized. In 1991, Arnold
Schwarzenegger flexed his way through the box-office hit *Termi-
nator 2: Judgment Day*, fries were becoming supersized and SUVs
began hogging the highways. One half of the Oakland Athletics'
burly Bash Brothers—the muscular Jose Canseco—would regularly drive to the Boys & Girls Clubs of Miami to say hello from
the front seat of his red Jaguar during the off-season.

Alex was immersed in a culture of physical distortion and exaggeration. Though chemistry could enhance Alex, it didn't create
him. His skills and coordination separated him from peers who
were taking performance-enhancing substances. Until his junior
year in 1992, Alex's reputation had been that of a slick fielder with
good range, a sure glove and a quick release, flicking his wrist like
a lion tamer.

Now he was an uncommon teen focused on a mission to make himself a great baseball player. By reading workout magazines, he learned to cut out Big Macs and fries and eat healthfully. "We took his coach and him out to eat," says Roger Jongewaard, the former head of the Mariners scouting department. "He was very careful with his diet. He'd just eat chicken and vegetables."

All of those muscle powder mixes and supplements—many of which are banned by Major League Baseball now—favored by Alex didn't create his diligence. It just added to his distance.

"Hit it in the pool!" fans would shout whenever Alex came to the plate during home games. "There was a swimming pool in left field," Jongewaard recalls. "I said to his coach, 'I bet he has hit some in the pool,' and he said, 'Actually, he's never hit a ball in the pool; he hits them over the pool.'"

Alex was one of the few high school players in the nation who could drive a ball more than 400 feet. The added muscle alone did not account for his newfound power. His pitch selection, which he had worked on with Hofman through the off-season, gave him an edge. "He had only hit [.256] as a sophomore," recalls Hofman. "So he worked on his swing. I talked him into not hitting pitcher's pitches but looking for his pitch to hit. And then it seemed like he hit a home run almost every game that summer."

Hofman became Alex's protector, the new male voice in the teen's head. "I think he confided in me a little more [that year]," Hofman said. He was the one who handled the scouts and media requests that began piling up during Alex's junior year. "You always hear that something is wrong with a player from scouts," Hofman recalled, "but never, not once, did I hear a scout say something negative about Alex."

Suddenly, no one could throw a fastball past him. He was gaining a reputation, hit by hit, as the complete package. He was a national star, often mentioned in major publications. Soon, pitchers were perversely challenging him, craving an Alex Rodriguez strikeout as a personal trophy. "When pitchers pitched to him, scouts told me that most of them amped it up about four to five miles per hour more than they did for the next batter," Hofman says. "There was a personal vendetta to get him out. He didn't have an easy road."

He more than merited the attention of major-league scouts during his junior year, when he earned All-American honors by batting .477, with 52 runs scored, 42 stolen bases and 6 home runs. Scouts who were nosing around Westminster would usually find Alex in the weight room—usually alone. They would see him take extra fielding reps and linger in the batting cage long after everyone else had stopped hitting. "I think his work ethic was something special," Hofman says.

The scouts swarmed the Westminster team—ranked number one in the country by *USA Today* in 1992, with a national championship banner—with as many as 100 scouts watching its tournament games.

Alex handled the attention, the scrutiny and the adulation well. He acted, spoke and thought like an old soul. He knew what people wanted to hear. "He was almost always like a grown man," Hofman says. "He seemed to understand the whole process and his destiny."

Hofman says he told Alex: You'll be in the big leagues soon; you'll be in the Hall of Fame before it's over.

In late August 1992, regular TV programming was interrupted throughout south Florida by the sight of Doppler radar screens showing an ominous orange mass twice the size of the state churning toward the coastline. Hurricane Andrew, feeding on the warm waters off the talcum-powder beaches of Miami, was heading for landfall. On August 23, a Sunday extra edition in the *Miami Herald* called Andrew the "hurricane of our nightmares."

The paper warned of 20-foot waves and winds powerful enough to flip buses over. Residents who didn't heed the bullhorn warnings to evacuate rushed to supermarkets for Spam, tuna and pinto beans—anything that could be served by can opener—and cleaned out ATMs.

Alex Rodriguez was far removed from this disaster, playing at a world youth baseball championship in Monterrey, Mexico—and playing well; he was the best player on the U.S. team. "He was the star shortstop on a pretty darn good team," says Fernando Arguelles, a Mariners scout who would soon be the team's coordinator of scouting throughout Latin America. "I think all those kids got drafted, and he was their three-hole hitter and shortstop. And he was playing against some of the better seventeen-year-olds in the world. That's when I first thought, This kid's got a chance to be a big-time player. He was hittin' balls out all over the field. He was putting on a show in batting practice, and we were thinking, This guy could be the next Cal Ripken, Jr. He was a man as a child."

Alex was playing out of his mind, but he was burdened with worry about the safety of his family. He had no idea where they were when Andrew hit with 145-mph winds. There were 65 deaths as stucco homes were lifted from their foundations and tossed like tumbleweeds. More than 250,000 people in Miami–Dade County were left homeless. There were mad scrambles for food and water as desperate residents filtered water in the street through cloth rags.

Alex had no way to reach his mother or Susy. "I frantically called home," he said. "I couldn't get through for three agonizing days." Finally, he made a connection and was told they were okay. His home had been beaten up by flying debris; trees were down and phone lines were lying in the streets of Kendall, but his family had hunkered down and ridden out the storm several miles away from the blast zone.

Westminster's campus was a devastation scene after Andrew. Windows were blown out, and there was structural damage to almost every building and wall. When Alex got back to Miami, he learned that there was $3 million in damage to the school, including $100,000 to the baseball field. That meant his senior season was in jeopardy. Would the school be ready when classes were scheduled to start in just a month? Would they have to cancel the baseball season? Alex knew that a season undercut by an abbreviated baseball schedule could hurt his draft status.

An angel in a hard hat materialized just in time: A local contractor donated his services to repair the ball field. Just weeks before the start of the season, a ballpark was unveiled with new dugouts, backstops and bleachers. They would need those bleachers to accommodate all the scouts coming to scrutinize every move Alex made on the baseball diamond.

Years later, Alex would fluff up his high school legend by telling this tidbit about how meticulously he had prepared for the pros: "I decided to use a wood bat in high school instead of the more powerful aluminum so I'd be ready for pro baseball," he said. Yet in game photos from his high school years, he is swinging an aluminum bat. The opening sentence of an article from 1993 in *Sports Illustrated* reads, "As the ball left Alex Rodriguez's aluminum bat . . ."

He didn't need the exaggeration. As far as the scouts and baseball writers were concerned, Alex Rodriguez was a demigod at age 17.

Alex knew what was coming as far as attention from the media and the scouts. As his senior year approached, he asked his sister for help. "At the end of his junior year Alex said, 'Susy, I'm really going to need you next year,'" she recalls. "He said 'It's going to get really crazy. I need you at most of my games. They're going to want to talk to me, but I can't talk to them.' When he said 'crazy,' I thought it would be just a couple of people here or there. I came from a family that just watches baseball." She could not imagine the frenzy that lay ahead for her family.

Alex, though, was ready for the press. He welcomed their attention, their inspection, and their affection. In fact, he craved it and did his best to please writers from the *Miami Herald*, the *Los Angeles Times* and even *Sports Illustrated*.

The pamphlets, packets and questionnaires from major-league teams hit coach Rich Hofman's mailbox almost daily during Alex's senior year. "At his first home game of the season, there were at least ninety scouts or agents or representatives in the stands," Susy says. "People had those machines—radar guns—and stopwatches out every time Alex ran. Some were scouts, some were agents. At that time I didn't know the difference. They were all sitting right behind the fence, and I remember thinking, They're not letting me see my brother play! Can't they sit the way the rest of us sit?"

Susy could see enough of Alex on the field that day to know he went three for four with a home run. Seventy-two scouts showed up for his second game. "Newspaper headlines called me Superman," Alex once recalled of his high school days. "It was a crazy time. Everyone wanted a piece of me."

Who was looking out for him? His mother cared deeply about Alex's welfare, but she was working two jobs. His siblings—Susy and Joe—were there, but they were also trying to establish themselves after college.

Alex relied on a circle of adults, from Eddie Rodriguez (no relation) at the Miami Boys & Girls Club on Southwest 32nd Avenue to an array of youth coaches, from mentors such as Jose Canseco to agents trying to woo him. His natural impressionability as a teen was heightened by the fact that he had no father standing sentry between him and the many adults who saw a payday in Alex. He was about to make millions. That was clear.

Alex played to the media craving for a player who was fresh and grounded despite the crush of attention. As Ed Giuliotti wrote in the Fort Lauderdale *Sun-Sentinel*, "Alex Rodriguez, the object of their desire, smiled, called scouts by their first names and teased many." He carried himself with modesty and an air of innocence, often telling reporters how lucky he was to have played in the United States instead of the D.R., where the poverty means no leather gloves or green fields.

The media were enamored of his charisma and awestruck by his numbers. He hit .505 with nine home runs, 14 doubles, 6 triples and 35 stolen bases in 35 attempts over 33 games during his senior year at Westminster. The stats ensured that he was all but a lock to go number one in the June draft. Detroit Tigers scout Steve Souchoki said, "He's got instincts you can't teach. I wish we had a lot of players in our area like him. It would make our job easier, that's for sure." A top college baseball coach, Cal State Fullerton's Augie Garrido, said at the time, "If you were to sit down in front of a computer and say, 'How would I construct the perfect shortstop?,' you'd put all the data in and then you would see Alex Rodriguez."

Covering all his bases, Alex had signed a letter of intent to play for the Miami Hurricanes before his senior season, but nobody expected him to walk away from the big money that would come to the number one pick. Every agent worth his Rolex wanted a chance to land Alex. They came with presents and slick talk. "Alex knew not to break the NCAA rules," Susy says.

They arrived with pitches and promises. "We interviewed the top four agents," Susy says.

The list was then cut to two: Ron Shapiro and Scott Boras. They could not have been more different. Boras was a rumpled, hard-core negotiator, relentless in squeezing the last penny out of owners even if it meant fabricating rival offers from phantom teams. He would later be depicted by the media as the man who had ruined baseball by driving salaries beyond the reach of small-market teams.

Almost always dressed in a tie, Shapiro was a Harvard law school graduate with a reputation for nurturing his clients. He cared about their happiness and always factored in emotional well-

being when signing his stars to lucrative deals. He was the agent for
Cal Ripken, Jr., and he seemed to be the favorite of the Rodriguez
family.

Shapiro realized that Alex was malleable, vulnerable. "To me
it looked like a particularly appealing situation because not only
would Alex benefit from some representation but maybe having
someone guide him and help shape some of the values that he
would have," Shapiro says. "One of the things I feared for Alex
early on—and I told this to my partner Michael Maas and later
shared it with Cal Ripken—was that while he had this tremendous
talent, he might be persuaded to take steps that might not build on
the happiness quotient for him, on the satisfaction quotient."

One adviser Alex leaned on when making the decision between Boras and Shapiro was a family friend who was a fixture in
the Miami community as a businessman and public official. Joe
Arriola had been a youth-league coach of Alex and was the uncle of
major leaguer Alex Fernandez, a client of Boras. "Alex's first choice
was Shapiro," Arriola recalls. "And I told him, 'Look, I know Scott
pretty well, and maybe you should talk.' And that's how Scott got
the client."

Boras didn't come to Alex bearing gifts. One agent had taken
Alex to Hooters, where he tried to entice the young star with an
equipment bag full of goodies: balls, bats and gloves. It was insult-
ing to Alex. Boras promised a more cunning inducement: a job at
his agency for Susy. "Boras got to her," says Hofman. "That's really
the key."

Seattle Mariners scout Roger Jongewaard had devoured all the video
of Alex and had no doubt he was seeing something special. He'd
sold his impressions to the highest levels of the organization. "We
knew what Roger believed, and he was very convincing," recalls
Woody Woodward, the general manager of the Mariners in the

1990s. "We knew Alex had potential to be unlike anything we'd seen before." Jongewaard's scouting report from May 10, 1993, makes that clear. Under PHYSICAL MATURITY, he wrote: "Similar to Jeter only bigger and better." Under PLAYER STRENGTHS: "Better at 17 now than all the superstars in baseball were when they were seniors in H.S." Under PLAYER WEAKNESSES: "Tends to jump at the ball." Under ADDITIONAL COMMENTS: "Generates a special feeling when watching him play. Premium prospect with potential to be an impact player. . . . [Darren] Dreifort would be good pick but Rodriguez is better!"

Rodriguez had already stated his interest in joining the Mariners as the number one pick, but Boras was at work well behind the scenes, advising the family from afar. He couldn't be directly involved because that would jeopardize Alex's amateur status—and eliminate the threat that he might play for Miami rather than go pro. After being coached by Boras, Alex called Jongewaard at his Seattle office on the morning before the draft. With his assistant in the office and the phone on speaker, Jongewaard heard Alex speaking in a way he never recalled before. His voice sounded odd, weirdly rushed. "It was like he was reading from a piece of paper," Jongewaard recalls.

"Roger," Alex told Jongewaard. "Please don't draft me. I want to go to a National League team, and Seattle is too far away, and I don't want you guys to draft me."

"Alex," Jongewaard said, "it's too late. We already have your number and we plan on drafting you."

"Uh," Alex said, having to put his script down and improvise. "Bye."

Jongewaard wasn't stunned by the bizarre conversation. Alex wasn't the endearing kid from Kendall in that moment but something manufactured. "I figured it was probably a Boras thing, where they would try to get him to a bigger-market team," Jongewaard says. "So I was somewhat expecting that."

He was right. Boras had begun his famous game of cat and mouse with teams vying for his clients. He was an expert at creating divisiveness from unity, at gaining emotional separation from club and player so he could work the cold numbers of a contract. Boras capitalized on Alex's need for someone—particularly a male figure close to him—to define his identity for him. Boras liked to grind teams up for every dollar, so Alex was sure to be a holdout.

The Mariners knew what they were up against but made the call, anyway. A few minutes into the 1993 draft, around 1 p.m., the phone at the Arteaga home rang. This was where Alex wanted to be on draft day: where his memories of Mr. Arteaga were fresh, where his best friend J.D. lived, where his family could surround him . . . and with local TV cameras on hand to record it all. There were more than a hundred people packed into the family room and kitchen. It was a festive atmosphere with cupcakes on the table and a family cruise to the Bahamas planned for later that week. Alex had gone on a shopping binge with his mother. "We bought $1,000 worth of suits," Alex told the Fort Lauderdale *Sun-Sentinel*.

Where had Alex gotten that kind of money? Or had he just fudged the number? Anything was possible with Alex. On draft day, he wore a denim button-down shirt with a cartoon-colored tie decorated with baseball card images that read STRIKE and HOME RUN. All week, Alex had been flooded with inquiries about whether he would feel pressure to do too much as the probable number one pick. "I know I'll be able to handle it, because I keep attacking people," he said. "I think I'm the best. If they think I'm the best, I'll go and take it to them early. Then they're mentally whipped."

The phone in the Arteaga house rang again. The crowd let it ring twice. It was Jongewaard on the line, delivering the news that Alex Rodriguez was the number one pick. Inside, he'd wanted this despite his ramblings about the National League and the distance to Seattle. Numbers would always form Alex's identity. In effect, he liked being a number—as long as it was number one. Top salary, best stats, highest draft pick.

There was an explosion of cheers and then relief as everyone drifted toward the cupcakes after the call from Seattle. Later that day, there was another phone call. It was Victor. "I wanted to tell him I was so proud of him," Victor says. "He was busy, I know."

Lourdes was angry that Victor had called. " 'It was *my* special day,' my mom thought," Alex said in 1996. "He had no right to be a part of it."

Alex didn't want to look back. He didn't want his excitement clouded by the most injurious loss of his life. He only wanted to look ahead.

Chapter Four

LIKE A VIRGIN CLIENT

THE ABANDONED BOY WITHIN Alex Rodriguez made him particularly gullible to the influence of successful, authoritative men, so it was easy for Scott Boras to manipulate him like a sock puppet. The bigger challenge for Boras was that of orchestrating Alex's negotiations with the Seattle Mariners from behind the curtain, out of sight.

Alex said whatever Boras told him to say during the summer of 1993, even though Boras wasn't—officially—his agent. That public role went to Alex's mother, Lourdes, and his half sister, Susy, in a cynical ruse to conform to NCAA rules so the number one draft pick could maintain his college eligibility, a bargaining chip Boras cherished.

Boras represented many of the top players in baseball, and he had a reputation for keeping prized amateurs off the market to maximize his leverage in negotiations. "Trust me," he would tell them, "I know what's best for you." Alex was an ideal client in that regard. He performed on cue, sounding hypnotized when speaking to reporters the afternoon the Mariners called J. D. Arteaga's house to tell Alex he was officially their man. He had rehearsed his message to the club in the bathroom mirror six times. As the thrill of being the top pick dissipated, he fired a warning shot at the Mariners through the media.

"Right now, I'm going to the University of Miami, and every day I'm unsigned means I'm closer to going to college," Alex told reporters. "But if circumstances are right, I wouldn't mind going pro."

The latter part of that statement was an ad lib. Alex was nervous and longing to sign because, despite his enviable position as the top pick, he didn't want his mother to work as a waitress anymore; he didn't want to risk injury; he didn't want to destroy his family's dreams of wealth and comfort. But Boras played on the flip side of Alex's insecurities, telling him the Mariners were lowballing him, that it was a bargain-hunting organization that didn't deserve his special talents. He told Alex he had a chance to make history for the kind of money a top pick could command. He told Alex he deserved to be paid more for his extraordinary gifts. He told Alex what the insecure teen wanted to hear.

"Boras was messing with his head," says a Rodriguez family friend. "Alex didn't know what hit him, but all he'd heard from everyone was 'Boras is the best.' He'd seen his picture in a magazine."

Boras was accustomed to being bad-mouthed by GMs, other agents, and even family members of his clients. "The greedy agent," he once said mockingly of his reputation. "When you bring a player to a team, they don't reward you for it—the team recruited him. But if you take a player, the team didn't lose him—the agent took him away. For money. Everything is about money; nothing is about anything you do to accentuate the performance of the player. None of that is ever talked about. It's money. It's contract. It's not talent assessment. It's not doing things that help the player—his career, his life, his family. It's money. I used to fight that battle early on. I stopped. I go into a city now, and I say, 'Okay, where's my horns?'"

Boras relished his blackhat reputation, and Alex admired his fire, his taste for confrontation, in part because those were qualities Alex knew *he* didn't possess. Despite that, Alex spent the summer of 1993 in anguish, tormented by an internal tug-of-war between the security he sought for his family and the disrespect Boras had convinced him the Mariners were showing him. Ron Shapiro, the agent who had nearly landed Rodriguez, thinks Alex might have made a bit less money in his career but been much happier. "This is strictly my reflection, but as I've watched his career progress he has fulfilled everything I thought he would as one of the great players to play this game, but I think he's gotten sidetracked along the way by the lights," Shapiro says. "I hope he ends up a happy person, but I sometimes fear that may elude him."

Boras hardly fit the suave image that usually appealed to Alex. He had mousy hair and short, thick fingers that made opposing parties feel as if they were gripping a ham when they shook his hand. Often dressed in jeans, he would come to meetings carrying a weathered leather satchel that looked as if it had been found un-der the desk in a lit professor's office. It had ferried the paperwork for dozens of megadeals over the years, and the handle had been replaced repeatedly. "I'm close to that leather," Boras once said.

He didn't introduce his clients to Hollywood stars or seduce them with invitations to music industry award shows. He was all about bottom lines, driven by a philosophy that dictated elimi-nating frills because they would diminish his persona as a bare-knuckled deal maker. Boras once boasted to *Sports Illustrated*, "I don't cater to clients."

Instead, he massaged their self-esteem by pumping them up with grandiose evaluations of their worth. Bigger-than-life images always appealed to Alex. Boras was a master architect when it came to building myths. "He knew how to play to his client," Woodward recalls. "He was an expert at knowing what strings to pull." At times, Boras sounded like a proud father psyching his child up for the biggest game of his life—*Nobody can beat you; nobody's better*—in a voice that resonated deep within Alex. "His father had left the family," Jongewaard recalls. "His dad was an ex-player, so . . ."

Boras liked to remind his clients that, unlike his rival agents who'd been born in office swivel chairs, he too had played professional baseball. He used this line on his résumé to goad the competitive egos of his clients. For him, negotiations were about winning, hardball style. Other agents brokered conciliatory contracts to keep their clients in the good graces of management. Boras bragged that he broke teams' backs. "My identity should reside in my players' wallets," he said. Some organizations had been so stung by Boras that they steered clear of draft picks represented by him.

"We were familiar with Scott Boras," Jongewaard says. "But we really felt Alex was worth whatever we had to go through."

Boras was directing Alex's campaign against the Mariners, but Lourdes's signature was on the endless stream of faxed contract negotiations between her son and the Mariners. It was Boras who, through Lourdes, set the early parameters for Alex's contract demands: $2.5 million over three years; a guaranteed quick ascent through the farm system; a major-league contract. And a key requirement: while negotiating, no one from the Mariners was to contact Alex personally. Ever. For any reason.

This was a classic Boras ploy. He knew that detachment removed emotion from the process. This meant avoiding face-to-face meetings, where eyes could be studied, souls could be searched, minds could be read, the price could be whittled down, in this case by Alex's desire to please. Boras would have none of it. "Scott tries to divide you away from the client," Jongewaard says. "He wants control from the client and to portray us as really bad guys. And that way, any personal ties are eliminated. There's nothing personal about it anymore."

Alex and his family took these rules of separation seriously. The Mariners called Alex's home 50 to 60 times in the first five days after the draft, but not one call was returned. A week later, Jongewaard and team representatives from the Mariners flew to Miami and knocked on Alex's front door. They were not greeted warmly, but they were allowed to step inside, where they presented their opening offer: $1 million over three years. They said that was about $20,000 more than what the college All-American Jeffrey Hammonds had signed for a year earlier as the fourth pick of Baltimore.

Lourdes cut Jongewaard off before he could explain more about the offer, which was a major-league deal, as the family had requested, and included the September call-up to the majors they had demanded. Lourdes put her hand up as if to stop traffic. "It was kind of like 'Get out, you're wasting our time,'" Jongewaard recalls. "We said, 'This is a great offer that nobody else has ever had.' But Scott wanted to be a pioneer with this guy."

•　　•　　•

The tractor bumping along the furrowed fields of the farm in California's fertile Central Valley was equipped with a single amenity for the teenager behind the wheel: a radio. On most days, Scott Boras had it tuned to KSFO, dialing in the crackle of a San Francisco Giants game as he worked among the dairy cattle grazing on land with soil rich enough to grow alfalfa.

He was reared in a family of farmers just south of Sacramento and could have easily left that life by virtue of his academic achievements, not to mention his skills as a high school center fielder. The

Ivy League schools wanted him after his senior season in 1970, but Boras took a scholarship to play for the University of the Pacific, located outside San Francisco. He had a disciplined eye at the plate and a knack for blistering liners into the gaps. He was a student of baseball—of its in-game nuances and strategic odds—but his mind demanded more fodder than the calculation of RBIs and ERAs. He was into Hg and Zn, too, applying his curiosity about life toward a major in chemistry.

He was the lone ballplayer in his Calculus III class, and in a nod to the demands of his baseball schedule, the faculty at Pacific allowed him to take lab exams privately from 9 p.m. to midnight. "I was the first athlete to ever have, like, a premed type situation [there]," Boras once told *The New Yorker*. By his sophomore year, in concurrence with his undergraduate coursework, he had begun pursuing a degree in industrial pharmacology.

He signed with the St. Louis Cardinals as a free agent in 1974 and got an $8,000 bonus. "You think it's the greatest privilege in the world, because now you don't have to go work on the farm anymore," he said about signing a professional baseball contract. "You get that check the first week, and you can't believe anyone's paying you to play."

After surviving a round of spring training cuts one year, Boras saw 50 of the vanquished gathered in the parking lot, left with nothing in their pockets but the dregs of their per diem. They were just kids, many with barely a high school diploma, and suddenly it was over. "It was stunning to me," Boras said. "I saw number one draft picks who had rusted-out vans. There were wives crying and players with kids. I saw the other side out there, the ending of careers. I mean, in college baseball, you had cuts, but you still stayed around the school. This was, for these guys, just the end of the road."

He quickly came to see the business of baseball as a brutal model of social inequity in the marketplace.

He still loved the game, of course. Although he often hid his physics texts beneath men's magazines as he worked on his degrees during his downtime, Boras played until his knees betrayed him. At age 26, after a four-year stint in the minor leagues, he left the game to return to school. He finished up a PharmD in industrial pharmaceuticals, and briefly, before he went to law school, he worked as a pharmacist in a Sacramento hospital.

"Scott was an excellent pharmacist, and he and I would frequently discuss med management and drug interactions of patients going into surgery," says Burton Goldstein, an anesthesiologist who worked with Boras. "We would engage in conversations, and I really enjoyed talking to him about that because he was a very knowledgeable pharmacist. He really knew his drugs."

Boras went off to law school. After passing the bar, he spent five years defending drug companies against product liability claims, although that seemed paradoxical, given the zeal for class warfare stoked by his stint in the minors.

He soothed his social conscience by moonlighting for ballplayers in need of legal advice. He struck his first major score when an old minor-league teammate, reliever Bill Caudill, hired him to handle his contract negotiations with the Toronto Blue Jays in 1985. Eight minutes before a scheduled salary arbitration hearing, the unruffled Boras, who neither cursed nor yelled to make his long-winded points with management, landed Caudill a five-year, $7.5 million contract.

A note about the signing landed Boras's name in *Sports Illustrated*. When his Chicago law firm forced him to choose between defending corporate America and representing ballplayers, Boras sided with his inner vigilante. "I enjoyed working for people instead of big companies," he said. "It's like you're working for David against Goliath."

He enjoyed making masters of the universe squirm. In this respect, Boras was the soul mate of Gene Orza, the associate general counsel for the Major League Baseball Players Association. Orza was an almost maniacal civil libertarian who defended players even when they seemed indefensible. It didn't matter how many times pitcher Steve Howe was cited for drug and alcohol abuse—which led to seven suspensions during a career that spanned from 1980 to 1996—Orza was unflinching in his fight to keep the troubled player in baseball. Like Boras, Orza loved a good war. Like Orza, Boras adored the game.

It was the owners neither man had use for. When Boras chose to get back into baseball, he decided to get back at baseball. "It's that chip on his shoulder that he still wants everyone in baseball to pay for," says one major-league general manager. "His client becomes secondary to his anger against the baseball gods. It's always about Scott."

And the contract is his scorecard.

Alex protected himself against a long summer of negotiations by buying an insurance policy with Lloyd's of London that would cover him if he suffered a career-ending injury. In June, he was working out for Team USA in Tennessee when Fernando Arguelles, the Seattle scout who had known Alex for two years, started talking with other baseball officials on the practice field. Alex walked up and joined the conversation. Arguelles did not mention a word about Alex's contract, but word filtered back to Boras that he had spoken to his client.

On June 22, Alex unleashed a rant against the Mariners organization that had been dictated by Boras. "They're low class," Alex told reporters. "They disrespected my mom. We told them not to contact us in any way, and they contacted me. Right now, I'm very upset with them. I'm 17, and they're going beyond the limits. I'm in no need of money. And it's not that the minor-league life is so great, anyway."

Boras liked to turn his clients against a team even if it meant that he had to cook up the illusion of hostility. "Scott wanted to be the guy on the white horse," Jongewaard says. Boras accused the Mariners of stalking Alex and harassing the teen everywhere he went. "It wasn't true," Jongewaard adds. "But Scott wanted Alex and his family to think that. It was very, very aggressive on Scott's part."

The timing of Alex's "low class" riff was also a diversion from the other issue surrounding the top draft pick, who, with every passing day of stalled negotiations, was being characterized in the press as a diva.

Team USA had no use for Boras's games. He had advised Alex to refuse to sign over his rights to Team USA's trading card company, Topps. "That would have cost me at least $500,000 in lost income with another card company," Alex later wrote. "I told team officials I couldn't agree to the card deal. I got cut [from Team USA]."

It was an embarrassment for Alex. It was business as usual for Boras.

As the summer ground on, though, Alex started to waver. Lourdes couldn't sleep. She had heard all about draft disappointments and busts. "C'mon, your mother is working as a waitress," Arguelles told Alex in August. "How can you turn down a million dollars when your mom is struggling and has worked her tail off to put food on the table?"

How could he? Alex wondered that himself. He knew nothing was guaranteed.

In 1966, the Mets had picked catcher Steve Chilcott as number one, but he had never played a major-league game. Back injuries had plagued Jeff King, the draft's top pick in 1986. In 1991, the Yankees had selected the hard-throwing lefty Brien Taylor as number one, but he had never pitched in the big leagues. Taylor could throw 90 miles per hour before he was 14 and was the surest thing anyone had ever seen. In December 1993, in a trailer-park brawl, Taylor took a swing at a man and missed everything except

the side of a car. Just like that, it was over for Taylor. The last anyone heard, he was laying bricks.

"Everybody said, 'Oh, he's going to make it, he's going to make
it,' but only two percent make it," says Joe Arriola, who advised the
Rodriguez family. "And there've been people with as much talent
as Alex that have not made it, you know? So as a mother you have
to be worried."

This game of chicken involving Alex made Lourdes very nervous. What if the Mariners called his bluff? What if Alex had to
start taking classes at Miami? She'd lie awake at night, staring at
the ceiling, wondering if Boras wasn't going overboard. Despite her
fears, she hid her nerves from the Mariners, playing the bad cop on
those faxed offers from Seattle.

"She was programmed," Jongewaard says. "If we would've
said ten million dollars, she would've said, 'I'm insulted; that's
not enough money for my son.' Scott once told me, 'You never
know what you'll do until the eleventh hour. When you might find
people afraid of losing the guy, what they'll come up with it.' So I
figured it would take all summer to sign Alex."

By August, the faxes sent to the Mariners by Lourdes—as the
stand-in for Boras—had grown terser. On August 4, less than a
month before Alex was to begin classes at Miami, the Mariners
received a faxed letter that laid out Alex's drop-dead demand: $2.5
million over three years.

On Mariners letterhead, in a fax dated August 16, 1993, Mariners team president Chuck Armstrong, wrote:

Dear Ms. Navarro:
    Your August 4 letter asks me to respond "honestly"
to your proposal, which you have now characterized as a
"final" and "non-negotiable" position.

I had thought that we responded to this proposal in our prior letters, and in putting forward the Club's offer to Alex. So that you and Alex will know exactly where the Mariners stand, let me try to be more clear and direct:

1. *We remain interested as ever in Alex and are committed to offering him a competitive contract.*

2. *We believe our previous offer to Alex was highly competitive for all of the reasons stated in my July 26 letter. It remains the best offer made to anyone in the past two years.*

Again, we are desirous of sitting down with you, your family and advisers, to discuss these issues and to see common ground. I share your sense of frustration with our exchange of letters. Certainly, Alex's professional future is important enough to justify a face-to-face discussion, before we think about pursuing other alternatives. In this regard, we invite you to Seattle. We think you will find a visit to Seattle to be both interesting and worthwhile. You are welcome anytime. We have an exciting homestand coming up with Toronto beginning Thursday, August 26 which should be a lot of fun. Just let me know when you would like to come.

I hope Alex is recovering well from his recent injury. If we can help in any way with his medical arrangements, please call.

Very truly yours,
Chuck G. Armstrong.

Lourdes was crying into the phone receiver. It was Saturday, August 28, two days before Alex was scheduled to attend an 8 a.m. Introductory Psychology class at the University of Miami. Two days until the $1 million offer from the Mariners would officially turn to dust.

The injury Armstrong mentioned in his letter had unhinged Lourdes and Alex and made them eager to make a deal with the Mariners. On July 28, as Alex lounged in a dugout during a junior national tournament in San Antonio, Texas, a fluke throw—a wild warm-up toss by a second baseman—had smacked him in the face. Alex's right cheekbone collapsed. Three days later, a surgeon had to treat Alex's face like a dented fender and pop it out with a screw.

The injury was not serious or long term, but it scared Alex. It was a reminder of how fragile a career can be. The panic it churned up for him and his mother prompted Lourdes to put in an emergency call to a family friend.

She always leaned on Arriola. He was listening to Lourdes and could hear her voice tremble as she asked him for advice. He was a well-respected former city manager of Miami who worked for a $1-a-year salary because, as a self-made man who had sold his business, Avanti Press, for millions, he didn't want to take taxpayers' money. "I'm a wealthy guy," Arriola says of his decision to get involved in Alex's stalled negotiations. "I had nothing to gain."

He was a doer, not a talker, a selfless man with a rescue gene, and Lourdes needed him. "We're poor people; we can't just turn down a million dollars," she sobbed into the phone. "Joe," she pleaded, "do the best you can. Screw Scott. Screw everything. You gotta help us."

Arriola promised to do what he could. He rented a hotel room at the Marriott next to the Miami airport and huddled with Boras in a marathon session, looking for some flexibility in the agent's position. "We talked for hours," Arriola recalls. "I don't know how many hours, but, like, zillions of hours."

Arriola finally had to call Lourdes and tell her Boras wouldn't move off his numbers. "She said, 'No, you gotta get this done for me.'" Arriola walked down the hallway to Boras's room and said, "You guys are out."

Boras was furious. He called Arriola a traitor, even though he had brokered the introductory meeting between Boras and Alex. "They were really pissed," Arriola says. "I was like, Hey, I brought you into the game; so what the hell are you talking about? I didn't care; I was doing it for the family. If the mother would've said, 'Stay out of it,' I would've stayed out of it, but when she said, 'I want you to help me,' I did."

That evening, Arriola moved to a different hotel, the Grand Bay in Coconut Grove, and met with the Mariners. He negotiated with team officials, including Arguelles and Benny Looper, a scout director, well into the night. They drank coffee and rubbed their tired eyes. By 3 a.m. Monday, five hours before Alex's first college class was scheduled to begin, they agreed on a three-year deal worth $1.269 million. The package included a $500,000 bonus, a major-league deal and a guaranteed call-up in September 1994.

Alex was relieved and gave Arriola the green light. The deal meant that Lourdes could finally exhale and concentrate on her dream: owning her own immigration assistance office.

Arriola picked up the phone and called Boras to tell him Alex had decided to sign.

"They're fucking crazy," Boras fumed. "He should've gone to school. I could have gotten them $3 million in a couple of years."

"Don't you get it?" Arriola said. "These are poor people. They've never seen this kind of money. They're starving."

It was a pointless argument, because Boras never factored emotion into his deals. The teen's insecurities, which had worked in Boras's favor for three months, ultimately undermined the superagent. Alex looked up to Boras, was in awe of his celebrity, but he wanted to please his mother. She had been through so much. *They* had been through so much.

Alex wasn't like so many other teens, who withdraw from their parents in order to establish their independence and identity. As soon as he was able to afford it, he bought Lourdes a home with a nice driveway and put a Mercedes in the garage. For years, Alex would find sanctuary in her home, returning to Kendall during the off-season to be with his mother. "She's my best friend," Alex once said. "I love spending time with her."

On August 30, Mariners executives, including team president Chuck Armstrong, were pacing the marble floor of the Grand Bay Hotel. It was 2 p.m. and their press conference to announce the signing of Alex Rodriguez had been scheduled for 1 p.m., but Alex was nowhere to be found. This was Boras again, taking one last piss on ceremony.

He hadn't made the deal—which had prompted Alex to tell him he would get only a 2.5 percent commission instead of the usual 5 percent—but he was still in the ear of his client: Make them wait, he said. A few minutes before Armstrong was about to bolt for the airport, Alex walked in—75 minutes late.

He was wearing a sleek suit in the faintest tint of green, with a crisp white shirt and red-and-white tie. His mother wore a Christmas tree–green dress with pearl and gold buttons down the middle. Susy had looped a double strand of pearls around her neck, and Alex's brother, Joe, wore the colorful baseball-card tie Alex had had around his own neck on draft day.

"I was twenty-nine when this began," Arguelles joked on that day. "Now I feel fifty."

Alex cheerfully (if belatedly) slipped on a Mariners cap in front of a bank of TV cameras. "I'm glad the negotiating is over," Alex said. "I never wanted this to be a bad thing and have people think wrongly about me."

He knew his image had been tarnished by his summer of sometimes clumsy machinations, even though most of the media's ire had been directed at Boras. Not that Boras cared. He came out swinging the day Alex signed, with Susy as his mouthpiece. "I'm not that excited about it because I don't think he got a fair deal,"

Susy told a reporter after she had returned home from the press conference. "He wants to play professional baseball, and I guess that's the reason he signed."

From start to bitter end, Susy had been played expertly by Boras. He knew she wanted to go to law school, and he had flattered her endlessly about her negotiating skills with the promise of a job at his firm. "Every time he talked to Susy, it was, 'Oh Susy, I'm going to do this for you; I'm going to do that for you,'" recalls Arriola. "She was important to him then. And he didn't do anything for her."

Alex had made his deal with the Mariners by breaking from Boras, but he kept him as his agent. He was not the nurturing father figure Alex craved, but he was calculating and smart, ruthless and fearless. Together they would make many more big deals and generate many more headlines. And controversies.

Screw Arriola, Boras thought. His impulse for revenge seemed to know no limits. Not long after Alex signed his contract with the Mariners, Boras stepped in to have it voided. Boras filed a grievance with baseball against Arriola. He convinced Alex that his deal had been wickedly mismanaged by Arriola and his son, Rich, who had just graduated from law school.

Arriola was mystified. How could Boras file a grievance against him? And for what his son had done, which, in fact, was nothing? "He said that [Rich] had misrepresented to Alex that he was a lawyer," Arriola says. "And he didn't."

Boras claimed that the Mariners and Arriola had misled Alex into believing his deal was guaranteed for five years, not three. The players' union was on Boras's side—specifically, his dear friend Gene Orza was on his side. "Sometimes you get the feeling that Boras is more important to the union than the players," says one major league player familiar with Boras. "It's that screwed up."

In a memo to Chuck Armstrong from Roger Jongewaard, dated February 28, 1994, Armstrong said:

> I have come by some information that has run the gamut before actually falling into my hands. The chain so far runs like this: I was told by a reporter who spoke with Peter Gammons, who talked to Gene Orza who said that we [Orza] will definitely not lose the Rodriguez case. He goes on to say that he's never been so sure of anything in his life.
>
> *How he intends to win the case, nobody knows. I realize this is second hand information but thought you might be interested in hearing it.*

Orza was wrong. Boras couldn't win. The grievance languished in baseball's arbitration system but was eventually dropped in 1996 when Alex signed a contract extension with the Mariners. In hindsight, Arriola had negotiated a good deal for Alex, which got him to the majors and onto his next deal more quickly.

"You can say whatever you want, but at the end of the day that meant an extra $25 million for Alex, right?" Arriola says. "By the way, I have never even accepted a cup of coffee from either one of them."

Alex never apologized to Arriola.

Chapter Five

THE PERFECTIONIST

ALEX RODRIGUEZ WAS SUFFERING from a writer's block of sorts in forming his own baseball identity, wanting badly for his career to be a living folktale but completely frozen on how to start the narrative.

By the spring of 1996, the now 20-year-old Alex had earned a major-league roster spot in fewer than three years after draft day, but now what? The accelerated promotion of Alex from minor-league outposts such as Appleton, Wisconsin, and Calgary, Alberta, to a certified Mariner was a bit dizzying, enough to induce errors and whiffs.

He was foundering. At the outset of his first full season with the Mariners, Alex was hitting a dismal .105. He needed a faith healer for his psyche. Fortunately, he knew who to call.

In a downtown Milwaukee hotel room, with April nearing its

chilly end, a motivational guru in a sharp, tailored suit asked Alex to close his eyes to envision his future. Visualize three goals, Jim Fannin told Alex in a sedate voice lightly flavored with a southern drawl. Alex responded instantly: "I want a batting title this year."

"He took possession of it in his mind," Fannin recalls. "He saw it. He felt it."

Alex next visualized himself being selected to the All-Star team three months away. "What do you see?" Fannin asked him.

"I see Cal Ripken, Jr., walking across the diamond, sticking his hand out and telling me, 'I couldn't wait to meet you. I've heard so much about you.'" This was an odd bit of crystal ball reading by Alex, because as a high school player, he had in fact shaken the hand of Cal Ripken, Jr. He just never believed Cal would remember that moment. Alex was just another upstart. He wanted to be famous enough for Cal to approach him. Not the other way around.

Finally, as Fannin listened further, Alex imagined himself becoming a household name. He conjured a moment in which a voice on a soundstage of a late-night talk show introduced him: "Ladies and gentlemen, please welcome Alex Rodriguez, the major league's newest superstar." Alex laughed at the vision but could hear the applause.

Fannin told him if he could hear it in his mind, he could make it real.

Jim Fannin believed in the power of visualization in part because of what it had done for him. He was making a very comfortable living as a mental coach for some of the biggest sports stars in the country. Contrast that to his childhood: he'd been reared among the working poor in Appalachia, where his home had plywood sheets covering the floors because termites had attacked the floorboards.

"At age twelve, I met this awesome guy who was a custodian at a YMCA tennis facility outdoors in Kentucky," Fannin recalls. "He was an eighty-three-year-old African-American man, and he showed me some things about energy that were life-changing. He taught me how to visualize success."

Fannin says the development of his mental strength complemented his athletic gifts and gave him a way out of eastern Kentucky. In the 1970s, with his tall frame and surprising agility, he earned a tennis scholarship at East Tennessee State University, where he majored in marketing and psychology. After graduating, he began working with tennis players as a life coach—long before that term gained both popularity and scorn—and later developed his S.C.O.R.E. System, a way to achieve success rooted in what can only be described as magical thinking: Just believe.

In the 1980s, an ophthalmologist for the Chicago White Sox spotted Fannin preaching the gospel of positivity at a workshop and asked him to help the players on his team.

After that introduction to major leaguers, Fannin quickly became a cult figure in baseball, worshiped by some and derided by others. One major-league player sarcastically calls Fannin "Doctor Feel Good for the weak," but players who relied on him include pitchers Orel Hershiser and Randy Johnson. But no one was as devout a follower as White Sox second baseman Joey Cora, who was traded to the Mariners in 1995. His new double-play partner the next season? Alex Rodriguez.

"Alex marveled at Joey's discipline," Fannin recalls. "And he should have. Of all the athletes I've coached, and I've coached some of the best, probably no one was more disciplined than Joey Cora. To the point of being anal, to the point of being obsessed. He really got the most out of his talent."

Cora had bought into Fannin's strategy of finding the perfect state of mind for performance, what he calls "the zone." "The zone needs stress," Fannin says. "You can't get into it without stress."

To get into Fannin's zone an athlete applies his acronym for success: Self-Discipline, Concentration, Optimism, Relaxation and Enjoyment. S.C.O.R.E.

"As important, if not more important, than anything else, is optimism, which includes trust and confidence and belief," Fannin says. "But you also need relaxation."

In his first full season in the majors, Alex wasn't loose at all. He was tight, his mind was spinning. He couldn't S.C.O.R.E. if he couldn't breathe.

At the start of spring training, Alex had been anointed the Mariners' starting shortstop, the presumptive heir to Ken Griffey, Jr.'s, legacy at the plate and a can't-miss idol on Madison Avenue. Alex tried to downplay expectations, even trotted out a bit of toe-scuffing humility for the beat writers. "I never want to crowd him," Alex said of Griffey. "I want to be a guy who helps him win. I want to be the guy in the background. Whether fans like me and my personality, that's up to them."

This, of course, was far from the truth. The need for adoration fueled Alex's ambitions, and he thought he was destined to be baseball's best player. But he understood that the fans liked humble players, so he became a student of how to play the media. He worked on perfecting his answers, as if each interview were an audition. On occasion, when his answers were ill received or sounded awkward or he appeared to have been rambling he would say, "I didn't mean it that way. My English isn't very good."

After four years of schooling in the Dominican's ABC school and the rest of his education in the U.S. system, Alex's English was just fine. But unlike players who shrugged off malapropisms and peppered their speech with profanities, he was self-conscious and overly deliberate when he spoke in public. (Jose Canseco once wrote that Alex spoke as if his answers had to be filtered through a "focus group.")

The media trainer Andrea Kirby was Alex's public speaking coach. At his rookie orientation, she began to work with him at the request of a Major League Baseball official. The league recognized that Alex could be a huge draw for them—a handsome, bilingual prodigy with big-play flair and studio-quality charisma at a time when fans were sick of surly sluggers like Albert Belle, who spewed out expletives in live interviews and upended clubhouse buffet tables out of anger.

Alex was angelic by comparison, baseball's boy-band idol. He was the youthful antidote for a sport still hobbled by the labor strife of 1994, when the entire postseason was canceled. Fans were disgusted by greedy players and owners, and attendance plunged.

The fans who did go to the ballparks often booed the players whose behavior, they felt, had tarnished the sport. Barry Bonds and Bobby Bonilla habitually preened after hitting home runs, while Darryl Strawberry and Steve Howe were cited for repeated drug offenses.

Alex could be the savior. He was neither too urban nor too country; he was smooth and stylish, unlike the players who sported gold chains as thick as lassos ("I don't like to wear gold," Alex said) or chewed on wads of tobacco that made their cheeks puff out like Dizzy Gillespie's.

There was a genuine, lovable core in Alex, the part of him that was acutely sensitive to what others wanted him to be, the part that made him so popular with children. Kids of all ages wrote to Alex, requesting him as their show-and-tell project in school. He was fastidious. He was meticulously inoffensive. He had his hair trimmed once a week and brushed his teeth obsessively to polish his smile. He claimed to floss four times a day. "He knew that people were looking for him to be, well, I want to use a phrase that I've never used before: a clean hero," Kirby recalls. "He knew there was an expectation for him to be one of the good guys, and he wanted to live up to that." He wanted to be good at being good.

Alex would watch taped interviews he'd done and scan the morning papers, looking for his name. "He liked to read the papers and all that stuff," Cora says. "So he knew everyone was talking about him." He rehearsed out loud answers to easily anticipated press questions while driving in his black Jeep Cherokee—his only splurge buy from his signing bonus. His salary was $109,000—the league minimum—but it was plenty of money to buy video games and his high-end suits and to pay for all those long-distance phone calls to his family. He had budgeted $1,000 a month for incidentals and saved most of it.

Alex was hardly a shut-in stuffing his money under his mattress. He explored the city, walking through Seattle's art galleries and its music district, trying to get to know his new surroundings. "He was mature for his age, mature and confident," Mariners former scouting director Roger Jongewaard says. "He wasn't afraid to try things or do things. He went to places and did things that young kids just don't go to, just don't do."

When Alex was asked back then how he stayed away from trouble, he said, "What I try to do is stay busy. Believe it or not, I went to Stanford University the other day and just walked around campus. I tried to picture myself being a junior in college and what it would be like. Stanford is one of the places I had a chance of going to school." When asked what he did on the road, he said, "When we go to Anaheim, I like to go to Newport Beach in the morning, relax, hang out and read a book."

In the years to come, he would tell the Seattle reporters how impressed he was with Leonardo da Vinci's genius. "He wrote his notes backward so that people wouldn't take his ideas," Alex said. "People like me would have to put them up to a mirror to read them. He says you can learn seven facts every second for the rest of your life. That means we are using only two percent of our brain. It fascinates me."

And he fascinated everyone who followed baseball. They all agreed: Alex was just what the sport needed.

He liked shopping for Frank Sinatra tunes. He was old school. Sometimes, as Sinatra's music flowed through the speakers of his Jeep, his mind would become preoccupied with his image. He would get lost in replaying his flip throws on a double play. He would go over again and again what he had said in the postgame interviews. Had he remembered to make eye contact? Had he engaged the reporter in personal conversation? Had he answered with authenticity?

"Some of the training methods are technical things," Kirby says. "But they come across to people at home as 'I'm seeing a genuine person,' and he really wanted that. I think he really wanted people to see the best of who he is."

The irony is that all this self-consciousness only added to the pressure he placed on his performance on the field. During spring training, each at bat, each catch, each throw felt pinched by pressure because he knew he was the starter and that everyone was watching him. "It's not easy making that transition from high school," his manager, Lou Piniella, said. "But Alex was a special talent. We knew that in a short period of time, this guy was going to be an All-Star player."

Alex was overwhelmed for the first time in his baseball life by the very thing he craved: attention. He had come down with a case of the uglies. The yips. He struggled to field normal hops. He struggled to put the bat on the ball. He struggled to find himself in February and March. "He was lost," Cora recalls. "He had no idea what he was doing, especially when hitting. I don't want to say he was scared, but he was *concerned*. He was concerned that he wasn't going to live up to the hype."

Alex picked apart his ungainly plate appearances—was his pitch selection that off?—and he obsessed over his misplays. Alex confided his fears to Cora, and Cora introduced him to Fannin. Cora told him that Fannin had taught him that self-criticism wasn't a noble pursuit; instead, it was a destructive diversion. "I have the phone number of a guy who can help you," Cora told Alex in late March. "Give him five minutes. I know it's going to work."

Fannin met Alex in mid-April and immediately confronted

him with questions: "What do you want, and why am I here?" There was no hesitation in Alex's voice when he stared Fannin in the eye and said, "Hall of Fame." Over the next few minutes, Fannin asked Alex if he realized how much a life lived by S.C.O.R.E. would cost him. Alex thought he meant money, since Fannin's rates ran from $10,000 to $50,000 a year per client. But Fannin was referring to the discipline needed to succeed. His S.C.O.R.E. program required Alex to be selfish. He would have to isolate himself from his family. "You'll miss birthdays," Fannin told him. He would have to cut himself off from undisciplined teammates.

The ideology seduced Alex. He craved guidance. He wanted to know: What is the secret to greatness?

Bill Haselman, a backup catcher in the majors for 13 seasons, was a teammate of Alex twice: in the minors, playing in the frozen reaches of Canada and then, years later, in Texas. He was a friend who thought of Alex as a good guy but could see his neediness. "When he came into the league, he wanted to learn as much as he could, almost too fast," Haselman says, "instead of just letting the game take its course and learning it as you go. It's like he wanted to drink from a fire hose. And that's good, because he wanted to learn a lot, but it's also hard to do when you're coming up and wanting to be successful at the same time. He was always trying to find out what was going to make him better. That's what he's driven by."

Fannin provided easy-to-remember, easy-to-use answers. "I have a lot of tools, a lot of routines on how to attract the zone," he told Alex. "I have preperformance tools; I have adjustment, quick tools you can do in fifteen, thirty seconds."

What others might consider fortune-cookie philosophy, Alex devoured as wisdom. Fannin soon persuaded Alex to begin reciting a catchphrase in his mind before every at bat: "I hit solid with an accelerated bat head." For the next 12 years, Alex would say these exact words to himself as he stepped out of the on-deck circle. For a dozen years, Alex would either talk with, text or e-mail Fannin before every game.

The results would, in Alex's own words, change his baseball life. "Jim is my sounding board, guide, advisor, mentor, therapist, baseball strategist, life coach and Zone coach. And my friend," he once wrote.

This sounded so *Oprah*, but Alex grew up during the boom times of the self-involved, self-help culture. He watched the daytime talk goddess on occasion and saw Al Franken's Stuart Smalley character mock the popularity of therapy on *Saturday Night Live* with his "doggone it, people like me" routine. Alex grew increasingly into himself.

"He'd put one of those self-help books on the chair in front of his locker," says one former Mariner. "He wanted us to see it: 'Look, I'm improving my inner self.' It was different, I'll say that."

Alex also kept a scrapbook of newspaper and magazine articles about himself in his duffel bag. He would read them from time to time as if to absorb a hit of self-affirmation. As if Fannin weren't enough of a self-esteem prop. Funny thing, though, it worked.

"He changed," Cora recalls. "It was almost right from the get-go." By the time Fannin sat down with Alex in Milwaukee, his stats were slowly inching up. In April, Alex had been hitting ninth as he groped for singles. His spot at the bottom of the order was part of Piniella's plan to ease him into the big time. "Sweet Lou was great for Alex," says Fernando Arguelles. "I told Alex when we signed him that Lou spoke better Spanish than we did. Sure enough, Alex said, 'Oh, man, you were right.' Lou was a great father figure."

Piniella was not known for patience and sensitivity toward youth. The good humor and lovable side of Piniella could, at any moment dissolve into a dirt-kicking rant at an umpire that would inevitably end with Sweet Lou's spittle dotting the uniforms of everyone within the blast zone. Yet he truly liked Alex. "Like his own son," Arguelles says. Some wondered if Piniella had the deft touch to deal with young players, but he was careful with Alex. He tucked Alex away from scrutiny, sticking him at the bottom of the lineup. Within a month, with Fannin in his head, Alex began performing. By May 8, Piniella had seen enough maturity in his young shortstop that he moved Alex into the number two spot, right in front of Griffey. In the 49 games after the switch, Alex hit .360 with 13 homers and 46 RBIs.

Rodriguez gives a lot of credit for this hot streak to Fannin, but baseball observers know that Ken Griffey, Jr., played a large role. He hit right behind Alex in the third spot, which meant that pitchers went after Alex, throwing him strikes, needing the out because they didn't want to face Griffey with a man on base. That meant Alex saw a lot of fastballs that, with his uncanny bat speed, he was able to feast upon. "The most obvious thing Junior does for me," he said at the time, "is get me better pitches."

There were other factors. Mariners hitting coach Lee Elia taught the young shortstop to square his body at the plate to create a solid foundation. He also moved Alex's pinkie off the knob of the bat for a better grip. Small adjustments, but they had a major impact for a hitter this talented. Elia knew he was working with a special player. "I had Mike Schmidt in Philly, Don Mattingly in New York, Ryne Sandberg in Chicago," he said, "but I haven't seen too many guys who can get their bat through the hitting zone any faster than Alex. With his ability, there's no telling what he can accomplish."

The league's best players were scheduled to play the 1996 All-Star Game in what most people felt was the worst stadium in Major League Baseball. Veterans Stadium in Philadelphia—the Vet—was old, decrepit and ugly. The turf was the phony green of an artificial Christmas tree. The smell of garbage, an unsavory mix of half-eaten hot dogs, beer-soaked popcorn and discarded cole slaw, permeated the corridors, and the workout room was literally full of gym rats—scurrying, not lifting. The place was a dump, and Alex Rodriguez was thrilled to be there.

A few days earlier, *Sports Illustrated* had hit newsstands with Alex on its cover. With a backdrop the color of hot lava and an achingly trite headline, "Hot Player," the cover featured a shot of Alex in a gray Mariners uniform with a blue sweatband on his left forearm bearing his jersey number: 3, in honor of Braves outfielder and perennial All-Star Dale Murphy, another spotless hero Alex had worshiped. In the photo, Alex was smiling, with streaks of eye black high on his cheekbones and his flip-style sunshades under the brim of his Mariners cap. He was 20 years old and appeared to be happy and completely relaxed. And why wouldn't he be? He was coming to the All-Star Game with a .336 batting average and on the cover of the nation's biggest, most respected sports magazine.

The story inside was a paean to Rodriguez so effusive that it might have been written by Alex's mother—or his agent. In the opening paragraph, Gerry Callahan wrote, "By 10 p.m., he is nestled in bed with his Nintendo control pad. He makes Roy Hobbs look like John Kruk, and he makes you wonder if you're missing something: A guy this sweet has to be hiding some cavities."

Callahan tried to find a flaw in Rodriguez, *anything*, but it was a futile search. "He doesn't just sign autographs for anyone who asks in the hotel lobby—he thanks the pests," Callahan wrote. To close the piece, he added, "Someday, Rodriguez may bat .400 and hit 60 home runs, but for now he is doing the next best thing: He is living up to expectations."

On the day before the game, the All-Stars were taking batting practice at the Vet when Cal Ripken, Jr., walked up and introduced himself. Alex later told Fannin that the legendary shortstop had said, "Hi, my name is Cal Ripken, Jr. I couldn't wait to meet you. I've heard so much about you."

Those were the exact words Alex had heard in his mind back in April, when he was visualizing his dreams of success. He immediately phoned Fannin from the stadium locker room, excited and in awe over the power of S.C.O.R.E.

Alex, who still had a poster of Ripken at his mother's home, later described the thrill of that moment to reporters: "Imagine a teenage girl going out to dinner with Madonna," he said. "That's kind of what it felt like for me during batting practice."

Turning on the charm and modesty, Alex added, "You can compare me to high school kids, but not these guys."

A good quote, but Alex Rodriguez knew he belonged. After all, hadn't he envisioned all this back in his Milwaukee hotel room.

August was a cruel month for the Mariners. They went 12–17, while their division rivals, the Texas Rangers, got hot, winning 9 of 10 games in one stretch. The worse the Mariners played, though, the better Alex played. He hit .435 in August, with nine home runs.

He was on everyone's "get" list. The newspaper reporters, ESPN correspondents and radio talk-show hosts all lined up for time with him. This was his opportunity to maximize his visibility in markets far bigger than Seattle. And he understood the power of exposure.

On August 19, he was in a limo on his way to the *Late Show with David Letterman*. He called Fannin from the car to tell him where he was heading—again, just as he had visualized.

What he hadn't foreseen was the hectic schedule he'd have to endure. He had flown from Seattle to New York on a midnight flight to be on Letterman's show. Then, a few hours after sitting on Dave's couch, he was in a helicopter, zipping over the Hudson

River to Cherry Hill, New Jersey, where he sold autographs and memorabilia on QVC.

Griffey, who'd been swept up in the same kind of publicity whirlwind nearly a decade before, was concerned. He saw that he needed to help Alex understand that being fresh for the team and at his peak mentally and physically were the most important elements of being a superstar. At Yankee Stadium the next day, before the Mariners played in a marquee matchup on national television, Junior sat down with Alex in the cramped visitors' locker room.

"The only question with him is: Will he burn himself out with all the extra stuff? So far, he's handled it well. I just wanted to make sure that baseball comes first," Griffey said later. "He did Letterman and QVC. That's not an off day, especially when we have a big series coming up. I just tried to get an idea where he's at. I wanted to make sure he's okay. He's a big part of our lineup."

It turned out that Junior had little cause for concern; the Mariners beat the Yankees three out of four on the road, and Alex went 8 for 20 with two home runs.

By September, marriage proposals started filling the mailboxes at the Mariners' front offices, some written in crayon, other spritzed with expensive perfume. All were addressed to Alex—or A-Rod, the handle that was quickly becoming a favorite of headline writers.

The nickname first appeared in the spring of 1996 when Alex was spotted writing "A-ROD" in capital letters on his equipment to mark it. His teammates picked up on the moniker and so did Dave Niehaus, the longtime voice of the Mariners. "It just seemed natural to me," he said. "And it stuck like glue."

It was marketing genius. Alex was now a one-name wonder boy. Crowds gathered just to marvel at his batting practice swings;

at team hotels, the line of fans for his autograph was now as long as—if not longer than—the line for Ken Griffey, Jr.

Griffey knew what Alex was going through. In 1987, Junior had been a 19-year-old drafted out of high school as the number one pick. He was the son of Reds legend Ken Griffey and had an uppercut swing so smooth it appeared to be happening under water. Junior generated awesome power with his bat and amazed fans with his ability to suspend himself in the air as he stretched his body full out for highlight-reel catches in centerfield.

So Junior knew what it was like to be the talk of baseball and the great hope of a generation. He also understood the perils of a fawning press eager to deify you on your way up and just as eager to bury you on the way down.

"There was an interesting dynamic growing between Junior and Alex," recalls Woody Woodward. "I think Junior wanted to protect him but I'm not sure how that was perceived by Alex."

Junior tried to reach out to Alex. They played video games such as Mortal Kombat together, but there was always a distance between them. From his leather lounge chair in the Mariners' clubhouse, Junior witnessed the season unfold and the adulation of Alex grow. Junior was on his way to a 49-home-run season despite missing 22 games with injuries, but he knew who the new prom king of the clubhouse was. "He's a heartthrob because he's this young, clean-cut, handsome dude, just like I used to be," Griffey told the *Los Angeles Times*. "Cute, you know. . . . I hope he doesn't get some of what I get: 45 or so bombs and 135 ribbies and people say, 'Just Junior having a Junior year. Nothing special.' I accept it and don't worry about it, but I don't want him feeling he has to do this every year or he's come up short."

A rivalry developed over the next three years. The more popular Alex became, the more passive-aggressively Junior reacted. He groused about a T-shirt night for A-Rod, pointing out that the Mariners had never feted him on a special giveaway promotional.

He was upset when, as both players inched toward free agency, he was constantly being compared to Alex. "We are on totally two different pages," Griffey told reporters. "He's young, single. He doesn't have to worry about certain things. Besides, he gets to hit in front of me. One day, I'd like to hit in front of me, too."

"There was definitely tension in the clubhouse because Junior had been the king for so long," one former Mariner says. "A-Rod said all the right things, but I believe Junior never trusted him. Maybe he saw something he didn't think was real."

Junior acted as if Alex were hoarding all the adoration from fans, as if Junior were last year's model. He clearly resented it. He told *Sport* magazine, "When a player gets more than their share [of attention], then they say about me, 'You're not the star of this team.' But I'm the guy who has to take responsibility."

The implication: Junior helped the team win while Alex helped himself to the endorsement money. He was in milk ads, was plugged into Nike's ambitious advertising and marketing plans and was being feted for signing over large checks to children's charities, including the Miami Boys & Girls Club.

Alex knew he was in danger of being overwhelmed by all the demands on his time, and he regularly called people he trusted for advice and reassurance. He reached out to Jose Canseco all the time, sometimes talking to him for four or five hours about baseball and life and the demands of fame. "I knew him as well as anyone back then," Canseco says. "What do I realize now? He was never who he pretended to be."

Junior seemed to have sensed that as well. His petulance toward Alex was clearly rooted in distrust. One former teammate of both players says, "[Alex] always said publicly how much he looked up to Junior, but Junior knew Alex was playing both sides in the clubhouse. He wasn't honest during that MVP shit."

The MVP voting for the 1996 season exposed in Alex a dichotomy between the media-trained darling who measured ev-

ery word and the hurt child who needed to hold the trophy. The
Mariners were contenders for most of the season but sputtered in
September, losing six of their last eight games and squandering a
10-game winning streak that had pulled them to within one game
of the Rangers for the division lead. Alex also lost steam at the end,
hitting .259 over the last 14 games of the season.

Even with that stumble at the finish line, Alex put up astounding numbers his rookie season. He hit .358, with 36 home runs and
123 RBIs. At 21, he had put up the best batting average ever for a
major leaguer so young. Alex was 11 days younger than his nearest
competition for the record: Shoeless Joe Jackson, who hit .408 in
1911. He won the batting title—beating out Frank Thomas, who
finished with a .349 average. Again, just as Alex had envisioned it
back in April. Now many people were touting him as the American
League MVP.

Alex deftly and diplomatically discouraged such talk, pointing
out that a large part of his success was due to the fact that he was
hitting in front of a great hitter and a great leader, Ken Griffey, Jr.
"I don't see how I can be MVP when I'm not the MVP of my own
team," Alex said as the season neared an end.

With that brilliant and calculating ploy, Alex hoped to appear
modest and magnanimous—but he didn't mean to lose MVP votes
because of it. He was furious when he learned that he'd finished
second to Juan Gonzalez, who'd led the Rangers to a division title
with a .314 average, 47 home runs and 144 RBIs. Gonzalez took
the MVP by a record slim margin—290 points to 287—which
meant that Alex missed out on being the youngest player to win
the award by one first-place vote. The cruelest twist: writers in Seattle who voted for the MVP had placed Griffey—who was fourth
in the voting with 188 points, including four first-place votes—
ahead of Alex.

"It hurts not to get a first-place vote from my own town after
the season that I had," Alex said.

A couple of reporters challenged him: Wasn't it Alex who had proclaimed Junior the MVP of the Mariners? He seemed shocked that he would be held accountable for his words, but, in a brilliant but perverse twist on modesty, he declared, "If I can lose the MVP every year because of my humility, I will lose it every year."

Somewhere, a media trainer slapped her forehead in exasperation: Humble people don't say they're humble.

It was a romance born in sweat and pursued on a treadmill.

Alex Rodriguez trained diligently out of dedication to his game but also out of vanity. Whenever he was in Miami, he could be found working out in a gym. He enjoyed the sweat and effort and reward intertwined in the gym culture of hard bodies. "Alex can't stand fat people," one friend says. "He really can't be around them."

The popular Body & Soul gym in South Miami was a veritable catwalk for buff and beautiful boys and girls, which was why Alex liked to work out there. One day, in the winter of 1996, a blond woman with expressive brown eyes caught his attention. Alex saw that Cynthia Scurtis wasn't like some of the other women in the gym—she didn't come to socialize or flirt, she came to push her body.

"I was on a treadmill," Cynthia once said. "And he came up to me. He [had] scouted out my plan in the gym. He said, 'I know you are gonna go over there and stretch. Do you mind if I wait for you over there?' So this kind of went on for a few days."

Cynthia was a 23-year-old psychology teacher at Gulliver Prep—the same elite academy she had attended while growing up in the affluent Miami neighborhood of Coconut Grove. After getting an undergraduate degree in psychology at Ohio State, she had moved back to Miami to be with her tight circle of friends and even tighter family, which was prominent in the local Greek Ortho-

dox Church. Her grandfather had moved to Miami in 1944 and
founded Florida's first Greek Orthodox church, St. Sophia Greek
Orthodox Cathedral.

She had grown up just 10 miles from Alex but in a much more
affluent neighborhood than the one Alex had been raised in. She
was Alex's type: smart, strong-willed, no-nonsense and uncom-
monly fit.

Each day, Alex grew more interested in her. She was disciplined and didn't seem at all distracted by his attention. "I wanted
to see her routine," Alex said. "And I wanted to see what time she
came in. See how consistent she was. Sure enough, she was like a
machine. She would come right after work and get on the treadmill
and do her abs."

She would pass him and nod. Cynthia wasn't returning his
affection, which only drove him to be more insistent. He was a
baseball player. She knew that but wasn't impressed. She could see
how everyone else in the gym reacted to him. "I knew he played
baseball because everybody in the gym would say, 'Do you know
who that is?' I didn't grow up in a sports-oriented family. I wasn't
aware that you could have an entire livelihood off a sport. So when
they would say, 'Oh, he plays baseball,' I would always think, 'I
wonder what else he does?'"

Alex circled her for weeks as she kept rejecting his unsophisti-
cated pickup lines. For all of Alex's media training, he was socially
awkward. "I can remember going out with him in Seattle," says a
former Mariners teammate. "He couldn't talk to a woman without another guy with him. He'd call me and say, 'I'm at this club.
Come help me.' He'd say the cheesiest stuff to girls—lines you'd
hear on bad TV."

All Alex knew he'd learned on TV. Alex hadn't had a father to
teach him the fundamentals of dating. This state of arrested development was obvious to Cynthia.

"One day I am leaving the gym, and there he is in the parking lot," Cynthia said. "And he says, 'Listen, you've got to help me. I have run out of gas.' And I'm going, 'Oh, yeah, right. *This* guy ran out of gas.'"

Alex wasn't asked to prove it, but he was prepared to look helpless. He had a small red gas can in his hand. "Can you just take me around the corner so I can get some gas?" he asked Cynthia.

She was skeptical—wasn't this guy trying a little too hard?—but she opened her car door and let Alex get in. They drove two blocks to the gas station and returned to pour a gallon or two into Alex's tank. Cynthia had done her Good Samaritan deed for the day and decided that she could now leave.

"Wait," Alex said. "Aren't you worried; aren't you gonna wait and see if I'm okay?"

Alex was accustomed to being rescued, whether the lifeline came from a family member, friend or self-help adviser. Cynthia, rolling her eyes, waited in the parking lot, slightly annoyed but a little bit intrigued, wondering what ploy Alex would pull out next. Instead, he went in headfirst. He told her that he didn't get it: How come she had never accepted any of his invitations to go out for a meal?

Cynthia explained that she wasn't the spontaneous type. She was structured and lived on a tight schedule. "Why don't you take my number, and this way you can call me and it can be planned," she told him.

"I don't want your number," he said. "I have literally asked you out a dozen times, and you say 'No' every time. I am very busy. I am leaving for Japan soon. If you want to see me, here is my number."

Alex was leaving for Japan on October 29th with a group of major-league All-Stars for exhibition games to promote baseball in Asia. He told her he'd be back in Miami by early November.

A few weeks later Cynthia called him. "And that was it," she said.

They dated for six years. Alex knew that she was good for him. "She kept his head on straight," says a friend of Cynthia's. "She told him 'No' enough so that he really paid attention to what she thought. He respected her."

Alex wanted her to move to Seattle to be closer to him, but, as a daughter of a traditional Greek Orthodox family, she refused to be his live-in girlfriend. Her family wasn't so sure of Alex, anyway, in part because he wasn't Greek.

Alex was sure of Cynthia, though. He valued her intellect, her moral compass and her dedication to her body. The last was important to him. Friends say he has always been obsessed with fitness, his own and that of others. The gym world of carved muscle and mirrors was a reflection of how much importance Alex placed on superficiality. Numbers and stats were like muscular bodies: the more definable, the better.

Alex seemed to fit a steroid user's psychological profile to a T. He wasn't simply interested in power and confidence but also in the vanity. He looked up to Canseco's brawn with awe, though he didn't want a thick look for himself. He liked sinewy. He liked definition. He was a virtual disciple of the Miss Fitness competitions.

"He definitely has an appreciation for fitness and what people in my industry do," says a former Miss Fitness America, Amy Fadhli, who, in 1998, met Alex through Canseco's wife, Jessica, who was also a fitness competitor. "He's into the whole fitness lifestyle. He knew who I was. He read the magazines, the fitness publications."

Alex flirted with women who made their living by building muscle, but, as Fadhli knew, he was planning to marry Cynthia one day. She was two years older than Alex. "He always said he liked older women," says Fadhli. "I do remember that."

Chapter Six

MR. TWO-FIFTY-TWO

THE ARC THAT TRACES Alex Rodriguez's rise to superstardom neatly parallels the one tracking the abuse of steroids in baseball. The popularity of performance enhancers among everyday ball players—not just sluggers but pitchers and utility fielders, too—began taking hold when Alex was in high school. As player stats became more inflated and the paychecks were distorted to match, Alex was emerging as one of the best players in the history of Major League Baseball. He could field for show and hit for power without fatigue. He was the product of an artificial bubble.

The Johnny Appleseed of Generation Steroid was Jose Canseco, the handsome, swarthy, Miami-reared superstar with action-hero pecs who dated Madonna in 1991 and, one year earlier, had signed a five-year, $23.5 million deal with the Oakland Athletics—the largest contract in baseball history at the time. He was a pioneer of steroid use, its shameless poster boy and a tireless proselytizer. As he moved around the league, from Oakland to Texas to Boston and then on to the Blue Jays and Yankees, he spread the gospel of Better Hitting Through Chemistry. Many of his converts became the top hitters and pitchers in the game.

His dependence on steroids was obvious, an open secret even in those early days before HGH was in the headlines and steroid abusers were called before Congress. In 1988, Canseco's hulking physique inspired the *Washington Post* columnist Tom Boswell to write, "[He] is the most conspicuous example of a player who has made himself great with steroids." Hostile fans began to taunt Canseco with chants of "Ste-roids! . . . Ste-roids!" but he laughed that off; he knew he'd lost endorsements because of the steroid rumors, but he also knew that performance enhancers had quickly transmogrified him from a skinny, 15th-round draft choice into the most feared hitter in baseball. As he would later write in *Juiced*, his first of two tell-all memoirs, "using steroids made me a better ballplayer—and, as everyone soon found out, my expertise on steroids could make other players around me a lot better, too."

Canseco even injected his wife, Jessica. After being urged for months to try steroids, Jessica allowed Jose to put the needle to her in 1996. "Finally, I let him do it," she wrote in *Juicy*, her answer to her ex-husband's confessional. "One shot wasn't going to do the trick. . . . He shot up my other cheek. It was even worse than the first time. I couldn't understand how Jose had withstood that kind of pain on such a regular basis over the course of so many years."

He endured that pain for obvious and substantial rewards: money, power, celebrity. He kept a stash in a duffel bag in his bedroom closet, and he would happily dip into that valise whenever a baseball buddy wanted a jolt of strength and confidence. Canseco was bold but not reckless: He advised players to buy their steroids over the border—from either Mexico or the Dominican Republic—and taught them how to mix, or "stack," performance enhancers to gain the desired effect. He preferred the steroids Deca-Durabolin and Winstrol, with a low dose of testosterone.

He boasted in *Juiced* that he had mentored Mark McGwire in the 1980s and then injected Ivan "Pudge" Rodriguez, Rafael Palmeiro and Juan Gonzalez with steroids in the 1990s. All of those players had morphed into awesome power hitters under Jose's tutelage—and needle. Pudge and Gonzalez won MVP awards in the late 1990s; McGwire was credited with saving baseball by drawing fans back to the game after the 1994 players' strike with his conquest of Roger Maris's single-season home-run record in 1998. Jose was a generous man—he was willing to help, he wrote, "anyone who was interested."

One of Canseco's youngest and most ardent acolytes was Alex Rodriguez. Friends say they got to know each other around 1993 when Canseco would visit his old stomping grounds at the Boys & Girls Club of Miami. Alex had grown up there, too. He was 18, a high school hotshot with pro potential everyone could see. Canseco was coming off an MVP-caliber season. In their own version of a Skipper and Gilligan relationship, Alex tagged along behind Canseco, taking all direction from him.

Alex was starstruck. He would, throughout his career, use Canseco as his template: Alex would use steroids, put up big stats, sign the richest contracts, and even date Madonna. "He wanted to be me," says Canseco.

For years, Canseco treated Alex like a little brother. They went everywhere together in the off-season. In 1994, when Alex was 19, Canseco flew him to his homeland of Cuba, where they visited refugees at the Guantánamo Bay U.S. military base. In the winter of 1996, a writer from the *Seattle Times* noted in an off-season story, without drawing the obvious implication, that he'd seen a cache of unidentified powders, pills and vitamins bunched on the kitchen counter at Alex's home. The reporter also described Alex and Canseco's bond: "So trusted is Canseco that if Alex had to go home to entertain some reporter, Canseco could head off to a restaurant and do the most intimate thing: order sushi (for the both of them)." The point? Only the closest buddies could know each other's tastes so well.

"He was seventeen, eighteen. I took him into my home," says Canseco. "He wanted to do everything I did. He wanted everything I had." Alex quickly came to treasure Canseco as yet another fill-in for his father. "Jose has taught me a lot about life and baseball," he once said.

In his late teens and early twenties, Alex worked out with Canseco in the off-season, often using the $1.3 million gym in Canseco's 20,000-square-foot Mediterranean-style mansion outside Miami, where he kept exotic animals on the manicured property and used the gym as both a training ground and a home chemistry lab.

Alex had just been introduced to the steroid culture. At Westminster High, between his sophomore and junior seasons, he transformed his body with an extra 25 pounds and added an eye-popping 200 pounds to his bench press.

There was no question that Alex's gym-rat ethos—in early, out late—was part of the reason for this change, but the added power and muscle seemed aided by synthetic means. "Was he on steroids in high school? I think probably so," says Canseco. "I worked out with him when he was 18. He could lift almost as much as I could." If Alex had any questions about performance-enhancing drugs, he knew just who to turn to: Canseco.

When Alex got to the big leagues, he hired Canseco's trainer, Joseph Dion, a no-nonsense ex–military man who had grown up in Miami. For almost four years each off-season, Alex rented a house near the beach in the Dominican Republic resort of Casa de Campo and trained with Dion. Alex, his girlfriend, Cynthia, and Dion spent days charging up nearby hills and churning through the beach sands on training runs. Dion and Alex worked on stretching and flexibility and used a medicine ball to create a retro-style workout glorified in the *Rocky* flicks.

"He worked the hardest of anyone I've ever had," says Dion. "He was very hungry."

After three hours of sweat, they would separate. Dion never socialized with Alex after their daily sessions ended. Alex had plenty of family and friends on the island, and scores of major leaguers gathered there in the off-season. Some went there to kick back, others played winter ball to stay sharp and more than a few made the trip to purchase readily available steroids in a country where they were legal. A player could buy Dianabol, Winstrol or Deca-Durabolin over the counter at corner pharmacies.

Dion says he never saw Alex buy steroids in the D.R. but admits, "Alex and I, we led two different lives there."

That off-season spent working out in the Dominican Republic produced tangible results: Alex added 10 pounds of muscle before the 1998 season. In April of that year, *Muscle & Fitness* magazine declared that Mark McGwire, Jeff Bagwell, Juan Gonzalez, Glenallen Hill and Alex Rodriguez had the "Best Physiques in Major League Baseball." This hot-bod list of 1998 would eventually become a handy guide of baseball's more prominent users—McGwire, Gonzalez, Hill and Bagwell would be linked to performance-enhancing substances in the media—but Alex managed to dodge public suspicion on that front for many years. Even his longtime critic, the pitcher Curt Schilling, would describe Alex as one of the few clean sluggers in baseball, attributing his success to the fact that he was a "genetic freak." Rodriguez was convincing as an untainted hero because of his awe-inspiring work ethic and the fact that, unlike typical steroid users, his body wasn't cartoonish in size.

Alex had no desire for the Paul Bunyan look. He didn't need to be a behemoth at shortstop, where his range would have been compromised by playing at the size and shape of a barge. He simply needed power to layer upon a hitting talent so distinct that baseball people could *hear* the difference when he took his cuts. "When we looked at his size when we signed him, we thought he could be a twenty-five-plus home-run guy," says Woody Woodward, Seattle's general manager when Rodriguez played there. "But then in batting practice, you could hear something special, like you could with Albert Pujols or Manny Ramirez. There was a different sound when the ball came off his bat. Alex is one of those guys that if you close your eyes you can hear a difference, something deeper."

In 1996, at age 21, Rodriguez, hit .358 with 36 home runs and became the youngest player to win an American League batting title since Al Kaline hit .340 as a 20-year-old in 1955. He also was the first AL shortstop to capture a batting crown since Lou Boudreau in 1944. And only Mel Ott, Ted Williams, Frank Robinson and Tony Conigliaro had hit more than 30 home runs at a younger age.

It was a wonderful season: 36 homers made a nice exclamation point. Yet it wasn't enough. All around him, players were getting stronger and more powerful as baseball's steroid era seemed to spread from obvious locales—like the Oakland A's—to other teams.

"Alex never looked up to the workmanlike guys on a team— the everyday, hard-nosed player. He idolized the sluggers because they got all the attention," says one former Mariners teammate of Alex. "They got all the press."

Alex was mesmerized by the fawning, nonstop ESPN coverage of Mark McGwire and Sammy Sosa as they riveted America with their race to top Maris in 1998. Alex saw a disco-ball effect as flashbulbs popped in stadiums during each home-run trot. McGwire, a redheaded lug who ran the bases on the tips of his toes, was striding closer and closer to Maris. Alex admired virtuosity and discovered it in himself.

Almost obscured by the McGwire-Sosa buddy flick, Alex, at only 23, had become the third 40–40 player in major-league history, joining Barry Bonds and Canseco by hitting 42 home runs and stealing 46 bases for Seattle in 1998.

He was unstoppable. He was the toast of Seattle. During the season, in private, he began to venture outside his choirboy persona. One teammate says he began jetting women from city to city to comfort him. He also began to indulge in the ultimate perk of stardom: he started building an entourage around him. Various friends—including one pal known to many of the Mariners as "Judy"—chauffeured him to and from different places

Judy's real name was Yuri Sucart, a pudgy man who would later be known as Alex's "cousin." His job was simple: to do whatever Alex told him to do. Judy didn't say much. He didn't engage other players. He was, in effect, Alex's manservant, washing his car and even laying out Alex's clothes each day.

Seattle players didn't think Sucart was suspicious, just weird. No one imagined then that he would one day be fingered as the mule for Alex's steroids. Alex's Mariners teammates had their doubts about Alex's power, but, as one player says, "No one that I know of actually saw him shoot up, but he did take greenies." In the late 1990s, before they were banned in 2006, amphetamines were placed in dishes inside clubhouses as if they were hard candy. Alex, who has admitted to using Ripped Fuel, a stimulant also later banned, was no different from many other players.

But some extra pep to get through a late-season doubleheader and injecting something that would give you the power to deposit a fastball over the opposite-field fence were perceived differently by players: many of them considered greenies a necessary survival tool when facing the grind of 162 games; steroids helped individuals inflate their stats as a way to get paid more.

Those who knew Alex believed his power surge was chemically enhanced in 1998.

"Look at Alex's body," Canseco says. "It was obvious: He was taking steroids."

In his 2007 memoir, *Vindicated*, Canseco wrote that he had hooked up Alex with performance enhancers in the late 1990s through a Canadian dealer turned fitness trainer in Miami he called Max. "That's me," Dion says. "And that's really funny because I hate steroids. I'm against them a hundred percent." Dion denied being a steroid supplier but does remember Alex asking him a lot of questions about steroids: What drugs were most toxic? Which were most effective?

Alex had a more sophisticated knowledge of steroids than he ever let on to the public. Throughout his career, he consistently played the naïf when this issue came up. As late as 2002 he asked reporters, "What are steroids?" His media training was paying off: Look everyone in the eye, he was taught, and turn on the faux sincerity. Not everyone was fooled. Teammates and competitors suspected Alex of taking steroids as early as 1992, when they saw his body change dramatically. The damning evidence that Alex Rodriguez had juiced during his career wouldn't surface for another decade. During those 10 years, he expertly—and cynically—spun tales to make himself seem too good to be true. He was a model of embellishment, depicting his upbringing as a mythical struggle, stretching his natural talent into something surreal and awe-inspiring. He craved being bigger than life.

By the fall of 2000, he was in a position to parlay his fable into a fortune. He was a free agent, ready to be feted. Alex and Boras were expecting to land a monumental contract, but they were looking for more than just a hefty payday. He had already trademarked a company name—AROD Corp.—in 1996 and planned to use his impending free-agent bounty as part of a grand opening that would extend his name and fame—his brand—throughout the Western Hemisphere not just through Nike commercials and car endorsements, but also through assets and acquisitions. Alex was angling to become baseball's Michael Jordan or Tiger Woods. He was going for transcendence.

It was the ultimate vanity publication. The 73-page binder was midnight blue; the gold lettering on its front cover read ALEX RO-DRIGUEZ: HISTORICAL PERFORMANCE. Scott Boras printed more than 100 copies of the tiny tome (at a cost of $35,000) and handed them out at the baseball general managers' meetings on Amelia Island, Florida, during the first week of November 2000. The binder was an elaborate sales brochure stuffed with glossy photos and glittering stats. The table of contents tells you that this was a book with a very limited audience, and a very narrow subject—All About Alex:

Ch. 1—ARod: Actual and Projected Performance
Ch. 2—ARod vs. Hall of Fame Shortstops
Ch. 3—ARod vs. Current Major League Shortstops
Ch. 4—ARod vs. Jeter and Garciapara
Ch. 5—ARod: History 40/40 Season
Ch. 6—ARod: Leadership Qualities
Ch. 7—ARod vs. All Current Major League Players
Ch. 8—ARod vs. Griffey and Bonds
Ch. 9—ARod vs. Top 10 All-Time Offensive Leaders
Ch. 10—ARod vs. Top 10 Paid Players of 2001

Boras ladled up a bushel of shimmering stats but also made his case with quotes from media and baseball types, giving the binder the feel of a movie poster plastered with rave reviews printed in bold type. Alex was the "Hope Diamond of baseball's free-agent jewels," said John Henderson of the *Denver Post*. "If you were to build a franchise, that's the guy you'd start with," said Phillies former manager Larry Bowa. Alex was compared to Michelangelo by Seattle center fielder Mike Cameron and to a "baseball da Vinci" by *USA Today*'s baseball writer. Dan Le Batard of the *Miami Herald* supplied the coup de grâce: "Rodriguez has nothing less than the game in his grip. He is everything you want in an athlete-

ambassador—graceful, charming, handsome, polite, hard-working
and absurdly, hypnotizingly talented. . . . Yes, Alex Rodriguez can
save baseball."

As Boras darted about the massive lobby of the Ritz-Carlton,
pressing his tendentious compilation on every general manager and
owner he could buttonhole, he'd explain that signing Alex Rodriguez was the smartest move they could ever make. "It's not about
value," he told them, "it's about presence. We believe Alex is the
best shortstop in baseball history at age twenty-four, and maybe
the best player. I don't think the average fan realizes that, and that's
what this book is for."

Scott Boras had thrown open the doors of his showroom and was
welcoming all shoppers, but the team he was really looking to hook
was the New York Mets. They had the money, the market and
the need. The franchise was suffering from an inferiority complex,
always looking up to the New York Yankees. The Mets played in
Shea Stadium, built on the cheap in 1964, where a Volkswagen-
sized Big Apple rose from behind the outfield fence like a gopher's
head to celebrate home runs. Just beyond the outfield wall of Yankee Stadium lies Monument Park, where fans can kiss the bronze
plaques of Joe DiMaggio and Mickey Mantle, Babe Ruth and Lou
Gehrig.

The Yankees attracted the elite from Park Avenue. The Mets
were beloved by Vinny from Queens. The Yankees had all those
rings, all that history and all that star power in Derek Jeter. This
last intangible would always be a maddening source of jealousy
for Alex; when people argued about the game's best shortstops,
Alex wondered how Jeter even got into the conversation. Statis-
tically, Alex trumped him in every category. Every category but
one. On November 12, with his Yankee contract almost certain
to be extended, Jeter's agent, Casey Close, spelled out the differ-

ences between Alex and Jeter in what would become the anthem of the anti–A-Rod Army. "Is the best player the most valuable player or the one with the best stats?" Close asked a *Newsday* reporter. "Derek's value increases because he makes 24 other players better. I think Alex in part does that. I know Derek does that. After a career is over, what is remembered is whether a player won or lost. Jordan will be remembered for winning. At first it was, sure he can score, but can he win? Michael never really got credit until he won."

The Mets hadn't won a World Series since 1986. The Yankees had won four between 1996 and 2000—that last one against the Mets in a five-game "subway series." The Mets had come so close that season, and they believed they were one superstar away from winning it all.

With a glee usually reserved for children on Christmas Eve, the Mets opened negotiations with Boras as soon as the free-agent signing period began on November 11. Two days later, however, Mets General Manager Steve Phillips issued a stunning update on how the talks were going: They weren't. The Mets no longer wanted A-Rod. Mets owner Fred Wilpon had decided that his demands for special treatment would make him a clubhouse killer, and Phillips agreed. "I have serious reservations about a structure in which you have a 24-plus-one man roster," Phillips told the press. "I don't think it can work, and those reservations are enough for me to back off. . . . I do buy Scott's arguments that we probably haven't seen the best of [Rodriguez] yet. It's not about an individual, it's about 25 players that join together as a team, and that is something that, when compromised, it becomes difficult to win. That's even before considering the 12-year contract and the escalators and the outs every three, four years."

Alex and Boras had badly overplayed their hand. In a meeting with club officials, Boras had handed Mets executives Alex's wish list: the use of a private jet, a hotel suite on the road, a personal marketing staff with an on-site office, unlimited use of the Mets logo, a catered luxury box for friends, a promise that the team's ad campaign would center around him, and a guarantee that his image would be plastered on more billboards around New York than Jeter's.

"That was the first I'd heard of anything like [those demands]," Phillips recalls. "I felt bad for the 'twenty-four-plus-one' comment because Alex got labeled. But we had Mike Piazza, who was a superstar in his own right, and he was the lowest-maintenance superstar you'd ever see. That's what we were used to. Every once in a while his dad and his brother showed up. There was no entourage."

The response was supportive of the Mets' decision to cut off talks. Bill Madden of the New York *Daily News* wrote, "Boras, in particular, has seemingly accomplished the impossible in changing the perception of Rodriguez from a class act, team leader and baseball 'purity' to a greedy, ego-driven private corporate entity."

Alex was crushed and over the next couple of days called Mets players, urging them to push the team to return to the negotiating table. "We never reengaged," Phillips says. That was it. Game over. Boras was stunned. Few GMs had the nerve and owner support to call him out. Suddenly, Alex's dream team was off the board.

Alex saw the Mets—and, more important, New York—as the ideal stage for him to perform on. He wanted the competition, not just on the field but in the streets. He wanted to go headline-to-headline with Jeter. He kept telling the press he wanted to be part of a winner, but, as one former teammate says, "Alex only wanted to be treated like number one, the richest player in baseball, in the biggest fuckin' city in America."

The Texas Rangers watched the fallout from Perk-Gate and cheered. Good, they thought, If Alex wants preferential treatment, we will give him preferential treatment.

In one afternoon of cruising around Dallas in a convertible Mercedes SL500 driven by Rangers owner Tom Hicks, Alex experienced the sensory splendor of big money. "Everyone was looking at us," an awestruck Alex later told a friend.

Hicks had shrewdly realized that Alex needed to be courted as if he were a titan of industry, not a prom king. Other general managers took Alex to dinner; Hicks ferried him to the world of power brokers.

At 54, Hicks was a tall straw of a billionaire at a slim six-foot-five, but he loomed even taller thanks to the thick heels on his embossed cowboy boots and his aura of success. He was a home-grown Texan, the son of a radio station owner, whose amiable style had made him a natural as a disc jockey during his teens. He had spun records singing about big dreams under his moniker "The Weekend Wonder Boy" and earned another nickname on the high school football field: Ice Pick, for his spindly frame. A master of leveraged buyouts, Hicks had made millions investing in distressed companies. He was already on the Forbes 400 list in 1998 when he purchased the Rangers for $250 million from a group led by George W. Bush. In some reaches of Dallas, Hicks was the more luminary name of the two.

"It's not every day an executive signs autographs at the ballpark," the *Texas Monthly* writer Skip Hollandsworth pointed out after watching Hicks being swarmed at Rangers batting practice. As the subject of glowing features in the *New York Times* and the *Wall Street Journal*, Hicks reflected the American obsession with charismatic corporate czars. Executive giants such as General Electric CEO Jack Welch—whose books would later be on Alex's nightstand—were gaining on Hollywood A-listers as household names worthy of *People* magazine profiles.

It was a heady time for CEOs as one conglomerate after another paid millions to celebrity execs to boost profits and, just as important, the company's image. In late 2000, Rakesh Khurana, a Harvard Business School professor, told *BusinessWeek*, "We've made this a superhero job. Boards look at the CEO as a panacea and get fixated on the idea that one single individual will solve all of the company's problems."

It was no different for some baseball teams. Hicks admired A-Rod as his stellar CEO, his savior-in-stirrups. In three seasons as an owner, Hicks had watched the Yankees dismantle the Rangers, sweeping them in the 1998 and '99 play-offs. The final indignity came the next season, when the Rangers lost 91 games and left Hicks wincing with embarrassment. "We had lost to the Yankees, and we had just signed a new $500 million–plus contract with Fox Sports Net," Hicks recalls. "So we were trying to take the next step."

It was a cool Sunday, November 25, 2000, when Hicks stretched out his hand to greet Alex and his girlfriend, Cynthia, upon their arrival in Dallas. That night they dined in front of an ornate fireplace and beneath coffered ceilings at the chic Mansion on Turtle Creek restaurant.

The next day, Alex had lunch with Rangers players Rafael Palmeiro, Rusty Greer, Kenny Rogers and Manager Johnny Oates, viewed video of the team's minor-league prospects and toured the team's tricked-out stadium, the inelegantly named The Ballpark in Arlington.

Alex then slipped into Hicks's Mercedes and they went for a leisurely drive, past the art museums and the bell tower of SMU and by the boutique stores of prestigious Highland Park, where Hicks resided in a mansion with a two-story pool house. Hicks had done his homework, so he knew a few of Alex's favorite things: Armani suits, fine dining, Picasso. That's why his tour of Dallas played up the sophisticated aspects of the city and ignored the strip malls, cheap suburban sprawl and every greasy spoon that decorated its entrance in a stagecoach motif. Hicks and Rodriguez rolled on to the wealthiest stretch of Texas, Preston Hollow, where oak trees formed canopies over gated entrances to $20 million estates. The neighborhood has been home to the billionaire oilman T. Boone Pickens, the Cowboys icon Roger Staubach, George W. Bush and Dallas Mavericks owner Mark Cuban. Hicks drove Alex past Walnut Hill, where renovations on the 30,000-square-foot French château he had purchased were under way. He told Alex its pristine, 20-acre grounds would soon be outfitted with a helicopter pad.

"Alex was really interested in real estate," Hicks says. "He was very interested in the price of housing." It was clear that Rodriguez was happy to envision himself living among the elite of politics, business and sports, and carefully gleaning from his neighbors the strategies of success. "Alex is a sponge," Hicks says. "He just soaks up information. He used to ask me all about leveraged buyouts." When it came to investments, Alex wasn't like other athletes. He wasn't looking to open a restaurant or fund a friend's business. He wanted to be a mogul.

Hicks was Alex's kind of owner: savvy, worldly, self-made, number 382 on the Forbes list of the 400 richest Americans. Another key selling point: Hicks made Alex feel secure. He vowed that he wouldn't abandon Alex, at least not through the life of their 10-year deal . . . or 12 years, if Boras got his way. Hicks perceived that the perks Alex demanded were less about entitlement than about confirmation of his status. Although most players probably thought Rodriguez had enough self-confidence to fill an ocean, he desperately needed a constant stream of validation. "He is a very insecure person," says Joe Arriola.

With the Mets no longer in the running, Boras now had to get creative in order to generate a bidding war for his client. He wouldn't allow Alex to sign with the Rangers without making them sweat and up the ante. Many teams, he insisted to anyone who would listen, were willing to pony up the 10-year, $200 million entry fee to put Alex into their uniform. He wouldn't specify which teams were ready to make that deal, of course. "When you dance with a lady, it's better to whisper in her ear than use a megaphone," Boras said.

He did have one ardent suitor, the Mariners. They wanted Alex to return to Seattle but had nowhere near the resources to make it happen. They offered a reported $130 million over five years; Alex called the deal insulting.

One by one, the competitors dropped out: the Mariners, White Sox and Braves. Yet Boras had the Rangers convinced they were bidding against another team, so Hicks kept sweetening his offer. On December 15, Alex was at the Mirage in Las Vegas, enjoying the cabaret act of the singer/impersonator Danny Gans. Alex loved Vegas in all its decadence, with its fake facades and phony flair. In later years, it would become his preferred getaway destination, a place where he didn't have to camouflage his sinner's side.

For now it was an escape from the pressure of the biggest deal of his life. About halfway through Gans's act, Boras called. Alex had put his cell phone on his lap and set it to "vibrate" because he knew an offer was imminent.

"Alex, Texas can get this thing done. What do you want to do?"

"Get it done," Alex said.

Boras, Hicks and General Manager Doug Melvin negotiated for more than eight hours in a Dallas hotel room. Hicks felt the adrenaline of the escalating numbers. Melvin put his head in his hands, fretting over the figures. "I think Doug knew things were getting out of control but couldn't stop it," says a person familiar with the negotiations. Some time after midnight, Boras stood beside an easel near the sofa, where he had written "252/10." It was over. "Anything else?" asked an exhausted and elated Hicks. "Any more to say?" He stood in his cowboy boots branded with a Rangers logo, reached out his hand to Boras and pulled him close for an embrace. "I think that's one of the first times Scott realized going to an owner can have a real benefit in negotiations," Phillips says.

The 10-year, $252 million deal would dramatically alter the business landscape of baseball—it raised the ceiling for superstar salaries, gave the players' union more clout and compelled owners to adopt a luxury tax that would help small-market teams compete in the otherwise lopsided free-agent market.

Two days after Alex Rodriguez signed with Texas, he held a press conference in Dallas (the delay gave the national press plenty of time to book flights). Alex entered the Diamond Club of The Ballpark in Arlington wearing a tailored black suit and gold tie, a wardrobe choice that purposefully reflected what he perceived to be the core of Texas: oil and money.

As he looked at the more than 300 reporters gathered at his feet, his first word was "Wow." He then spoke with his usual eloquence about how thrilled he was to be a Texas Ranger and flashed his beatific smile. He talked of building a champion in Dallas.

Alex then slipped a bit, let some bitterness break through the shield of studied humility that usually earned him latitude in his press dealings. "When I came here to visit, a lot of people were joking and asking, 'What's A-Rod doing?'" Rodriguez said as he looked at his new owner. "Nobody's laughing right now; are they, Mr. Hicks?"

He chastised the Mariners for making him a lowball offer that had left him in "disbelief" and threw a jab at the Mets and their GM: "I wish I could play against Steve Phillips' team and lead twenty-four guys to beat them up. I don't know Steve on a personal level. Obviously he has an agenda against me, but I'm not sure what it is. The Mets were a definite option until he started saying we were making all these demands that obviously were huge speculation. You eliminate them, and you move on with the process." No one in the room that day stopped to point out that the Mets, in fact, had eliminated *him*.

The historic deal was discussed on network newscasts and became fodder for the late-night monologues. *ESPN the Magazine* asked its readers to vote on Alex's new nickname: E-Rod, K-Rod, MVP-Rod or Pay-Rod. On message boards, Alex was depicted as Gordon Gekko with "greed is good" in e-mail subject lines. Some baseball columnists decried his contract, saying it would be the ruin of baseball. The deal came to define him for many people: 252/10 wasn't just another stat; it was the only stat. Instead of big hits and defensive gems, 252/10 became his bar code, the price tag stamped on his chest. During spring training Alex began to feel the burden of the scrutiny, saying, "There's this 252 tag over my head."

It was a splendid April 1 in San Juan, Puerto Rico, sunny and warm. Major League Baseball had come to the island for Opening Day of the 2001 season, hoping to build on its Latino fan base. One day earlier, Tom Hicks had stood in his soaked swimsuit at a resort hotel and declared the Rangers a lock to win the AL West. ESPN was on-site to broadcast the debut of A-Rod with his new team.

The atmosphere was electric. Crowds formed on the roads leading to the hotel the teams were lodged in, hoping to get a glimpse of the players. As the buses for the Rangers and the Toronto Blue Jays were escorted by police through the city, pedestrians clapped and cheered. "You felt like the president was coming," recalls Alex Gonzalez, who had played youth ball with Rodriguez in Miami and started at shortstop for Toronto that day. "It was overwhelming."

A-Rod was visibly nervous as he took grounders before the game. He misplaced his batting glove, talked a little too fast, and chewed his gum a million times a minute. "I think he was definitely feeling the pressure to come out and make a statement on Opening Day," says Gonzalez. "He was under the magnifying glass."

Before the game, writers referred to him as "Mr. Two-Fifty-Two." After the game, they called him something worse: a flop. He botched a throw for one error, slipped on the artificial turf to foil a double play and then tripped on his shoelaces on an infield hit. The game story in the *Fort Worth Star-Telegram* summed up his fiasco this way: "Oh, yeah, one more thing: The $252 million man wasn't even the best shortstop on the field Sunday. That distinction, at least for the day, belonged to the Blue Jays' Alex Gonzalez."

Afterward, there were parties for both teams back at the resort hotel. But Alex was a no-show. He was in shock. He had until now played in the shadow of Ken Griffey, Jr., and he suddenly missed that cover. He was more comfortable being an eager disciple rather than the man expected to lead. "I think people may have looked to him more as a leader and it didn't turn out that way," says the Rangers' former closer, Tim Crabtree. "Alex Rodriguez is not a leader. I perceive him as another guy who kind of is in his own world. There's no question about his work ethic, but as far as looking for a guy to lead a ball club, that's not him. He had too many things going on, too many priorities in his life. He wasn't really looked upon as a leader, although I think Mr. Hicks would've really liked for him to be."

That "252" became an inescapable disclaimer to everything Alex did, as if it were the surgeon general's note on each pack of cigarettes: *Warning: This player makes an ungodly $252 million!* "How much is A-Rod making per strikeout? Per hit? Per trip over shoelaces? Per sunflower seeds spit or not spit?" asked *Los Angeles Times* columnist Diane Pucin after Alex struck out three times during the Rangers' home opener two days later.

Alex had his motivational guru, Jim Fannin, on speed dial. "Pressure is good. Pressure is fun," Alex kept telling himself, but the heightened expectations made him pace around the clubhouse, tighten his bat grip and rush throws. In his first 10 games, he had just 11 hits, 2 RBIs and no home runs. "He felt it," says Rangers

teammate Bill Haselman. "He had the mentality of somebody trying to hit a three-run homer with nobody on base."

Alex had always worked hard, but he worked even harder now.
He would often be in the batting cage for an hour after games. He
studied all the scouting reports and exhibited a voracious appetite
for in-game nuances. He stole signs at shortstop to detect when
a hit-and-run was on. He practiced throws from every conceiv-
able position, right down to a bare-handed dive for a ball where he
would twist and throw from his knees. "I'm kind of like, 'Wow,
dude, why would you even practice that?'" recalls former Rangers
teammate Mike Lamb. "And then, that night, the exact play hap-
pens, and you're just like, 'What in the world?' That kind of thing
just boggled my mind. You watch these guys do stuff like that, and
it ruins it for us mere mortals."

Alex was in constant motion in the Rangers clubhouse from
the moment he arrived—at noon for a 7 p.m. game—until well
after the last out. He'd sometimes watch game videos till 3 a.m.
One ex-Ranger says Alex was "the only player I ever knew who
would turn up the volume on a game tape to hear what the com-
mentators were saying about him. If they said he was great, he'd hit
the rewind button to listen to it again."

Alex's self-obsession had on-the-field benefits.

"He was aware of everything," says Haselman. "He was aware
of guys trying to steal signs, of guys taking too big a lead. He was
aware how important it is to hold a guy on second with one out,
not letting him steal third. The little things that don't show up in
stats, kind of running the field. In that regard he was tremendous,
just on top of everything. He knew the pitches coming, the pitches
being thrown to the hitters."

Alex's in-game attention to detail cut both ways, though, during his three seasons in Texas. Former Rangers say he would also
use his insider's information *against* his team in what they describe
as a stunning display of devious behavior. In games that were

lopsided—and with the Rangers, there were plenty—Alex would occasionally violate a sacred clubhouse code: From his shortstop vantage point, he would tip pitches to the supposed opposition at the plate in a quid pro quo. It would always be a middle infielder who could reciprocate.

"It was a friend of his . . . a buddy who maybe had gone 0 for 3 and needed a hit," says one former player. "Alex would see the catcher's signs. He'd signal the pitch to the hitter, do a favor for him. And down the line, Alex would expect the same in return."

According to ex-Rangers, here's how the pitch tipping worked:

The game is out of hand—one team has an eight-run lead in the late innings. Alex picks up the pitch and location signs being flashed by catcher Pudge Rodriguez. This is a normal routine for shortstops, the quarterbacks of the infield, who often use the knowledge to align the defense. If a scouting report indicates a hitter will pull a curveball, a signal by a shortstop to his defense can help infielders adjust.

The key questions are: *When* is the signal given? And, *How* is it delivered?

A shortstop's cue to the defense is usually subtle and sophisticated—a hand slipped over a kneecap, a jab step forward—and it coincides with the pitcher's windup. This way, the hitter cannot pick it up. His eyes are on the pitcher's release.

Some Rangers say Alex's cues appeared to be more conspicuous when conspiring with the opposing batter.

Before the Texas pitcher's windup, Alex, with his left arm hanging by his side, would twist his glove back and forth as if turning a dial on a safe's lock. Then the hitter knew: a changeup was on the way. Alex would also sweep dirt with his cleat to tip a slider to the batter.

The location of a pitch is vital to a hitter, too. Alex would stretch his back and lean left or right, depending on where the catcher laid down his sign, to let the batter know if the pitch was going inside or outside.

"It wasn't like he did it to throw a game—that wasn't it at all—but he did it to help himself," says a former Ranger. "He probably thought: 'Hey, it's a few times, no harm.' He didn't care if it killed his own guys. It was about stats for Alex—his."

Alex expected the same courtesy. If he were having an off night near the end of a meaningless game, Alex could look to a buddy in the middle infield for a sign. "Here was the game's best player—and yet he felt he needed this," says a former player.

Neither the Rangers nor an opposing team were ever in on these tipping conspiracies. In fact, it was only detectible because of repetition over many games and because Alex's mannerisms were so animated. Few Rangers were aware it was going on, but those who did were maddened by it.

Team chemistry is built on trust. Camaraderie is based on the premise that everyone in the clubhouse is in it together. Cheating and baseball are historically entwined—from corked bats to spit balls to pine tar—but the object of gaining an edge is never to sabotage your own team.

Even if the buddy-ball Alex was playing with a small circle of opposing players only meant a dozen extra hits for him and his pals during a long season—a home run here, an RBI there—that's a dozen moments when an inning may be extended or a pitcher's psyche may take a hit.

It was destructive on many levels. So if a small group of Rangers believed Alex was betraying his own guys, why didn't they do anything about it? Most saw a great risk in confronting Alex. They were certain Alex would go running to owner Tom Hicks to squeal on his accusers.

One Ranger at least questioned Alex.

"I think you're signaling a little too soon out there," he said.

"What are you talking about," Alex replied.

"The batters, they see you."

The conversation continued, and on the surface, Alex accepted the critique. Behind the scenes, he was enraged at being scrutinized by anyone in *his* clubhouse. He didn't change his ways.

The Rangers pitching staff struggled mightily during the Alex era in Texas. (There were other factors besides giving up extra hits off an Alex tip, but it did not escape attention when the staff ERA dropped from 5.51 from 2001 to 2003 to 4.53 in 2004—the year Alex left.)

"He talks about how pressure in Texas made him do certain things," says one former Ranger. "Well, plenty of guys have faced pressure without doing what he did . . . without undermining his own team."

Often, the pressure on Alex was self-induced. He had only himself to blame for an interview he had done with *Esquire* that ran in its April 2001 issue.

Again, he forgot to pretend to be gracious and revealed his Jeter envy/obsession. "Jeter's been blessed with great talent around him," Alex told the *Esquire* writer. "He's never had to lead. He can just go and play and have fun. And he hits second—that's totally different than third and fourth in a lineup. You got into New York, you wanna stop Bernie [Williams] and [Paul] O'Neill. You never say, 'Don't let Derek beat you.' He's never your concern."

Alex clearly didn't get it: Jeter had four rings, which in the baseball version of paper-rock-scissors, beats individual stats every time. Alex talked of winning titles, of rolling into Texas in pursuit of a World Series, but Jeter had *done* it fourfold as a Yankee. "It bothered him," Haselman says. "He wants to win really bad. He really wants a ring. Everybody does. But I think what Alex really, really wants is to be able to *say* he's a champion."

Alex had always wanted a World Series title as résumé stuffer, as a chapter in his autobiography, as an engraved line on his Hall of Fame plaque, as the final validation of his status as The Greatest Ever.

That ring must have seemed very far away during his first month as a Texas Ranger. On April 6, just days before Alex was to visit Seattle for the first time since he had dumped the Mariners, a letter was published in business journals, addressed to officials at Boeing, which was contemplating a move of its base operations from Seattle to Chicago or Dallas: "I moved to Dallas-Fort Worth to improve my future," the letter began, "so should you." Signed, Alex Rodriguez.

The letter was a clever promotion for the city of Dallas, but it incensed many Seattle fans who didn't need much to kindle their A-Rod animus. He arrived in Seattle on the Rangers' jet on tax day, April 15, braced for boos when he went out to dinner that night. He was greeted graciously—at first. "I don't care what comes out of their mouths," Alex said before the game. "I still love them."

The feeling was not mutual. When Alex walked onto Safeco Field on April 16, its retractable roof was open, open as wide as the cranks and pulleys would allow. "Alex doesn't like to hit with the roof open," Mariners president Chuck Armstrong told reporters early in the week. "If we can possibly leave it open, we'll leave it open."

Alex had a fitful night of sleep and talked to Fannin several times that day. In the first inning, as the number three hitter, his name was announced. It was greeted with a cascade of boos . . . and thousands of counterfeit bills that fluttered down to the field from the upper balconies. It appeared that every stack of Monopoly game money within 30 miles of Safeco Field had been tossed his way. Signs written in Magic Marker, crayon and craft paint were flashed from the seats: ALEX, BUY ME A HOUSE and WHO LET THE DOG IN? and A-FRAUD.

As Alex approached the on-deck circle, he kept his head down, which may be why he didn't see a spectator, Jeff Heckman, who was sitting near the field, raise a fishing pole. On the end of the line he had hooked a dollar bill, and it was now dangling over Alex's head. "I didn't even get a nibble," Heckman said later. "Maybe the denomination wasn't up there for him."

After the game, Alex tried to laugh off the boos, but they seemed to have tied him up at the plate. In that three-game series in Seattle, he went 3 for 12 with 2 strikeouts and 1 RBI. The Mariners won two of three and led the AL West with an 11–4 record. The Rangers were second at 8–8, but they went on to lose 20 of their next 26 games.

Not even A-Rod could lure people to watch a team this bad. Texas sports fans turned their attention to the upcoming Cowboys season, local TV ratings slid and the Rangers' team ERA ballooned to a league-worst 6.38. Johnny Oates resigned as manager after the first month when the team that had been touted as a pennant winner.

Alex shook off his slow start in mid-May and got his average up to .308, but skeptics delighted in pointing out that it was only .260 with runners in scoring position. Such shortcomings in his team stats didn't go unnoticed. On a tour of the Hall of Fame, the legendary Minnesota Twins slugger Kirby Puckett said of Alex, "He can't get in here with $252 million. We won't let him in. You can't buy into this team here. You have to earn it."

On June 8 the Rangers were 27 games behind the first-place Mariners and getting pounded on the field and in the papers. Thomas Boswell of the *Washington Post* called the Rangers' lone-star plan built around A-Rod "idiocy." Jack Curry, of the *New York Times*, wrote, "This is the home of the Texas Rangers, the team that can't. Can't win, can't pitch and can't fathom how a season that they thought would be exciting, perhaps memorable, has been a disaster. Can't believe this debacle happened after they signed Alex Rodriguez for 10 years, for $252 million."

Alex internalized every word of almost every article that depicted him as the fool's-gold purchase of the Rangers.

Years later, he would say that this burden of expectation
had driven him to inject a steroid he referred to as "Boli" in secret
from 2001 through 2003, though teammates say his use was not
entirely discreet. In the D.R., "Boli" was short for at least three
steroids: Dianabol, Deca-Durabolin and Primobolan, which was
the one steroid not sold in Dominican Republic pharmacies. However, it was easily obtained through the D.R.'s underground drug
trade.

Alex knew the differences between the steroids and was capable of using them expertly. In 2001, Alex was believed to be
taking a combination of Winstrol and Deca-Durabolin with a low
dose of testosterone under the guidance of the Dominican trainer
Angel "Nao" Presinal. In other words, as one player put it, Alex was
stacking steroids like a pro. He was ensuring that his stats would
stand up to the Texas heat—and all other forms of fire.

Alex Rodriguez is blessed with an angler's snap of the wrist on his
throws, a museum worthy swing and an impeccable instinct for
damage control. He needed all three of those special attributes to
survive his return to Seattle for the 72nd All-Star Game in 2001.

He deftly defused hostilities with a heartfelt—but also
ingenious—plan he had hatched a week earlier. Alex told American League Manager Joe Torre about it, but few others. In the
first inning, as Safeco Field fans were getting comfortable in their
seats, the "home team" AL players jogged out to take their posi-
tions. Alex was the starting shortstop for the AL, and beside him,
at third, was Cal Ripken, Jr. This was his final All-Star Game—his
19th in his 20-year career—but his selection to the All-Star team
this year had been based more on sentiment than on merit. One
of the greatest shortstops in baseball history, he had switched to

third base this season to accommodate a changing of the guard in Baltimore. Ripken was stirring the dirt around third with his cleats when Rodriguez walked over and nudged Ripken ever so gently toward his old shortstop position.

"Here, this is yours," he told Ripken. "Why don't you go play an inning at short?"

Ripken looked at Torre in the dugout waving him over, saw the Seattle fans snapping photos, felt Rodriguez's glove on his back, knew the TV crews were onto the scene—and had one searing thought: "I didn't want to play short," he recalls. "There was a realization that I was mic'ed and he was mic'ed. I really wanted to tell him get out of here and stop bothering me with this."

He was more flustered than flattered by the offer. He had prepared himself to play third that night, not short, in front of millions of people. Cal and Alex were alike in their polish and poise and had another major thing in common: Neither man ever wanted to look bad. "It's the focus; and no player wants to go out there, be unprepared, and potentially be embarrassed," Ripken says. Cal had added length to his shortstop's glove when he moved to third to flag hot grounders to his right or left. And he knew the roomy webbing would make any fast-twitch double-play attempt from shortstop feel as if he were reaching into a mailbox for the ball.

Ripken looked at Alex in disbelief but knew what he had to do. As he walked over to the shortstop position, Ripken turned to AL starting pitcher Roger Clemens and yelled, "Okay, looks like you gotta strike everybody out."

Ripken wasn't tested at shortstop that inning, and he moved back to third base the next time the AL players took the field. "The deeper meaning was that it was a wonderful gesture," Ripken says. And, as he would later acknowledge, the switcheroo played well with the audience. Everyone got what they needed: Ripken was rightly honored; the crowd got to savor an emotional moment; and Alex was feted for his generous spirit.

The Rangers were a toxic dump on the field and going nowhere fast, so Alex had plenty of time to fill his depressed spirits with spending sprees. He housed buddies such as Yuri "Judy" Sucart and Gui Socarras in style. He would eventually buy a 7,500-square-foot neoclassical-style home in one of Dallas's most exclusive neighborhoods, Highland Park. The two-story house had a beautiful red-tile roof, gracious arches on the front porch, a 52-inch television in a spacious family room, a semicircular drive to welcome an elite guest list of politicians and business tycoons, and a Chagall above the bedroom fireplace. Alex prized his studio-sized, custom closet, which contained rows of charcoal gray suits that were separated from black suits that were divided from cream suits, most purchased through New York's Bergdorf Goodman. Polo shirts were folded into rectangles and placed on shelves. A motorized tie rack kept his Versace silks neat. Each pair of Ferragamo shoes had its own cubbyhole.

"Alex was getting his stats and living the life," says one ex-Ranger. "He was in a different universe, like he was above what was going on."

The Rangers were losing ugly and often. Veterans such as Ken Caminiti broke down physically, a weak pitching staff became laughably bad and rifts started to form over who was in Alex's posh camp and who was not. "I think that we would all recognize that things like that can stir up within us jealousy," says Chad Curtis, a Rangers teammate of Alex's. "Unfortunately, we all probably battled with that a little bit, saying, 'Aw, Alex, he's got his own private plane.' Well, that's a by-product of who he is and what he's done, so, way to go, Alex. Now if he chooses to take a few guys with him and go do something, good for them. If he chooses to not invite others, they may feel a little put out."

Alex did have friends among his teammates. He knew Pudge and Palmeiro from their off-seasons spent around one another in Miami. He formed a bond with Michael Young, a promising second baseman. Other players, though, took their cue from his cool attitude and distanced themselves from him, irritated by their prima donna. A clubhouse attendant was required to place toothpaste on Alex's toothbrush after every game. A hotel suite had to be outfitted with a basket of Alex's favorite foods when he arrived for road games. It was to some Rangers—as Mets GM Steve Phillips had predicted—a 24-plus-1 clubhouse. In previous years, the Rangers had been a close team, back when Will Clark had held them together. "If [Will] told a player to jump off a cliff, there's a good chance he'd jump off," Crabtree recalls. "If Alex Rodriguez told me to jump off a cliff, I'd say, 'You first.'"

The Texas baseball fans never seemed to take to A-Rod either. They were mostly of the boot-wearing, truck-driving culture that loved Troy Aikman's toughness in the pocket as a Dallas Cowboy and Nolan Ryan's gunslinger snarl on the mound. They sensed that Alex Rodriguez wasn't a player's player, that he held himself above the tobacco chewing, the jock scratching and the daily ribbing that bonded a team.

Even Hicks knew that his big investment wasn't paying full dividends. "Alex, he's a strong personality," the owner says now. "I think he's been coached along the way, and he's very smooth in how he handles the media. And I think when you compare him to hometown heroes, like Pudge Rodriguez or Nolan Ryan, they're just not that way. They're much more direct and just talk like an athlete. I think at least in our case our fans warmed up to that style more than Alex's."

Alex never seemed aware of his sliding Q rating. As one friend explains it, Alex equates his popularity to All-Star and MVP votes—status markers. As his debut season in Texas ground on, he felt pressure to keep his voting bloc happy by retaining their awe with big numbers. "What changes is, the expectations keep getting higher," Alex said upon his arrival in Texas. "People expect you to be superhuman."

With the right steroids, in the right clubhouse, Alex met that expectation.

Chapter Seven

THE "B-12" CODE

FROM THE FIRST DAY of spring training for the 2001 season, it was clear to his Rangers teammates that Alex Rodriguez wasn't even going to pretend to be a calloused, good-ole-boy Texas rough-neck. The inside of his large designer duffel, often lugged by a club-house attendant, looked more like a woman's carry-on: Clinique scrub for his face, emery boards for his nails, skin lotions, dental floss, hair products, lip balm and a self-help book.

The beauty products reflected Alex's "Look good, feel good" philosophy and dovetailed with an obsession about what he put into his body. He rarely drank alcohol, did not eat fried foods or sweets—preferring skinless broiled chicken and vegetables—and chugged down protein powders, supplements and vitamin packs to increase his fitness, sculpt his body and boost his energy. He would soon find that the Rangers clubhouse offered plenty of other ways to help him look good, feel good and crush baseballs. It was a virtual pharmacy for players, full of performance enhancers. There, on the shelves of lockers and sometimes stacked on the floor, sharing space with shoes, fan letters and batting gloves, were FedEx boxes stuffed with unmarked packages of syringes, steroids and growth hormone. This doping culture had been prevalent in Texas ever since 1993, when Jose Canseco had been traded there from Oakland.

Rafael Palmeiro, Pudge Rodriguez and Juan Gonzalez had all been avid students in Canseco's graduate seminar on steroids. They would frequently duck into a bathroom stall or a video room and inject each other with Deca, Winstrol and testosterone, combining water-based and oil-based steroids to create the desired effect: power and, just as important, confidence.

Steroids weren't exclusive to the Rangers—there were sirens going off all around the league, though no one wanted to heed them—but this team had many of the most profligate abusers. In 1993, Texas led the American League in home runs and in Mr. Universe physiques. Canseco played in Arlington for only a couple of years, but his impact lasted a decade. The Rangers became an offensive juggernaut, putting up astonishing power numbers. The question wasn't "What's in the water in Texas?" but "What's in the bag?"

Some major-league players have estimated that up to 50 percent of their teammates were on steroids from 1998 to 2003. The number might have been higher for the Rangers. Dressing next to Alex in that clubhouse were many players who would be tied to steroids, including Palmeiro, Gonzalez, Pudge Rodriguez, Randy Velarde and former NL MVP Ken Caminiti. More resolute than remorseful, Caminiti first talked publicly about his use of steroids with *Sports Illustrated* in 2002. He laid out the doping self-justification of many players when he said, "Look at all the money in the game. You have a chance to set your family up, to get your daughter into a better school. So I can't say, 'Don't do it,' not when the guy next to you is as big as a house and he's going to take your job and make the money."

Most players trust few people outside their inner circle. And Alex was no different. He spent most of his time with childhood friends—such as Gui Socarras and Yuri Sucart—and his girlfriend, Cynthia. Teammates say he purposely isolated himself because he was using steroids. "He didn't let people in," says one former Ranger. "He didn't want anyone to know—especially Hicks." In the Rangers clubhouse, Alex mostly hung out with the same crew, often speaking in Spanish with Palmeiro and Pudge. They would talk baseball, family and, in more cryptic tones, doping. "They didn't say anything in the open—they weren't telling the world or anything," says the former Ranger. "But when you hear 'B-12,' you hear it."

A "B-12 shot" was known as the code for an injection of steroids.

Some nights during the 2001 season, scoreboards seemed as if they would overheat from the barrage of hits and runs the Rangers put on them. Of the league-high 246 homers the Rangers hit in 2001, 47 came off the bat of the 36-year-old Palmeiro and a stunning 52 were launched by the 26-year-old Alex Rodriguez. "I think Alex is the kind of guy motivated not by the money but by putting up the best numbers he can put up," said Bill Haselman, his former Rangers teammate. "I think he wants to be the home-run king of all time."

Alex joined Babe Ruth, Willie Mays, Mickey Mantle, Ralph Kiner and Jimmie Foxx—all Hall of Famers—in hitting 50 home runs at such a young age. "At times, I forget how young I am, because I've been playing for so long," Alex said.

It might have only seemed so long because the Rangers were so bad. All those hits didn't translate into wins; the team had a league-

worst 5.71 ERA and finished last in its division, with a 73–89 record. The *Los Angeles Times* said A-Rod "[played] out a season for
the ages in virtual obscurity."

In the papers and on *SportsCenter*, he was also being buried by
Barry. In 2001, Bonds hit a single-season record 73 homers, breaking Mark McGwire's mark set just three seasons earlier. Seattle's
Ichiro Suzuki lit up Japan and America with his running swing,
which he used to lead the league with a .350 batting average.

Far from the national spotlight, Alex not only pounded balls
over the fence but also had a .318 average and 135 RBIs. It was one
of the greatest offensive seasons ever for a shortstop, and for what?
To finish 43 games behind his old team, the Seattle Mariners?

Just one year into his monumental 10-year deal, and the Rangers were already looking like a mistake for A-Rod. Attendance was
sagging, and television ratings were plunging. Someone had to
take the fall: Hicks fired General Manager Doug Melvin and hired
John Hart. "I think the landscape is littered with train wrecks that
have never made the postseason," Hart said when he took the job,
"clubs that are in large markets and have floundered around and
never had a clear path. We are not going to become one of those
train wrecks."

In October 2001, Hart was at the end of a successful 10-year run
as the respected and dashing general manager of the Cleveland Indians. Before the season began, he announced that it would be his
last with the team. Time for new blood.

The Indians gave him a nice send-off, winning the American
League Central title. Juan Gonzalez, two years removed from his
glory days in Texas, was in the midst of an astounding revival: He
hit .325 with 35 homers and a team-high 140 RB. He finished fifth
in MVP balloting.

The team's final regular-season road trip ended in Toronto, where, three weeks after 9/11, airport security was especially tight. All bags, whether from commercial or charter planes, were scrutinized by the Canadian Border Service. As reported by the New York *Daily News*, agents noticed that an unidentified gym bag had come off the Indians' charter flight. Wary, they unzipped the bag and discovered five ampoules of anabolic steroids, pills containing the adrenergic agonist clenbuterol, and hypodermic needles. Agents alerted Toronto police and called Indians executives, who were checking in at the Westin Harbour Castle hotel. Canadian officials then stepped back and waited to see who claimed the bag.

A short time later, a member of Gonzalez's entourage picked it up. When questioned by Toronto police, he said it belonged to a man who worked for Gonzalez: Angel Presinal, a 48-year-old trainer who had built an almost mystical reputation in the Dominican Republic for his healing touch with injured athletes. He worked with the D.R.'s national boxing and basketball teams but was better known for his involvement with some of baseball's greatest players, including David Ortiz, Pedro Martinez, Vladimir Guerrero and Miguel Tejada. He was also on Gonzalez's payroll. Presinal made most of his living off bonuses, such as the $50,000 he received from Gonzalez after his client was voted MVP in 1996.

Presinal arrived in Toronto that day on a later flight, and Canadian border agents were there to greet him at the team hotel, along with Cleveland's security chief, Jim Davidson. Presinal told Davidson the bag and its contents belonged to Gonzalez; he claimed he had packed the steroids for Gonzalez and had come to Toronto to help him administer them—a task he said he had performed many times for high-profile players.

The authorities then talked to Gonzalez, who had a different story: he said he had no idea who had packed the bag or what it contained. Both men were questioned for hours, but officials could never determine who owned the bag. "I didn't do anything [wrong]," Presinal would claim years later. Canadian authorities finally confiscated the bag and released Gonzalez and Presinal.

MLB officials were livid—and frustrated—when they learned of the Toronto bag incident. They were increasingly sensitive to the growing suspicions about steroid use by many of the top sluggers, but with the Players Association resisting every effort to devise a policy for testing, there was little they could do to a player caught with steroids. MLB could go after the enablers, though. Before the 2002 season, Rob Manfred, the executive vice president of Major League Baseball, banned Presinal from every major-league ballpark. All clubs were notified and sent a description of the musclebound trainer.

Hart never disciplined Gonzalez, and a few weeks after the incident, the GM left the Indians behind and settled into his new job with the Rangers. Unlike the other GMs, Hart didn't need a picture of Presinal. He knew his face well.

Hart had a busy off-season in Arlington. Rodriguez leveraged his close relationship with Hicks to weigh in on personnel moves. He knew the Rangers needed more pitching, not more hitting, and Hart tried to please him by signing Chan Ho Park, Ismael Valdes and Todd Van Poppel. In an effort to shake up what he perceived to be a complacent team, he brought in some notorious misfits with problematic baggage of a different sort: He signed Carl Everett despite the hotheaded outfielder's feuds with management in Boston; he signed the closer John Rocker, even though the former Brave had insulted almost every minority in New York with a homophobic, race-baiting rant in *Sports Illustrated* in 2000; and he brought Juan Gonzalez back to Texas. Apparently Hart wasn't put off by Gonzalez's bad attitude, his bad back or his blatant connection to steroids.

The new slogan for these new Rangers was "America's game. Your team." Based on the rampant use of steroids by some members of this group, the marketing department might have considered labeling them "The Dirty Dozen."

Despite his major-league ban, Angel Presinal was busier than ever. He was working with Gonzalez, and he had picked up another big-name client in 2001: Alex Rodriguez.

They'd met on one of Alex's many off-season trips to the D. R.

They quickly formed a close bond, with Presinal working on Alex's strength and conditioning. The Rangers weren't especially concerned about steroids. They rewarded Gonzalez with a nice contract and turned their heads when a doctor from the players' union showed up at their spring training facility and was seen pulling players aside and lecturing them on how to use steroids safely, as one player says. John Rocker confirmed the same scene in a 2008 radio interview. Rocker described how the union doctor had told them, "If you do it responsibly, it's not going to hurt you." The reliever says there had been just three players in this personalized how-to session: himself, Rafael Palmeiro and Alex Rodriguez.

The union was especially protective of Alex and knew of his relationship with Presinal. The Players Association did not interfere. Alex's image as the game's one true thing was important to many people. This included a league that craved an embraceable star to one day take the place of the serially surly Barry Bonds as the all-time home-run leader; a union empowered by Alex's record-breaking deal; and the agent Scott Boras, who, with A-Rod as his trophy, was validated as the planet's best deal maker.

"In an entertainment industry, there are good guys and bad guys," says former Ranger Carl Everett, who was branded as a villain by the media and will point out that A-Rod was ejected from more Texas games than he was. "Alex was the shining star. He's baseball's darling."

Boras was also the union's precious ally. In the backdrop, in sync with his longtime friend Gene Orza, the union's COO, Boras was a quiet force behind the Players Association's resistance to steroid testing. His biggest client—the most important player in baseball—was on them. As one player describes it, "You can't have a guy sign for $250 million and him hit 26 homers. Then the deal is shit. C'mon now, Boras was the bagman and Alex was the bag. [Orza] had both their backs."

A major-league player says union officials enabled the steroid era two ways: first, by declaring war on testing and dismissing the hazards of steroids; and second, by warning players not to purchase steroids in the United States in an effort to avoid authorities.

Alex knew every trick, but he was still sloppy about hiding his associations with steroid suspects. Repercussions seemed to escape his logic. Or maybe he felt protected from them by his handlers.

There are sign-in sheets in front of MLB clubhouses where security attendants require anyone not employed by the team to sign in. On several of these sheets from the 2002 season, the name Angel Presinal was listed on the docket. He flouted the ban. His star clients ignored it, too.

Far from being concerned about Presinal, the Rangers did what they could to make his job easier. They regularly reserved—though did not pay for—a room for him during Texas road trips. From 2001 through 2003, Presinal trained Alex at home, on the road and even in a chartered plane. One former Ranger described him as a "gnat by Alex's side."

When MLB officials learned that Presinal had been at The Ballpark in Arlington and the stadium in Anaheim, they ordered him removed. No matter. He worked in the shadows, seen by his players but not by MLB officials. Alex never skipped a beat.

The Ballpark in Arlington was built in 1994 as a kitschy homage to the American pastime—a popular conceit at the time. The same year The Ballpark was under construction, Disney was building a planned and canned town called Celebration, Florida, which was supposed to be an ode to the sock hop era, complete with a town square with old movie marquees on its theaters and chirping bluebird sounds pumped through loudspeakers near an old-fashioned soda shop. The Ballpark in Arlington was just as phony. It had multiple-personality disorder: the roof porch was like that of the old Tiger Stadium; the white steel frieze surrounding the upper deck resembled that of the original Yankee Stadium; a hand-operated scoreboard mimicked Fenway's; the arched windows came from Comiskey Park; the red brick veneer was lifted from Camden Yards. It was a patchwork stadium at best, a tacky monstrosity at all other times.

Alex liked it, in all of its artificiality, because he loved hitting there.

He hit .323 at home during the 2002 season; he was good almost every night and great on many of them. Unfortunately for Rangers fans, he was the only Texas star who shined. Setting the standard for slow starts, the Rangers were 11 games out of first place before April 23. The team was as bad as it had been the year before, but the farther behind the Rangers slipped in the standings, the more dominant Alex became—and the more irritable. In the first 990 games of his career, he had been ejected from a game only once. In a span of 12 games in June, he was tossed twice.

The rage Alex displayed was born of frustration, but he managed to channel that anger. By July, the Rangers were 16 games out of first place in the AL West, and Alex could not have been more impressive. He hit 12 home runs that month. His torrid hitting, however, did not bring fans to The Ballpark in Arlington. He was not, as Boras had promised in his gilded A-Rod portfolio, a boon to the Rangers' bottom line.

In July, Hicks told reporters that the Rangers had lost $31 million in the past year and might lose more in the 2002 season. He sounded very much as if he had buyer's remorse. "I'm not doing it anymore," Hicks said of his profligate free-agent purchases. "We're going to play within our means from now on, at least break even."

He wasn't getting a return at the gate from Alex despite his star's inspired production, and he was getting nothing from the $24 million he had invested in Juan Gonzalez. "Oh, God, Juan never played," Hicks recalls. "I mean, it was a big contract; he was hurt; he was injured; and in hindsight he probably had things in his body that weren't healthy."

Such hindsight is now common in baseball and always comes with a self-serving blind spot. Hicks was new to baseball—the neon sign of steroid use during the Canseco years in Texas had been under the visage of owner George W. Bush—and was hardly educated on the world of performance enhancers.

"I swear, I don't think he knew about Alex," says a former Ranger.

Alex was under Hicks's nose each day. They were constant breakfast partners and dinner companions. At times, in a manipulative attempt to build up his holy image while demolishing others, Alex would whisper names of dopers into Hicks's ear.

"Alex used to tell me negative things about other players around the league that were suspected [of steroid use]," Hicks says.

As a new owner, Hicks was naive about the prevalence of steroid abuse. But it's hard to explain GM John Hart's selective ignorance. Hart knew about Gonzalez's Canadian fiasco before signing him. But baseball in the steroid era was full of people doing moral backflips, professing willful ignorance and embracing contradictions—as in *Steroids are bad for a player . . . unless they are good for a player.* Increased production on the field made contrarians of almost everyone in the game. Home runs squared the ethics of cheating.

All that mattered to owners and GMs, to the union and agents, was one question: Did the player deliver?

And no one in baseball delivered more in 2002 than Alex Rodriguez did.

The oppressive heat of a 97-degree afternoon fell to a more merciful 91-degree Saturday night at The Ballpark when the Rangers took the field against the Blue Jays on August 17. The day before, he'd gone four for four, with a game-winning home run. Pitches looked as big and slow as soap bubbles to him, and he could see the seams spinning toward him.

Alex had never faced tonight's Blue Jays' starter, Steve Parris, but he had scoured the scouting report and was one of the best at reading pitchers from the on-deck circle, taking mock swings, noting release points and tics. In the first inning, with the sky darkening, Alex belted a 1–0 pitch into the left-field stands for his 40th home run of the year, 404 feet by the measuring tape. Undeterred, Parris was feeling good two innings later when he battled Alex to a 2–2 count. The next pitch turned into Alex's 41st home run, traveling 416 feet. When Jays reliever Corey Thurman got his shot at Alex in the seventh inning, he was met with a 366-foot blast for home run number 42. "I was possessed by the moment," Alex explained later.

This tape of performance set off the steroid alarms. In the dog days of the season, when players are wilting, A-Rod had fresh legs and a fresher bat. "It's that stuff that makes you say no fuckin' way," said one Rangers teammate.

The Rangers won their third straight that night but still trailed first-place Oakland by 20 games. Evan Grant of the *Dallas Morning News* wrote, "He is stuck on a team going nowhere, so Alex Rodriguez passes the hottest, most tedious part of the summer with a game of 'Can you top this?' He plays against himself."

And against ghosts. Alex knew of those who had gone before him and counted the game's living legends, such Cal Ripken,

Jr., and Pete Rose, as intimate advisers. He often declared that his mission was to compete with the record books. He loathed the Rangers' deadbeat existence because he didn't want to be associated with a loser. How would history judge him if he never won a World Series? Or, worse yet, never even made it to the play-offs as a Ranger?

He muscled out a league-high 57 home runs and 142 RBIs in a season that started a hot debate: Can the MVP trophy go to a player on a bad team? As the votes were tallied, Presinal was anxious—he had a big bonus riding on this vote.

Alex placed second in the balloting for the second time in his career, with the AL MVP going to Oakland's Miguel Tejada, another Dominican player who would be linked to performance enhancers. Another Presinal client.

Alex Rodriguez had a strong ally in Rangers Manager Jerry Narron, who recognized that the game's best player was happiest when allowed to create his own work environment. He knew that Alex—like his boyhood idol, Cal Ripken, Jr.—valued routine and structure and was wary of change. Narron was an amiable man who would stay up with Alex until 1 a.m. talking baseball in his office. Narron was also happy to accommodate the special perks A-Rod demanded. He was even allowed to pick his own clubhouse attendant, Tommy Bolin, a friend from Miami who had worked in the Anaheim clubhouse. Bolin was much older than his coattendants in the Rangers clubhouse—generally 18-year-olds on an $8,000 salary, plus tips—and he was virtually Alex's personal valet.

Narron was fired after the 2002 season, when the $100 million payroll yielded a worse record (72–90) than the team had posted in 2001. Hicks and Hart turned to a no-nonsense manager with plenty of baseball gravitas: Buck Showalter.

"Alex and I had a healthy respect for each other," says Showalter. "Some of my best times were sitting down and talking baseball with him."

Showalter was the son of a high school principal from a small mill town in Florida who valued discipline and authority. After three strong years managing the Yankees, he joined the long line of capable managers who had butted heads with the Yankees' owner, George Steinbrenner, and were quickly shown the door.

It was obvious to even casual fans that the Rangers needed a mental makeover, and Alex said little about the change. He had other issues on his mind. He was finally getting married. A year earlier, he had proposed to Cynthia Scurtis in a romantic Art Deco South Beach restaurant with the elegant ambiance of Sinatra-era Miami.

She had said yes, but her Greek family wasn't completely on board. Alex was viewed as a bit of an outsider to their faith, but, as the November 2 wedding date approached, Cynthia's 82-year-old grandfather, the respected Demosthenes Mekras, who had founded the first Greek Orthodox cathedral in Miami, agreed to preside over the ceremony.

Alex had actively prowled Dallas's club scene as a bachelor while dating Cynthia, but he relied on her for structure. She planned his days, oversaw his philanthropy and helped him formulate a corporate allure. "She was the rock in the relationship," Hicks recalls. "I think she helped him be a man."

Cynthia had left her job as a high school teacher and was working as a pretrial counselor, championing hardship cases, trying to keep the poor and underrepresented out of prison. "She was dealing with bottom-of-the-barrel people, but she loved doing it," Cynthia's sister told the *New York Post*. "Cynthia is intelligent and eager—she can read you up and down after your first conversation."

She grew up among the affluent near Miami's tony Coconut Grove. Her father, John, was an importer/exporter, while her mother, Evangeline, did volunteer work at local hospitals. She was serious but popular, a sorority girl and an ambitious woman.

Hicks hosted the rehearsal dinner at his home; he was famed for throwing lavish parties, having once hired Whoopi Goldberg to perform at an investors' retreat at the Ritz-Carlton near Palm Springs, and he spared no expense for Alex and Cynthia. A band played at his mansion. Champagne flowed all night. "It was a pretty grand evening," Hicks recalls. "All her family are Greeks, his family are all Dominicans, and we had Cal Ripken and Michael Young and my family there. And after everybody left, Alex and Cal and my son and I—and Boras—stayed up and talked baseball till about three in the morning."

Alex seldom drank, but on the night before his wedding, Hicks says that they all did a couple of tequila shots. The groom-to-be was buzzed and happy. "Just hearing Cal give big-brother kind of advice to Alex about what would lie ahead of him in baseball was a special treat for me," Hicks recalls.

A few hours later, they were all pressed, polished and ready to await the bride at the altar in a ceremony performed at Alex's Highland Park home. Cynthia looked beautiful and, as always, fit. She had just begun training with the pro bodybuilder Jenny Worth, who was a Fitness Olympia contestant in Miami, working under the celebrity trainer Dodd Romero.

Cynthia looked sculpted in an Amsale gown sparkling with Swarovski crystals sewn into the fabric. The vows were exchanged, and Alex was now a married man.

"He came to me after the wedding and asked, 'What do married people do?'" a former teammate recalls. "And I'm like, 'Wow, this guy needs someone to tell him how to be in every way.'"

What did it mean to love someone else more than himself? What sacrifice did that require?

"I think there was love," says a friend, "but there was also need.

Alex needed her to ground him from what I guess you'd call a dark side."

In the winter of 2003, at the start of spring training at baseball facilities in Arizona and Florida, major-league players were greeted by lab technicians with plastic cups. Drug testing in baseball had officially begun.

Major League Baseball and the Players Association were forced to do it. In the summer of 2002, politicians alarmed by Ken Caminiti's sordid steroid confessions in *Sports Illustrated* had dragged baseball officials before a Senate subcommittee and browbeat them into adopting a testing policy.

The union balked. As one former Rangers player says, "Why would the union sign off on a test that would kill the golden goose—steroids? Guys were making a killing with it."

Money meant power for the union.

"The union knew about [steroids] for quite some time, there's no question in my mind," says former Ranger Tim Crabtree, who was a union rep in Texas. "And because of the numbers people were putting up, putting more people in the seats, better for the game overall, better for bargaining, and all that . . . it was just kind of, 'Look the other way.'"

And as Canseco once wrote, "The [Players Association] never lifted a finger to stop it."

Two players who would end up being named in the Mitchell Report in 2007 say the union kept telling superstars the same thing: Don't worry about the testing; we'll take care of it.

Players Association Executive Director Donald Fehr didn't want testing but knew he had no choice but to deliver some reasonable facsimile of a plan to dislodge politicians from his back. The compromise agreement he made with MLB stipulated that every player on the 40-man rosters would be tested at least once, and throughout the season 240 players would be tested again. All results would be anonymous, and if fewer than 5 percent of the results were positive, no mandatory, punitive testing program would be imposed. The anonymity, of course, was considered a joke. Players were asked by administrators of the test to sign their names next to the code that corresponded to their specimen containers.

"The idea [behind the testing] was to get a feel for how many people were doing it," says Crabtree. "Yet every test had a name attached to it. So in that regard did the union screw up? Yeah, I'd say they did, because I don't know how you can attach a name to a sample if it's truly anonymous."

The union never imagined that the players would need the anonymity. Officials did everything they could to diminish the potential number of positive tests and keep them from reaching the 5 percent threshold that would trigger mandatory testing with punitive measures for cheaters. Keep the number below 5 percent— and the 'roid life would go on as it had. Players were told they'd be tested in spring training, so it would be easy for them to cycle off steroids to avoid detection. The handful of others tested in-season was given a heads-up because doping officials had to apply for parking passes and clubhouse credentials in advance. Drug-testing officials believe that teams used that gap to serve notice of the officials' arrival. That gave cheaters time to flush their system.

Players also became students of trickery. Some would disappear from the stadium when lab techies arrived. Others were known to use a device called a Whizzinator—a faux penis in five different shades of skin color that players kept tucked in their boxer briefs. The device contained a heat pack that kept a substitute urine stream at a temperature meant to fool the test administrators and ultimately dupe the lab tests.

"There are all sorts of mechanical devices—like catheters—

athletes use," says Dr. Gary Wadler, a member of the World Anti-
Doping Agency. "These methods still go on."

It would seem a good bit of chicanery was going down for
MLB testing that was pitched to players as anonymous. The union
tried to calm its players—and their agents—by telling its members
that if anyone did test positive, the results would be destroyed. No
harm would ever come of it.

Alex was well aware of the upcoming tests and, like many players, made an adjustment in his steroid routine. By 2003, a large number of players were switching from Deca-Durabolin to Primobolan
with a low dose of testosterone. Alex was believed to have moved
from Deca to Primo during the spring. Quest Diagnostics, which
analyzed the tests, was not a sophisticated Olympic-style lab—it's
the kind of place you send your cholesterol tests to, says one antidoping expert—but it did have the capability to detect the obvious.

One of the benefits of using Primobolan is that the steroid
produces maximum strength with minimum bulk and, even when
a player goes off it, there is a long retention of power. "I've taken
it," one former player says. "It's not an Incredible Hulk steroid."
The drug also has relatively few side effects and, most important,
it is detectable for a far shorter period of time than the steroids
previously favored by players, Deca-Durabolin and Winstrol. One
player trainer puts it bluntly: "Players could piss it out quicker."

At least 104 players and as many as 115, as federal agents would
later discover, either did not flush their systems adequately or didn't
even bother, never imagining that their test results would not be
destroyed. Apparently, Alex never thought twice. He felt that the
union—and thereby, Boras—had his back.

Spring training had one more twist for Alex: in mid-March, he felt
stiffness and fatigue in his left shoulder. He hadn't felt anything

pop or strain, so he tried to play through it, but a CT scan revealed a microscopic tear in the C6–C7 disk. He sat out for two weeks but was ready for the season opener. Alex felt his hefty contract obligated him to play every game, and he had not missed one in two seasons with the Rangers.

There was someone new with the Rangers watching over Alex's workouts: the Rangers new strength and conditioning coach, Fernando Montes, an antisteroid advocate who had worked with the Cleveland Indians for nine years. He knew right away that Alex was a steroid user—and he wasn't afraid to say so.

Obviously, the Rangers had their suspicions. One day Assistant General Manager Jon Daniels pulled up to Montes in a golf cart.

"Out of the clear blue, he asked, 'Do you think Alex is juicing?'" Montes recalls. "I said, 'Yes.'"

Montes didn't base his opinion on seeing a needle. He could tell from two decades of experience. "I watched him in the weight room," Montes says. "He was complaining about work level and intensity. What he was doing didn't match up to the numbers he was putting up and his ability to recover 162 games playing the way he does."

He also noticed how removed Alex was from the other Rangers. Alex was known to shower separately in an effort to hide steroid side effects from teammates. "You see it with steroid users: they act like they have a secret," Montes says. "They only talk to certain people inside and outside the clubhouse. They withdraw."

Buck Showalter tried to clear the Rangers' workplace of pals and posses. Showalter had seen Presinal—and didn't know much about him—but he didn't want player flies buzzing around. At one point, Showalter, hoping to declutter Alex's baseball world, suggested he pare down his entourage. Alex listened, but nothing changed.

There were fewer and fewer people in Alex's life who tried to bend his will—even a little. Eddie Rodriguez (no relation) had

THE GREATEST* "I haven't seen too many guys who can get their bat through the hitting zone any faster than Alex," said Rodriguez's first professional hitting coach, Lee Elia, of the Seattle Mariners. "With his ability, there's no telling what he can accomplish." RONALD MARTINEZ/GETTY IMAGES

THE SUPERNATURAL
Rodriguez hit .505 with 9 home runs and 35 stolen bases during his senior year at Miami's Westminster High. In 1994 he was the first draft pick overall for the Seattle Mariners. BILL FRAKES—

JUNIOR MINTED Batting in front of Ken Griffey Jr. ensured that Rodriguez saw a lot of fat pitches in the strike zone as a rookie. In 1996, his first full season with the Mariners, he led the majors with a .358 batting average while hitting 36 home runs and 123 RBIs. As Rodriguez's star rose, Junior got jealous: "One day, I'd like to hit in front of me, too." OTTO GREULE JR./ALLSPORT/GETTY

GARY BARBER/ALLSPORT/GETTY

MR. TWO-FIFTY-TWO Rodriguez, with agent Scott Boras *(left)* and Texas Rangers owner Tom Hicks, is introduced as a Ranger after signing his record-breaking, 10-year, $252 million contract in 2001. The Rangers were awful, but in 2003 Rodriguez was named the American League MVP. He later admitted to using the steroid Primobolan for the three seasons he played in Texas.

GREG FIUME/NEWSPORT/CORBIS

INTRODUCING C-ROD

Rodriguez met Cynthia Scurtis at a Miami gym in 1996. Over the objections of her family, they dated for six years before marrying in 2002 at the home of Rangers owner Tom Hicks. The couple, who have two children, divorced in 2008. KEVIN MAZUR/NFL FOR BRAGMAN NYMAN CAFARELLI/GETTY

DAMNED YANKEE

Desperate to leave Texas, Rodriguez joined Joe Torre's Yankees with great expectations and two humbling conditions: he had to switch his uniform number from 3 (which belonged to Babe Ruth) to 13, and he agreed to play third base in deference to Captain Derek Jeter, against whom Rodriguez had always measured himself. Rodriguez won two more AL MVP Awards, in 2005 and 2007, but has never won a World Series; Jeter has won four.

PETER MORGAN/REUTERS/CORBIS

ROBERT GALBRAITH/REUTERS/CORBIS

TOMASSO DEROSA—US PRESSWIRE

THE COMPANY HE KEEPS Rodriguez at the 2004 All-Star Game with Barry Bonds, baseball's all-time home run king, who has also been accused of using steroids. JEFF MITCHELL/REUTERS/CORBIS *Below:* Rodriguez is taunted by Toronto fans for his close friendship with Kaballah teammate Madonna. MIKE CASSESE/REUTERS/CORBIS

SHADOW OF DOUBT At a press conference in Tampa on February 17, 2009, Rodriguez admitted to steroid use from 2001–2003, saying, "I knew we weren't taking Tic Tacs."

AP PHOTO/MARY ALTAFFER

IN ROD WE TRUST
From left: Teammates Mariano Rivera, Andy Pettitte, Derek Jeter, and Jorge Posada watch Rodriguez discuss receiving injections from his cousin. At a similar press conference one year earlier, Pettitte confessed to having used human growth hormone (HGH).

CHRIS LIVINGSTON/ICON SMI/CORBIS

UNSTRUNG HERO Sitting next to Yankees general manager Brian Cashman, Rodriguez told reporters, "The last 15 months have been very, very tough. I've been through divorce, I've been through tabloids, you name it. I miss playing baseball and simply being a baseball player." AL MESSERSCHMIDT/GETTY IMAGES

THE HALL OF FAME QUESTION His prodigious stats suggest that Rodriguez will be considered one of the greatest players in baseball history, but voters for the Hall of Fame have shunned those who took steroids to prolong their careers. How will they treat someone who may have been "using" from day one? ANTHONY J. CAUSI/ICON SMI been Alex's go-to parent at the Miami Boys & Girls Club since he was seven years old.

He was one of the few people who would challenge Alex and set him straight. He would talk to him about sportsmanship and attitude. If Alex even tossed a bat in anger during a game, Eddie was there to call him out. "They drifted apart," one person close to Eddie says. "Alex wasn't listening to anyone anymore."

Alex stuck with Presinal. In the spring of 2003, Alex had ingested supplements and stimulants, injected steroids and rubbed on balms to prevent wilting. Presinal used every trick in his bag to heal Alex's neck. He wasn't completely at full strength, but on April 2, 2003, Alex hit his 300th career home run, making him—at 27 years and 249 days old—the youngest player to reach that milestone, breaking by 79 days the record set by Jimmie Foxx. His power was curtailed, though, and he was enduring more 0 for 4 games than usual. The Rangers didn't fare much better. They were 10–14 by April 26 and got worse from there. In June, the Rangers won only 7 games and lost 20. Hicks was simmering as he watched The Worst Team Money Can Buy flounder. In the *Atlanta Journal-Constitution*, Thomas Stinson wrote, "Strapped with a payroll that dedicates 34 percent of its $103.5 million to two players this year—A-Rod at $22 million and Gonzalez at $13 million—spending more for pitching help has become impossible. The road to insolvency is strewn with those who try to spend with New York's George Steinbrenner."

Hicks was not The Boss, but he was The Owner. He eventually stopped consulting with Alex on personnel issues (that direct line of communication had irritated both other players and Showalter) and began talking about ditching his marquee players for a younger, cheaper future. This was welcome news for Showalter, who preferred working with low-maintenance, young prospects. By the end of June, it was reported that Hart was in trouble. None of his 2002 signings was working out: Chan Ho Park was a disaster;

Rocker and Van Poppel had already been released. Hart's team was the "train wreck" he had once mocked.

By the All-Star break, there was trouble in the clubhouse once it became clear that Carl Everett and Juan Gonzalez, among other stars, were being shopped. Alex was still hurting. "I don't remember the last time I felt a hundred percent," he said in July.

Alex had plenty of people in addition to Judy and Presinal holding his hand. At home, Cynthia had flown the bodybuilder Jenny Worth in as her private trainer. She and Alex also welcomed in the trainer Dodd Romero and his wife, Sabina, on occasion. The guests cooked and trained Alex and Cynthia throughout 2003.

By Alex's standards, his .285 batting average and 22 homers by mid-July were a major disappointment. He didn't blame his neck injury, though. Instead, he ripped the Rangers organization. In the July 30 edition of *USA Today*, Alex told the columnist Jon Saraceno, "This is the first year where the performance of the team has actually affected my play—and there's absolutely no excuse. This is the first year I've felt like this losing is wearing on me. Mentally, I haven't been as honed in on my craft. I think it's three years of the same thing."

After digging himself a hole, he jumped into it: "At some point, if we don't turn it around, I will definitely be having a conversation with our owner. If he feels he has a better chance of winning without me, then I'd [discuss it]. I want what's best for both of us."

Note the "selflessness" of that last sentence, a perfect—and typical—A-Rod pronouncement. Those remarks did not sit well with his teammates, who already had a nickname for Alex—"The Cooler," as Ken Rosenthal of the *Sporting News* would later report. The moniker was rooted in this undeniable fact: He cooled off every team he played for. After Alex's *USA Today* interview, Rosenthal wrote, Alex had planted the seed of his discontent in the paper to take what "amounted to the first step in his new marketing campaign. He is as manipulative as the player he modeled himself after, Cal Ripken Jr."

The Rangers executives privately fumed about their petulant superstar. In early August, Alex made a clumsy attempt to backtrack, telling reporters, "I'm an employee, like everyone else."

His teammates rolled their eyes at this. Most employees don't have a personal clubhouse attendant wiping down their shower shoes or preloading their toothbrush. A lot of Rangers were fed up with the diva act. "It was a traveling sideshow. . . . I appreciated the way Alex played the game of baseball," Crabtree explains, "but I saw right through him as far as how fake he was."

Alex's reaction to the tension he had created was to go on a spectacular run. In August, he hit .340 with 15 home runs in just 29 games. No one had approached that mark since Barry Bonds had hit 17 in May 2001. How was he pulling this off? It might have been luck combined with tremendous skill. It might have been some "I'll show them" anger. Or it might have been just the right time—by August, almost all of the 2003 drug testing had been completed.

Alex Rodriguez rarely got nervous before a game, particularly one in mid-August for a team already planning for next season, but he was fidgety and bouncing around the dugout while preparing for his August 16 game against the White Sox. He wasn't worried about the starting pitcher; he was worried about a long-planned—and long-dreaded—reunion his wife had orchestrated. Cynthia had arranged for Alex's father, Victor, to attend a Rangers game. "I don't want to say Alex didn't have the emotional capacity, but it was difficult for him," Cynthia said of this rapprochement with his father. "There are two sides of every story. Things happen, people get divorced. It's hard on children. What Alex and I want to do is not rehash the past but move forward."

For Alex, moving forward meant coming to grips with the past and then letting go of it, which is why Victor Rodriguez, at age 73, was sitting in the good seats at The Ballpark in Arlington next to another special guest, Alex's half brother Victor Rodriguez, Jr. It was a double reunion for him. "My father and I hadn't seen each other in 23 years," says Victor Jr. It had been that long since he'd seen Alex as well.

Victor Jr. had left Miami in 1980 to serve in the U.S. Air Force. For the next two decades, he had led the military life abroad in Turkey, Egypt, Germany and Italy. He was far removed from the American daily diet of box scores and sports talk shows and knew nothing about the success of his half brother. "I'd come back to the States briefly, see 'Alex Rodriguez' in the paper, but, really, what were the chances?" he recalls. "I didn't know until my father said, maybe around 1994, 'Do you know your brother is playing in the major leagues?'"

Then, in a nice bit of geographical serendipity, Victor Jr. returned to the United States. In 2003, he was stationed at Dyess Air Force Base in Abilene, Texas, which is less than a three-hour drive from The Ballpark in Arlington. He wanted to see Alex play in person but didn't want to intrude on his life and had no plans to contact him when he purchased tickets for the Rangers game on August 16. A few weeks later, he got a call from Cynthia. "Alex's wife got in touch with us and said, 'Let's get together,'" Victor Jr. recalls. "She mentioned the date, and I said, 'Oh, no—that's too eerie. Because I have tickets for that very same day.'"

Victor Sr., his son and his grandchildren met Cynthia at the stadium, and they all watched as Alex, who found it hard not to look into the stands between pitches, went 1 for 3 with two walks, three runs scored and a stolen base. Afterward, they took a tour of the ballpark and then ventured down into the clubhouse to greet Alex. "It was an emotional day," Victor Jr. says. "Alex, you could tell he was emotional, too, but composed. He's very refined—like my father."

The similarities between Alex and his father were apparent to anyone who saw them together that day—the way they moved, the thoughtful cadence when they spoke, the wide, easy smile. Sometimes they would smile and tear up, joy overtaking them as they chatted in the Rangers' parking lot. Alex invited everyone to his home in Highland Park, and whatever awkwardness there might have been dissolved in a night of talking and reminiscing. "Cynthia was so kind that day," Alex's father says. "I will always have that day in my heart."

Alex didn't want it to be a one-day reunion; he invited Victor Jr. to throw out the first pitch of a game that fall. Victor gleefully took the mound that day, and Alex returned the favor by hitting two home runs during the game.

"That was really something," Victor Jr. recalls. "I have a son who loves baseball. And Alex took time with him and made him feel special. I really respect Alex, especially his discipline and generosity. He is a great player but an even better person."

Around his family, in front of Cynthia, Alex could be vulnerable, sweet and completely unselfish. *This* Alex didn't have to compete with anyone

On September 3, 2003 as the Rangers were getting ready to play the equally horrific Kansas City Royals, a phalanx of federal agents, narcotics detectives and Olympic antidoping officials zipped down Mahler Road in Burlingame, California. Their target was the Bay Area Laboratory Co-operative—or BALCO—located in an industrial park building next to Highway 101.

Just after 12:20 p.m. on the West Coast, Jeff Novitzky, a sinewy, bald federal agent, emerged from an unmarked Buick and led his fellow investigators through BALCO's front door, past the reception desk and the walls decorated with autographed photos of athletes such as Marion Jones and Barry Bonds. The Giants' slugger was a prime endorser of the BALCO supplement ZMA Fuel, pedaled by the owner, Victor Conte, who was the supplement supplier to Olympians and pro athletes.

Two days later, federal agents kicked down the door at the home of Greg Anderson, Bonds's personal trainer, and confiscated files and computer discs. Scott Boras, who had become Bonds's agent in early 2001, after brokering Alex's historic deal in Texas, told reporters that the BALCO case "really doesn't involve Bonds" and that he had no knowledge of any request for Bonds to testify before the grand jury investigating the company suspected of being an outlet for steroid distribution.

Boras erred in his prediction. Soon Bonds, along with Jones and Yankees first baseman Jason Giambi, were asked to testify in San Francisco in December 2003 on a scandal that mushroomed into a national debate on steroid use in sports. The questions about the authenticity of Bonds's inflatable stats were particularly heated because he had been voted the National League MVP a little more than a month after the raid on BALCO.

The AL MVP was Alex Rodriguez, which some considered more of a lifetime achievement award, since the Rangers were a dismal team that had lost 91 games that year.

A picture snapped a few days later shows Alex, wearing a pink shirt and tie, celebrating his MVP while throwing his arm around the shoulders of a muscular middle-aged trainer. In a note to Angel "Nao" Presinal, Alex wrote, "To Nao, the best trainer in the world."

Emboldened by his MVP award, Alex turned on the Rangers, dropping strong hints that he wanted to be traded to a championship-caliber team. He decided he'd had enough of losing. He refused to return calls from Showalter and Hart and would speak only to Hicks, one of many examples of why the *Dallas Morning News* columnist Gerry Fraley referred to Alex as the "assistant owner." Boras jumped into the mix as well, declaring that if Hicks slashed his payroll for 2004 it would betray a promise he had made to Alex to spend whatever it took to turn the Rangers into winners.

The same day Alex was named MVP, a story in the *Fort Worth Star-Telegram* detailed the rift between Alex and Showalter, which included the team's decision to fire Tommy Bolin, Alex's clubhouse valet. Showalter hadn't pulled that trigger, team officials did. Not only was Bolin the man who detailed Alex's car, but he was one of the few confidants Alex had in a clubhouse full of young players like Hank Blalock and Mark Teixeira.

Alex didn't want Bolin going anywhere. He fumed for days. He was always high drama. "In our clubhouse back then," Hicks says, "Alex kind of sucked the air out of the room and didn't leave air for other people."

This marriage was over, and the Rangers were eager to trade the best player in baseball. They moved quickly.

On December 17, reports surfaced of a pending deal between the Rangers and the Boston Red Sox. Commissioner Bud Selig, hoping A-Rod would help Boston compete with the mighty Yankees, granted a 72-hour window for the Red Sox and Rangers to restructure the shortstop's $252 million deal. Alex's potential exit from Texas was greeted with relief from the Rangers, who were sick of A-Rod's diva ways. "There's no doubt you have to question whether that's somebody you want in a foxhole with you on the day-to-day battle," Rangers outfielder Rusty Greer said.

The Rangers, Red Sox and Boras agreed on a plan to restructure Alex's deal, but the players' union nixed it because it didn't want to set a precedent of a player—even the highest-paid player in baseball history—giving back *any* money. "We had an oral understanding of what we were going to do, and at the last minute that changed," says Hicks. "I think it changed because [Boston] made some assumptions about what the union would allow, but from my

point of view, all I know is the deal we had discussed, they changed
the terms; and I don't do that in business, so I withdrew."

The deal to renegotiate Alex's contract downward broke up
when the Red Sox refused to come up with $12 million over seven
years. It was nothing to Boston, but GM Theo Epstein wouldn't
budge.

Alex was crushed. Returning to Texas after sniping at the team
all winter was an extremely unpleasant prospect. He knew that his
home fans would boo him, his teammates would shun him and
Showalter would challenge him. What could save him now?

Salvation arrived by a circuitous route a month later in a tipping point for the Yankee organization. In and of itself, the fateful
moment created only a small problem, but it would end up being
the loose pebble that starts an avalanche.

That fall, the Yankees' third baseman, Aaron Boone, had become a Yankees hero for the ages. On a cool autumn night, he
entered the team's pantheon when, in the 11th inning of the seventh game in the 2003 ALCS against the Red Sox, Boone lifted a
fluttering pitch by Tim Wakefield into the left-field stands of Yankee Stadium. With one swing he triggered a euphoric explosion,
perpetuated Boston's Ruthian curse and led the Yankees to a date
to play in their 39th World Series (the Yankees lost in six games to
the Florida Marlins).

Boone prepared for spring training in 2004 with lots of weight
training. "The crazy thing about it is, I never play basketball,"
Boone said. Playing hoops is a risk many ballplayers take, even
though MLB contracts usually forbid participation in any sports
riskier than Ping-Pong or golf. Just three minutes into a Friday-
night pickup basketball game with buddies, a loose ball on a re-
bound was tipped over Boone's head. Another player clipped him
from the side. "It wasn't like I was hustling for the ball," Boone
said.

His left knee collapsed, and he instantly knew he'd torn an anterior cruciate ligament (ACL). He had suffered the same injury on a baseball field in the 2000 season, so he knew his 2004 season was over before it had begun. He immediately notified the Yankees.

Three days later, Yankees general manager Brian Cashman, who was in Anguilla on vacation with his family, received a call from team president Randy Levine, who told him about Boone's injury. At first, Cashman and Levine couldn't think of a decent replacement.

But on January 25, Alex, seated at the Baseball Writers' Association of America dinner to receive his MVP Award in New York, began voicing his dismay over the collapse of the Rangers–Red Sox deal to Cashman. Days later, the Yankees GM wondered if Alex would switch to third. Boras would take credit for this brainstorm, but it was, in fact, good old Yankee ingenuity. Baseball sources say Cashman brokered confidential talks with the Rangers. They say Cashman realized the Yankees couldn't be the ones to ask Alex to move to third. It was too delicate a situation—and too flammable if it were leaked to the media. The question had to be posed by the Rangers. It was. And Alex said, "Yes."

He would do anything to get out of Texas. He'd give up shortstop and the glamour and power that came with the position. He'd also give up the ability to tip buddies. Third base was the hot corner—too tight of an angle to see and relay a catcher's sign.

So much for Alex being named the Rangers' team captain as a public makeup kiss for his near departure to the Red Sox. The trade to the Yankees was done two weeks later. The Rangers received Alfonso Soriano in exchange and agreed to pay $67 million of the $179 million left on Alex's 10-year, $252 million deal. "[Alex] was no longer right for Texas," Hicks says now. "I was relieved."

The news was greeted with hand-wringing by Yankee haters and outrage by most of the media. A-Rod's contract, even though it would be partially offset by the Rangers, pushed the Yankees' payroll to nearly $190 million. "I am very concerned about the large amount of cash consideration involved and the length of time over which the cash is being paid," Commissioner Bud Selig said after approving the deal. "I want to make it abundantly clear to all clubs that I will not allow cash transfers of this magnitude to become the norm."

Not that there was much danger of that. What team other than the Yankees, and which owner other than Tom Hicks, were rich enough and desperate enough to make such a deal? It was the deal of all deals—"The Beatles just got Elvis," one writer joked. The intriguing catch here was that Alex Rodriguez—whom many people, himself included, considered the greatest shortstop of all time—had agreed to play third base in deference to the Yankees' incumbent shortstop, Derek Jeter. Adding to the intrigue: the two men had once professed to be best friends but were clearly far less than that now. Alex's swat at Jeter's leadership skills in *Esquire* three years earlier had fixed that.

Alex knew he had some fence-mending to do. A day before the press conference announcing his trade in New York, Alex jetted to Tampa on his private plane to pick up Jeter, who was working out at the Yankees' spring training facility. Jeter still felt betrayed by the article. As Buster Olney wrote in his book *The Last Night of the Yankee Dynasty*, Jeter told Alex that that kind of public criticism wouldn't fly in a media market where every utterance is picked apart for days. The bottom line: Jeter would welcome Alex to the Yankees if Alex could keep his mouth shut.

Alex went overboard with Jeter, taking it to the point of awkward fawning. A week later, in a spring training site interview on the *Today* show, Alex smiled when Matt Lauer asked about his relationship with Jeter. He said, "He's like a brother to me. I mean, we've been out to lunch this week three or four times already. And I think they have to see us hold hands and go to a movie so they

know that we've made up. When we're fifty years old, they're going to say, 'Well, Alex and Derek: Are they arguing? Are they best
friends? Are they brothers?' We're just having fun with it now."

Alex was at it again. Overplaying his hand, embellishing. Trying to please everybody and pissing everyone off in the process.

Chapter Eight

THE TROPHY DATE

The curtains in George Steinbrenner's Tampa office, four floors above the Yankees' spring training diamond, were closed tight (as usual) and the thermostat was at 62 degrees (as usual), creating a vampire's paradise: cold, dark and foreboding. This was how The Boss liked his office. He loved wearing turtlenecks in June and windbreakers in August.

On February 17, 2004, Steinbrenner leaned back in his cave and watched a live feed from Yankee Stadium of the noon press conference announcing that Alex Rodriguez had been traded to his Yankees.

The joy Steinbrenner felt watching the scene—A-Rod in a pinstripe tie slipping into a Yankee jersey, with Derek Jeter and Manager Joe Torre by his side—sent a charge through him. Baseball's It Player was his. Yes sir, The Boss probably thought, I've still got it. By snaring Rodriguez, he had managed to outwit the Red Sox, dominate the tabloid covers (front and back) and reestablish his vitality as The Boss. Once again, he'd snatched baseball's biggest prize: the game's most talented player, a matinee idol–type Reggie Jackson had said was "so good-looking, he's almost pretty."

Steinbrenner, as one employee recalls, spent the day with his chest puffed out and a tear in his eye. He was increasingly tenderhearted at 73, and creeping thoughts of mortality forced even the mighty Boss to indulge in a bit of introspection. His friends were dying on him; how long did he have? Two months earlier, at the funeral of NFL Hall of Fame quarterback Otto Graham, Steinbrenner, fatigued from the heat of the stuffy church and light-headed from skipping breakfast, had collapsed. As attendants rolled him through the hospital corridors on a gurney, as described in *Sports Illustrated*, they pulled a sheet over his face in a well-meaning attempt to veil his identity from hallway gawkers and the media swarm. But The Boss wasn't dead—and landing A-Rod was proof that he was still a dominant force in baseball. *The* dominant force.

"I don't think there was any doubt about the talent we were getting," says Steve Swindal, a former general partner of the Yankees. "It felt like an emotional boost for everyone."

The Boss reveled in what was unfolding at Yankee Stadium from two thousand miles away. Steinbrenner knew that staffers there had already placed an audio loop of Alex's home runs against the Yankees on the phone for callers placed on hold. He knew Alex's new number 13 jerseys were being bought two at a time, that ticket sales had already spiked and that the ratings for his lucrative YES Network would soon be swept skyward by the A-Rod boom.

This deal was good for the Yankees and good for the game. Baseball needed a diversion grand enough to shove steroids off the stage in the same way it had once needed a big-money trade involving Babe Ruth to paper over a gambling scandal. The sports news this off-season had been dominated by the BALCO debacle. Superstar sluggers such as Barry Bonds and Jason Giambi were photographed outside of a San Francisco courthouse as they bolted through a wall of microphones and cameras to testify before a grand jury.

Alex was accustomed to being hailed as the savior of baseball—although he had been a little niggardly with the miracles thus far. He had been the Golden Boy in Seattle after the 1994 strike, the Mighty Turnaround Artist when he had signed with Texas, and now, in New York, he was A-God.

When Alex joined the Yankees, Dodd Romero had already been training him for a year in Texas at a fee of about $3,500 a month. But Alex had many caretakers for his body—he purposely kept a separation between them, hardly ever mentioning anything about Presinal to Romero. There were fewer tales to remember that way—Presinal was the private workout genie, and Romero was the well-known, highly regarded public cobbler of Alex's body.

Romero had grown up in a Miami neighborhood of small, low-slung houses, some with barred windows, close to the violence-scarred housing projects. The area's high crime rate wasn't enough to scare away college scouts, who were easy to spot driving up and down the local streets in rental cars, making visits to high school blue-chippers. Romero's neighbors in the late 1980s had included the running back Alonzo Highsmith and receiver Randall "Thrill" Hill—both first-round NFL draft picks out of the University of Miami. Romero knew a lot about the NFL through his father, Ray Romero, who had starred at Kansas State, and, according to league historians, had become only the 11th Hispanic player in the NFL when he played for the Philadelphia Eagles in 1951. He had lasted only one season.

Ray had moved his family to Miami when Dodd was in grade

school with little planning or even familiarity with the city—he had bought their home through the mail. It didn't take long, though, for the Romero family to become a focal point of a neighborhood. Everyone knew Dodd, a rippling six-foot-six with a body poured from concrete. "He was big like that for a long time," recalls Hill. "The side yard of his house was like a scene from a *Rocky* movie— he had all this weight equipment out there, used and rusted, but it worked. It didn't matter how hot it was, Dodd was out there lifting. You could hear it—the barbells rattled all day long, till sunset."

Dodd didn't follow his father into football, choosing to dabble in boxing, where, as one former competitor, Jim Warring, says, "He fought angry" and was thought by some to be on steroids. Everything changed for him when he found his calling as a fitness evangelist after his baby daughter Gianna nearly died of a liver disorder in 1999. He says he left her hospital bed and went to a church, where he prayed for three days. "I made a deal with God," Dodd once said. Days later, after an 18-hour surgery, he and his wife, Sabina, saw Gianna regain her smile, her skin color and her future.

The ordeal prompted Romero to incorporate spirituality into his training methods. He attracted many athletes as clients but was very selective, choosing only those he felt a connection to—and even then, he would work only on his own terms. "I had lunch with him," says the rodeo roper Stran Smith, "and he told me at the end of it, 'Not now, brother. I'll call you when it's right.' He did, and I couldn't be happier."

Alex passed Dodd's test of character in 2003. When Alex moved on to New York, Cynthia continued to work out with the bodybuilder Jenny Worth, who worked for Dodd. Although Dodd and Worth were steeped in the gym culture and surrounded by steroids, both professed to be clean. Many of Dodd's clients say he is a paragon of pure living, a product of manic workouts and a meticulous diet. He orders poached egg whites, no oil. He orders vegetables, no butter. Other observers are skeptical.

"I was surprised when he went to [Romero]," says Joseph Dion, who trained Alex in the late 1990s. "He was into that [bodybuilding] world, and that was a totally different thing."

As close as Romero was to Alex, he professed having only a cursory knowledge of Presinal in a series of interviews with a *Sports Illustrated* reporter in the summer of 2008. He noted how deft Alex was at living separate lives. "There's Alex," says Romero, "and then there is A-Rod. I knew Alex, I didn't know A-Rod."

Alex is the vulnerable one with a soft spot for people in need. A-Rod is the manufactured one with a ruthless business sense. Together, they seemed to form baseball's version of The Talented Mr. Ripley, able to assume whatever identity was required to advance, succeed and win. Alex was a clever chameleon with the New York media when he joined the Yankees, often whispering to tabloid reporters off the record even when he had nothing especially tantalizing to say, in a strategy to disarm them. How could they criticize him when he made them feel special?

Alex's reputation had been tarred and feathered in Texas, but his rehab tour was off to a terrific start in New York. He envisioned himself as a stylish, sophisticated New Yorker and aggressively played that role, striding along Park Avenue with Wall Street tycoons, dining at Nobu, shopping at Bergdorf, hanging out with the De Niro crowd. He convinced most members of the media that he was a perfect fit for New York. As part of that charm offensive, he invited *Sports Illustrated*'s Rick Reilly, one of the nation's most popular columnists, into his Manhattan apartment. Reilly was smitten. "In 2004 A-Rod is The Man," he wrote then. After praising Alex's exquisite taste, he added, "Where were the revolving beds? The tubs shaped like martini glasses? The home-wrecking French maid?"

Alex was putting on such a good show that some writers wondered if they had confused the dynamic of his relationship with Jeter. Perhaps it was Jeter who was jealous of Alex, not vice versa?

Alex pretended to be thrilled to talk about his relationship with Jeter, while Jeter mostly demurred. Alex happily reminisced about sleepovers the two had had during their first years in the league and earnestly referred to Jeter as his "brother." Jeter was clearly feeling less fraternal, and his responses to questions about A-Rod were polite but guarded.

Alex once said of his closeness with Jeter, "It's like we're looking in the mirror." Well . . . they both played shortstop, both were talented and handsome, and that's where the similarities ended. Beyond their divergent styles on the field—Alex had a long uppercut of a swing built for power, and Jeter slapped and poked to conjure up hits—they were disparate in demeanor and background. Alex, reared by a single mom, had leaned on a bevy of substitute fathers his entire childhood. Jeter had been raised in a disciplined home with a father who was a drug and alcohol counselor and where structure was a virtue. He had grown up seeing his parents in the stands for his games. At 28, Alex was already playing for his third team (and had gone through two ugly baseball "divorces" to get there); the Yankees were the only team Jeter, 29, had ever known.

Alex was as rootless as Jeter was grounded. "I think the biggest thing is that Jeet knows who he is," says former Yankee Jason Giambi. "He doesn't blow his own horn. He sets examples behind the scenes. He doesn't do something and then tell the media, 'Hey, look at me lead,' to be validated." Alex wanted to please everyone; Jeter suffered no fools. Alex put up stats that impressed even folks who didn't follow baseball; Jeter owned four World Series rings that he rarely wore in public. "The Jeter thing ate Alex alive," says one Rodriguez friend. "It was always about Jeter."

They also had different styles on the social scene. Jeter was famously cool, smooth and respectful, operating with the dignity of discretion; Alex was always trying too hard, pushing too hard, in the lens too often. The guys who went clubbing with Alex say there was one pickup line he used repeatedly, even on women who knew nothing of baseball: "Who's hotter, me or Derek Jeter?"

In conversations with his publicists and even during his negotiations with the Mets in 2000, it would come up again and again: "Who's more popular, me or Jeter?"

Here, Alex was the better hitter, the superior athlete, the richest player—and on and on. He would put his celebrity up against Jeter's. He would put his stats up against Jeter's.

He had put his body through *everything* to best Jeter. Yet he was consumed by one gnawing, galling, undeniable difference between them: Jeter was clean.

As the season began, Alex struggled both at the plate and in the field. His subconscious was bedeviling him. He talked daily to his motivational guru, Jim Fannin, religiously recited self-help haikus to free his mind and wore a focused look at the plate. Inside, though, he seemed to be coming unglued. The tip was the dramatic exhale he made every time he stepped into the batter's box. "When I saw him up at bat [in 2004], he used to blow out all the time," says Charlie Zabransky, the longtime clubhouse attendant at Yankee Stadium. "I said, 'What's wrong with this guy? He's got something on his mind. [He] can't concentrate.'"

In his most pressured moments—his first month as a starter in Seattle, his first month as Mr. 252 in Texas, and now as a new Yankee—Alex fought through fits of self-consciousness. Hyperaware of the photographers recording his every move, he would not make an ugly swing for a hit out of fear of looking awkward. (He is known to listen for shutter clicks while at the plate, while most hitters automatically block out the white noise.)

Teammates say he is the vainest hitter they've ever known. As former manager Joe Torre would later write, "When it comes to a key situation, he can't get himself to concern himself with getting the job done, instead of how it looks. . . . There's a certain free-fall you have to go through when you commit yourself without a guarantee that it's always going to be good. . . . Allow yourself to be embarrassed. Allow yourself to be vulnerable."

Alex couldn't abide vulnerability. Not at this point in his career. Even teammates who didn't like Alex felt sympathy for him as a player who was painfully self-conscious, who felt failure too deeply, who couldn't stop analyzing himself on tape.

The tension of the Spotlight Moment has always prompted Alex to squeeze the bat as if he's trying to twist the lid on a stubborn jar and to jump at pitches before his front foot is planted. "It's very subtle, it's not something that's horrible or terrible, but it's enough to throw your game off," says Cal Ripken, Jr. "And then it has a chance to build to a pressure point that makes you think, 'I gotta get a hit this time; I gotta get a hit this time.' "

The breakdown of Alex's mechanics under stress had dogged him in the past and would haunt him during each Yankee play-off run over the next five years, so it wasn't surprising that he struggled as a new New Yorker. "You can't put an Alex Rodriguez into a clubhouse and not think it's going to change," says Torre. "The only thing I tried to get across to Alex was, Don't try to be the guy all the time. It's putting too much pressure on yourself. New York is a unique place to play because with the recent history where we had the success, they're only concerned about wins. So [I told him] don't worry about anything else. Just go up there and do the best you can and they'll appreciate it."

The transition he was making had gotten the better of transient Yankees before him, including superstars such as Roger Clemens and Kevin Brown. Like them, Alex welcomed the attention and adulation but didn't want the pressure to lead that came with it.

Alex's teammates sensed his disconnect and left him largely on his own. The lack of a clubhouse support group—which he never reached out to assemble—left him leaning more and more on outsiders: advisers, spiritualists and opportunists. Looking back, it is easy to identify at least two of the reasons Alex hit just .196 for the first two weeks of the season: the pressure of New York, the new surroundings.

But Alex was also very likely preoccupied. There was always the steroid thing—this burden, this secret—that haunted him. He knew he had been juicing in Texas. But who else knew?

The union was supposed to protect any drug cheats by destroying the test results. In a dereliction of duty, officials waited too long to make that request.

On April 10, 2004, federal agents, armed with search warrants related to 10 players linked to the BALCO scandal, entered Quest Diagnostics, the lab MLB had hired to determine the results of the anonymous tests conducted in 2003.

Agents left the facility with documents and the urine samples of, among others, Barry Bonds and two players who'd recently signed with the Yankees, Jason Giambi and Gary Sheffield. The test results were not labeled, which meant matching them with names would be tricky—but not, it turned out, impossible, because players had signed their names to the specimen codes.

The same day Quest Diagnostics was hit, federal agents executed a search warrant for another lab, Comprehensive Drug Testing, which was responsible for cataloging the drug data. There they found a master list of doping cheats. Now the Feds had the results of the BALCO-linked players and a computer spreadsheet with the names of at least 104 players who had tested positive for steroids in 2003.

The BALCO Gang of 10 knew their 2003 test results were in the hands of the Feds the next day because the search warrants were issued to nab them, all of which prompted Sheffield to tell reporters, "I can't express how I really feel . . . but life is unfair."

The players who felt most wronged were the 104 who had not been involved with BALCO but had now been exposed as doping culprits to federal agents. Some players knew they'd tested positive. Others never had a clue. But every user in the major leagues—anyone who thought there was even a chance they'd come up positive—was nervous. They knew the list was sealed under a court order. *But what if the names leaked out?* The players' union went to court against the government in an effort to do what it should have done six months earlier: have the list put in the shredder.

For more than four years, the public had no idea that the feds had documented evidence that Alex Rodriguez used anabolic steroids the year he won MVP.

There was a long list of dopers in baseball and a short supply of answers as to why. Who was Alex's enabler? There was Boras, who had a PharmD in industrial pharmacology and who would end up having a long list of clients linked to performance enhancers. Of the 89 players listed on the Mitchell Report, nine were past or present clients of Boras. His response to the proportion has been to decry the findings as "hearsay." There were union officials who had obstructed steroid testing to help superstars like Alex keep on keeping on.

Alex would say in 2009 that his "cousin," later revealed to be Yuri Sucart, shot him full of steroids twice a month for six months from 2001 to 2003, when both men were fumbling around as steroid novices. Alex was no novice. He knew exactly what he was doing as a Ranger—and then as a Yankee.

Alex must have constantly questioned his reliance on steroids: Do I really need this stuff? Can I succeed without it? The pressure he felt in Texas was now magnified under the Broadway lights.

Alex couldn't square his mind, much less his body, in the batter's box. It was April 15, 2004, when the Yankees arrived in Boston.

That night, in the restaurant at Boston's Ritz-Carlton, Alex and Jeter were seen together, gamely trying to ease any tension between them. The odd couple had a few more things than usual in common that day: both had been horrific in April, with Jeter hitting .250 and Alex .212.

The next day, when Alex hopped up the steps of the dugout for pregame warm-ups, he heard hecklers screaming, "Who needs A-Rod? . . . Who needs A-Rod?" The mischievous sound technicians of Fenway Park were accused of having lowered the volume of the pregame music so the Yankees could hear every nasty barb hurled their way by fans leaning over the fences during batting practice.

The Fenway faithful would grow hoarse booing Alex during a 6–2 Boston win. They were giddy as he went 0 for 4, and in the sixth inning, with Alex aboard on an error by Red Sox shortstop Pokey Reese, they went nuts when he was thrown out trying to steal third with Sheffield at the plate looking at a 3–1 count, every hitter's dream. Cackles echoed off the Green Monster. "Every year," Red Sox pitcher Tim Wakefield said, "there is [a Yankee] over there that fans hate."

Alex was their target this day, but Jason Giambi also got an early taste of the scorn fans would show steroid cheaters for the next few seasons. Chants of "BAL-CO! . . . BAL-CO!" accompanied his at-bats. "At least I'm not him," Alex told friends, when he must have been thinking, At least they don't know.

What was it about Alex that produced such bad karma for others? In Texas, he had been nicknamed The Cooler for icing hot franchises—and it did not escape anyone's attention that, in 2004, Texas was 15–9 on May 1st. The Yankees, with a $190 million payroll, were shockingly average the first month of the season. The New York Post ran a back-page caricature of Alex sitting on a dugout bench in flames. The headline: A-ROD ON THE HOT SEAT.

Yankees General Manager Brian Cashman chews his nails when he's nervous, and in 2004, they must have bled from the constant gnawing. What pinstripe pandemic had Alex wrought? Jeter was flailing wildly in the midst of an 0-for-32 slump. "A streak like that, you wouldn't wish that on anyone," Jeter told reporters when he finally broke through. He was asked if the presence of Rodriguez had any effect on him. Jeter replied, "He's not in the box with me."

But he was, in a way. Alex smothered everyone. He alienated teammates with his constant neediness. He would, just as he had in high school, ask Yankee bench players of the lowest pay scale, "How did my swing look?" after he hit a home run. "He didn't ask you anything if he sucked that day," one former Yankee teammate recalls, "He only wanted to hear 'You're great! Best ever!'"

He didn't force the Yankees to hire a special clubhouse attendant for him, but he did poach one from the visitors' clubhouse. He was allowed to have this clubbie on call, which, teammates soon realized, meant all the time. The attendant regularly played wardrobe valet, laying out Alex's game clothes and warm-ups, played fetch, grabbing coffee for Alex, and dried his shower shoes for him.

Some things hadn't changed when Alex left Texas. He remained meticulously high maintenance and kept focused on his off-field image and empire-building.

At the 2004 All-Star break, Alex announced a business deal in the game's host city, Houston. In a conference room at the Four Seasons, he wore a charcoal Armani suit and $1,000-a-pair Borrelli shoes while discussing an exciting venture: He was opening a Mercedes-Benz dealership in the Houston area. "I've always been a big fan of cars," he said, "but I've never been able to afford them." He meant as a teen, of course.

This little diversion was yet another irritant for his teammates, who wondered, Who is this guy? "It's all part of him setting himself apart in an almost unknowing way," says one person with close ties to Yankee players. "And this need to be accepted and this superficial Alex emerging over the genuine Alex . . . um, if there's a genuine Alex left. I don't know."

By summer, the Yankees were on track, even though Alex was not. He was hitting an uninspiring .270 in mid-July even as New York was pulling away from Boston, up by 8½ games as the Yankees headed to Fenway on July 23. On July 24, they were in Boston, leading 3–0 in the third inning, when Alex came to the plate. Bronson Arroyo was on the mound. The night before, Alex had knocked in the winning hit against the Red Sox and christened it "my first official big hit to make me a Yankee." Arroyo stared into Alex's eyes, glanced down, then hurled a sinker that hit Alex in the left elbow. Alex thought the beaning had been intentional and was jawing at Arroyo when catcher Jason Varitek took over. His first shot was a classic put-down: "We don't bother hitting .260 hitters," Varitek told Alex.

"Fuck you," Alex said.

"Get to first!" Varitek shouted.

"Fuck you," Alex said again, then challenged Varitek, "C'mon!"

Varitek shoved his catcher's mitt into Alex's face and lifted him off the dirt. For an instant, Alex dangled in distress as the benches cleared in a scene that would be replayed on cable for weeks. (One interesting note: As the Yankees poured off the bench, Jeter was nowhere to be found. "I went into the dugout bathroom," he said. "I heard everyone running out, but I had no idea what had happened when I got back out there.")

A typical baseball fight ensued—a lot of yelling and circling, with few blows landed, but blood dripped from the ear of Yankee starter Tanyon Sturtze as the umpires separated the combatants and then ejected several players, including Alex and Varitek. In weeks to come, the Red Sox would point to that fight—the A-Rod Brawl—as the catalyst for their stunning revival in the second half of the season.

"The Varitek-Rodriguez fight would stand as the most important game moment of the Red Sox regular season," wrote Dan
Shaughnessy in his book *Reversing the Curse*. "It was bigger than
Ortiz's Easter homer, bigger than Mueller's walk-off winner late in
the same game. It meant more than any single home run by Manny,
more than any win by Pedro, and more than any save by Foulke.
Even though the Sox did not start playing better until a few weeks
later, most of the players and fans believed the season turned on the
violent play—just as the classic 1984 NBA Finals tilted in favor of
the Celtics after Kevin McHale's vicious open-floor takedown of
the fast-breaking Laker Kurt Rambis."

This ode to A-Rod made perfect sense: the curse was on Alex.

As one member of the Yankees organization conceded, "Everything he did to try harder worked in reverse—against us." There
was indeed an odd voodoo about Alex.

"When Alex left [Texas], it was probably good for both of us,"
Rangers owner Tom Hicks says. "And I think Alex is probably,
with his drive, his personality, his larger-than-life presence, better
suited in a market like New York."

The city welcomed him. The team, though, rejected him.
They did not like his haute couture flair, his high-maintenance
needs and his manicured quotes for the media. They also knew
that he was a hypocrite, playing the Boy Scout by day and the Bad
Boy at night.

On road trips, he hit provocative clubs other players shunned,
feeling they were at risk of image damage—or the wrath of their
teams—if they were seen in them.

In Texas, during an August series against the Rangers, Alex
was known to have ventured to Iniquity—a swingers' club in Dallas where a sign warns, "Be discreet and respect the privacy of others. No cameras or recording devices." Iniquity describes itself as a

"couples-only lifestyle club" but Alex's wife was home in Manhattan, pregnant with their first child.

Alex's peccadilloes were his own business until he started flaunting them. He was indiscreet about his many visits to Vegas, bragging to teammates and friends about his wild nights with strippers. But he could afford such indiscretions. "You can make a lot of mistakes with $30 million year," Jose Canseco says.

What Alex's money couldn't cover was the affect of his reckless behavior on his teammates.

At Yankee functions, with players' wives and girlfriends in attendance, Alex morphed into the caricature of a hyperaggressive swinger. "He would use these corny pickup lines on a guy's wife," says one former teammate. "He just wanted to know that he could, not that he would act on it. Seemed like an ego thing."

The Yankees brass wasn't concerned about Alex's social skills, but they were distressed by his diminishing skills on the field. In 2004, he muddled along at .286, with 36 homers, 11 fewer than he'd hit the year before. What was wrong with him? the Yankees wondered. According to two people familiar with the team's inner workings, high-level officials discussed possible causes for Alex's 2004 swoon: Was he doping or in steroid detox? Was he on something or off something? "No one knew for sure," says a former Yankee staffer. "No one ever asked Alex directly that I know of, but there was a lot of suspicion in-house."

Fueling that speculation was the fact that 2004 was the first season MLB conducted steroids testing with penalties. One trainer says testing was easy to beat back then, but many players decided to junk the steroids in favor of human growth hormone. It was a youth potion of sorts. Players healed faster. Felt younger. Hit farther. HGH wasn't yet banned—it couldn't even be detected in a urine sample—and it was in plentiful supply through various anti-aging clinics and underground Internet sites.

Testing turned out to be not as rigorous in 2004 as intended.

In an agreement made between the Players Association and MLB, there was a moratorium on testing after the 2003 testing results for the 104 who came up positive were seized by federal agents.

The twist: those players were told about the moratorium but not told how long it would be in effect. But Gene Orza, the union's chief operating officer, was never one for decorum when it came to steroid rules. The exhaustive investigation of baseball's steroid era by George Mitchell stated that Orza was a known obstructionist. In March 2004, he openly mocked the call for a crackdown. "I have no doubt that [steroids] are not worse than cigarettes," he said. Some players say the union even tried to intimidate those who tried to warn that there was a steroid problem.

Between mid-August and early-September 2004, according to the Mitchell Report, Orza violated an agreement with MLB and tipped a player that the moratorium was over, that he would soon be tested. The player was not named in the report, but it would later be revealed in a book by the convicted steroid distributor Kirk Radomski that it was former Oriole David Segui. Radomski was an important figure during the steroid era as a supplier to major leaguers—including Yankees. Twenty-two former and current Yankees would show up on the Mitchell Report, edging out the Rangers as the clubhouse leaders in doping. Alex had always had trouble resisting peer pressure.

Seven of the documented Yankees would be directly tied to Radomski.

One of his clients was the volatile Kevin Brown. In 2003, as a pitcher for the Dodgers, Brown was suspected of using steroids, according to a Dodger executive memo cited in the Mitchell Report. As Radomski relayed to Mitchell investigators, he knew Brown well, sent several orders of performance-enhancing drugs to him over a three-year period and considered his client an expert on human growth hormone. In June 2004, when Brown was a Yankee, an express mail receipt addressed to Brown was on a package from

Radomski with a return address for Brown's agent, who at the time was Scott Boras.

In late 2004, one player says, Alex was seen with HGH in the company of Brown. It was possible, the player says, that Alex was interested in using growth hormone as a way to help him perform at a high level during the upcoming play-offs. Through his lawyer in the summer of 2008, Brown denied sharing HGH with Alex. When confronted with the same information by a reporter from *Sports Illustrated* in September 2008, Alex said he didn't want "to throw Brown under the bus."

Months later, he would deny ever having taken HGH—what some players viewed as the safe alternative to steroid use. Alex was certainly aware of how risky steroid use would be. According to three players, Gene Orza also tipped Alex about upcoming drug tests at the end of 2004. "The union was going to take care of the superstars," one of those players says. "The big boys made the big money, and that was the bread and butter for the union."

One more win. That's all they needed. In game four of the 2004 ALCS, the Yankees were just three outs from sweeping the revived Red Sox when an unexpected hiccup from ace reliever Mariano Rivera allowed them to push the game into extra innings. The Red Sox won it in the 12th. The next night, in game five, the Yankees missed another opportunity to clinch as the Sox won in the 14th inning.

The temperature for game six was 49 degrees, with a wind that made it feel 10 degrees colder; first pitch was set for 8:19 p.m. The Red Sox, leaning on the camaraderie that had been the source of their second-half return from the grave, did their best to stay loose—and occasionally, goofy—as they fought to keep their microscopically thin hopes against the Yankees alive. Their bleach-haired leader, Kevin Millar, remains a folk legend for supposedly passing a bottle of Jack Daniel's around to teammates as a pregame warmup that night.

Alex had done nothing against Boston, going 1 for 5 in game four and 0 for 4 in game five. Here was his moment: It was the eighth inning, and Red Sox ace Curt Schilling, pitching bravely and brilliantly despite a tendon injury to his ankle, had left the game in the seventh, leading 4–1. Bronson Arroyo was on the mound in relief when Jeter stroked an RBI single to cut the lead to 4–2.

Alex was up next, staring at the same pitcher who had plunked him in July to start that brawl. He exhaled, stepped into the box and then jumped at the first pitch with a long swing that just nicked the ball, squirting a dribbler to Arroyo's left. The pitcher fielded it and raced to the base path to tag Alex. As he put his glove against Alex's arm, Alex, like a cat pawing at yarn, slapped the ball out of his glove. Jeter raced home on the play to cut the Boston lead to 4–3. Yankee Stadium was trembling from the crowd's roar as Alex stood on second.

Alex's "triumph" didn't last long. The umpires huddled and then correctly called him out for interference. A run was taken off the board, and Jeter was ordered back to first base. "That was junior high baseball right there at its best," Schilling said after game six, a 4–2 win for the Red Sox. They would go on to become the first team ever to come back from a 3–0 deficit and then go on to win their first World Series title since 1918.

The Red Sox were the feel-good story of the postseason, and maybe the decade, but that one play left Alex labeled a bush-league player—the ultimate insult for someone obsessed with his image. In the locker room after game six, he feigned incredulity at the interference call. He acted as if he didn't know the rule. He acted as if he couldn't believe what had transpired. He acted.

Years earlier, he had told a reporter, "I'll even cheat to win."

Chapter Nine

THE RISK TAKER

PUTTING ON THE YANKEE pinstripes was very good for business at the headquarters of AROD Corp. (est. 1996), the umbrella Alex used for everything from such high-gloss investments as his Mercedes dealership in Houston to his charity, the AROD Family Foundation.

Whenever Alex was asked to justify his otherworldly paycheck, he would talk enthusiastically about the joys of entrepreneurship and the satisfaction gained from delivering hope to struggling families. "I can't run away from [my salary]," he said upon becoming a Yankee in February 2004, when his salary was listed at $22 million. "I think we've been put in this situation, Cynthia and I, from a philanthropic point of view, to help thousands of kids."

Alex wrote seven-figure checks for the University of Miami's athletic program and made more modest donations to Boys & Girls

Clubs and UNICEF. Over the next couple of years, as the richest Yankee ever, he promised to give a lot more. He clearly enjoyed portraying himself as a great philanthropist.

But Alex managed to complicate even the simple act of charity, which became yet another tug of war between Good Alex and Bad Alex. Good Alex sang "Do-re-mi" at FAO Schwarz with his daughter as he signed his children's book, *Out of the Ballpark*, for fans in July 2007. Bad Alex was captured by paparazzi that same month, sneaking around Toronto with the exotic dancer and fitness competitor Joslyn Morse. Good Alex yanked a young Yankee fan out of a car's path on the streets of Boston in September 2005. Bad Alex snubbed children he had agreed to greet at a Dominican baseball celebration outside Yankee Stadium in 2008. "The problem was that he had so many hangers-on, his entourage, that you didn't get within twenty feet of him," says Steve Winiarski, the coach of the travel team at that event. "You were walking by and they're all surrounding him, so not one kid got to see A-Rod there. Plus he wasn't paying attention. He wasn't waving to the kids."

There are photos of Alex that day in a brown T-shirt and jeans running from the children asking for his autograph. His bodyguards—mostly friends employed by Alex—repeatedly yelled at the youth leaguers, "Stay away!"

The dichotomy defined his life. Good Alex extolled the purity of baseball in front of the crowds. Bad Alex cheated the game by using steroids in the shadows.

He pursued his investments with the same conflicted soul. He projected a Mister Rogers benevolence, but he was more like Mr. Potter in *It's A Wonderful Life*.

The headquarters of Newport Property Ventures in Coral Gables, Florida, occupies a stucco building with a marble-tiled entrance. Alex has an office on the second floor, finished with granite, and he sits behind a fancy desk so large that one employee calls it a landing pad. This isn't just a front or a tax shelter or a place for him to duel with "The Boys" on PlayStation. Alex is in that office regularly during the off-season, but there is no mention of him, or even AROD Corp., in the company's brochures or on its website. But if you walk up to the receptionist and ask, she'll tell you Alex is the founder and CEO of this real estate empire, which in 2009 owned 28 apartment complexes in five states.

Newport has six properties in Tampa, most within a 10-minute drive of the Yankees' spring training site. One complex off Dale Mabry Drive is even called Villas of Legends Field, a reference to the old name on the Grapefruit League stadium now called George M. Steinbrenner Field.

The entrance of the Newport Riverside complex, several three-story buildings, is behind a stand of oak trees. The wrought-iron fence around the front of the complex had recently been hit with a coat of black paint, but missing spindles gave rickety white banisters on the staircases the look of a gap-toothed smile. A dishwasher without a door sat next to a window with cardboard duct-taped over a broken pane. Two residents showed a visitor a showerhead with only a trickle of water flowing and opened a closet to reveal a "smell that wasn't quite right" because of *something* inside the wall. "Probably something dead but we can't get anyone to look into it," says the tenant, Mira Bay.

Other residents told tales of cockroaches high-stepping through kitchen cabinets, of carpets stained a decade ago and never cleaned.

"My mom comes here and she ain't no rich person, but she thinks I live in the projects," says Miguel Ruiz on the landing of Building 201. "She's scared to come over here, for real. . . . Honestly, I was raised in a ghetto and I was brought up a little better than this."

Not all of the Newport properties in Tampa are in such shabby condition. One resident at Newport Villas said he believes the lawns there were being mowed more often since Alex's company had taken over. A tenant at the Villas of Legends Field was pleased to report that the parking lots seemed a little cleaner these days.

Other buildings showed signs of a slow-footed management team. Mattresses were stacked near Dumpsters at Newport Villas, screen doors were ripped at Newport's Normandy Park and the plumbing was a common complaint at Newport Horizon.

"My toilet hasn't worked right in six months," says Rosa Mendez. She and many of her fellow residents had no idea their landlord was Alex Rodriguez, but those who did had a simple question: Why would A-Rod, who has nearly unlimited investment options, choose to be a slumlord? "He's got everything, so why take money off our backs?" asked Roberto Santiago of Newport Riverside, adding, "Why screw with us?"

The answer is complex. Other athletes might be satisfied with conservative investments, happy to live on interest accounts and deferred income. But Alex didn't want to be "comfortable": he wanted to be a deal maker on par with the titans he reads about in *Forbes* and *Fortune*.

Alex was willing to gamble a sizable portion of his contract for the rewards of super-wealth and for the power and celebrity that come with that status. He wanted to be recognized as a savvy Master of the Deal in his corporate circle of high-flying friends. As one former business associate explains, "There is a part of him that is in a race to do something on a large scale with the money he has—like being his own Trump. He sees numbers in this case, not the people in the apartments he owns. Is he tone deaf? You could argue that, but, like any businessman, he saw an opportunity to grow his fortune and be a big player."

There is another impulse here: Alex wants to be viewed as the rarest of creatures: the thinking man's jock. His father was a smart, savvy, well-educated man. His half brother Victor Jr. is a decorated Air Force engineer. His mother and other siblings possess sharp minds.

Alex acts self-conscious about his vocabulary and his wit with reporters, often lamenting the fact he chose pro ball over college.

His lack of classroom knowledge bothers him, creating yet another niggling insecurity. Alex envies Ivy Leaguers—he once asked a reporter, "What kind of SAT do you need to get into Yale?" The reporter shrugged as Alex continued, "I'd like to see Yale."

The Ivy League connotes the kind of status Alex craves. When he was in Boston, he liked to walk among the textbook-toting brainiacs on the Harvard campus. His friends say he has tried on glasses to see if he'd look smarter in frames . . . despite his fine vision. "He seemed fascinated by my Ivy League degree, declaring that he would love to graduate from Harvard one day," Doug Glanville, a former Ranger teammate who attended the University of Pennsylvania, wrote in a *New York Times* op-ed piece. "He talked about it too much for it to have been just a fleeting thought."

Playing for the Yankees doesn't leave much time for pursing a Harvard MBA, so Alex got his business education elsewhere. In August 2004, he wrote the foreword for a book by Dolf de Roos, *Real Estate Riches: How to Become Rich Using Your Banker's Money.*

The book lays out a paint-by-numbers approach to capitalizing on the freewheeling lending practices of banks back then, a giddy time for loan institutions that were routinely chopping up low-interest, exotic mortgages. Values were peaking when Alex jumped in with both cleats. "When I landed my well-publicized 10-year, $252 million contract, I set about finding an investment vehicle that would ensure my financial fitness long after baseball," Alex said in his one-page foreword, adding that de Roos's book had given him the "confidence to form Newport Property Ventures. I began by investing in a small duplex in an emerging area of South Florida, which led to the acquisition of several other income-producing properties."

He purchased properties in bunches between 2004 and 2006. Alex's brother-in-law, Constantine Scurtis, who served for several years as Newport's president, signed more than $50 million in mortgages for properties in Tampa, according to county records. Scurtis once explained the Newport strategy to a business reporter in Tampa. "None of these complexes will be converted [into condos]," he said. "We have very high standards and plan to put a lot of money into fixing them to give the tenants a better place to live."

Tenants say they rarely witnessed such efforts and hardly ever saw their celebrity landlord. Alex was known to have made only a couple of scouting trips to the properties, with at least one drawing the attention of renters. As Scurtis recalled, "People were coming out on porches, yelling, 'Hey, that's A-Rod.'"

If they were to see him today, they'd probably be yelling, "Hey, A-Rod, can you fix my cracked toilet?" On a website that rates apartments in Tampa, one renter at Newport Villas wrote, "A-Rod fired all the nice people in the office and his crew knows not a damn thing they are doing; I'm leaving. At least the old management would not have lost everybody's rent. They sent me a letter stating they were evicting me five months after they lost my rent."

The recession in 2008 gutted the value of Alex's investments. By early 2009, Newport Property Ventures had lost about $10 million in paper value on its Tampa-area properties. A Dun & Bradstreet small-business analysis in early 2009 said Newport Property Ventures was not in danger of collapse but was rated slow in making payments to creditors.

Alex also took a major hit on his personal properties. He lost nearly $4 million on the listing of his Miami estate by 2009. Even the value of his personal jet plunged. He is blessed in that he can absorb such losses better than many other rich people, because he has his ironclad Yankees contract and endorsements pouring in at least a combined $27 million a year for the next decade. Alex didn't like to lose even a dime on anything, though, because all stats are important to him. He measures himself by numbers: his net worth determines his self-worth.

Alex was angry when the *New York Times* ran a story about his real estate holdings in the fall of 2007, but a year later he would tell the reporter of the piece in private, "You think you made me out to be an ass, but I should thank you. More people want to do business with me than ever before. I have a name."

His career as a slumlord creates a paradox that perfectly captures the Good Alex/Bad Alex war: He pinches the needy with substandard housing, then tries to help those very people with his AROD Family Foundation—at least until the charity stopped being charitable.

Alex launched the foundation in 1998, updating its activities over the years via a shimmering website that had photos of Alex reading to children and handing over donation checks the size of surfboards. The foundation's motto read, in part, "dedicated to positively impacting families in distress."

From 1998 to 2008, Alex Rodriguez earned more than $200 million in salary alone. Over those 10 years, according to available 990 tax records, his foundation contributed, on average, $13,000 a year. By 2008, the foundation was an untended garden. The state of Florida temporarily dissolved the charity in September of that year for failing to file an annual report and for not paying a penalty of $61.25. The fine was later paid, and the foundation was shuttered a short time later. By the winter of 2009, the once-glossy website for the AROD Family Foundation was no longer accessible.

Alex isn't the first athlete to watch his noble ambitions fizzle, but this failure must have been particularly galling for him, if only because the thorn in his psyche, Derek Jeter, has had so much success with his charity. Quietly, over an 11-year period dating back to 1997, Jeter's Turn 2 Foundation had donated more than $15 million to community education programs. According to 10 years of tax records, Jeter wrote checks for a total of more than $2.3 million to help underwrite the foundation.

There was Jeter again, always besting him, even as the humble do-gooder. It never ended.

Alex was finally convinced that he'd put some distance between himself and the Yankees' Captain Perfect in 2005. During his off-season in Miami, after pushing the misery of the ALCS loss to the Red Sox out of his mind, he attacked his training regimen with a new fervor. He went on endless bike rides with his trainer Dodd Romero on county highways, through orange groves and across waterways that fingered toward the Atlantic.

He was serious about everything. He was now a father with the birth of his daughter, Natasha, in November, and he was determined to grow up. Alex adored Natasha but was also taken aback at how much of Cynthia's attention was funneled to their newborn, not to him. Alex knew it was wrong to feel that way. *What kind of man has these thoughts?*

He found comfort in his workouts among training partners who offered him constant assurance and attention. "How do I look?" he'd ask them, standing with his hands on his hips, feet shoulder-width apart.

"You look great, man," they'd say.

Alex let nothing disrupt his rigid routine. Early one morning, not much past dawn, he was driving to the gym when he got a flat on his luxury ride. He didn't yank out a spare or wait for the AAA; he phoned a friend. Within minutes, he was on his way to a workout in that friend's car while someone else handled the tire jack. Just another perk that comes with having friends paid to provide a 24-hour valet service. Alex never made himself a sandwich; never fetched his own coffee; never picked out his own clothes. He didn't even order his own soup.

"His wife always ordered for him," says a waitress at the Bagel Emporium, Alex and Cynthia's favorite breakfast and lunch spot in Coral Gables. "He never said a word. He never made eye contact with any of the waitresses."

Employees there describe him as increasingly dismissive over the years. Not so much as a "hello" when he walked in. This was a sign of what friends describe as Alex steadily "drifting completely away from normal."

Alex didn't have time for chit-chat with waitresses; he was obsessively focused on reclaiming his status as the best player in the game. He pushed himself hard in the gym, ran daily against the resistance of thick bungee cords and added more protein to his diet—anything to improve on 2004. "By far the toughest year of my career," he said, adding, "New York is a handful, and I just felt I tried to please too much. I'm more comfortable now."

When the gates to the Yankees' spring training facility were swung open in February, Alex was ready. He'd packed an extra 15 pounds of muscle onto his six-foot, three-inch frame. As George King of the *New York Post* wrote, "Thanks to a winter of pumping iron, Alex Rodriguez's chest looks like something out of an NFL locker room"

Not that anyone had kicked sand in his face in 2004. He weighed 210 pounds that season. Now he was at 225. Alex's extreme winter makeover heightened suspicions among Yankees—some of whom knew of his steroid use in Texas.

Some teammates began to privately call him "Bitch Tits," a reference to what they perceived to be his now slightly rounded breasts. These players had been around enough dopers to know that this disconcerting side effect—what doctors call gynecomastia—was common among steroid users. Look at Alex's shirtless photos and the 2007 *Letterman* skit on YouTube, Canseco says. "That's where you see the bitch tits. It's right there."

In Texas Alex had used a variety of steroids, including

Primobolan—a drug, experts say, that isn't associated with gyne-comastia. Which means he must have been using something else now. There were several other candidates—including Winstrol and Dianabol—but those drugs weren't easy to flush from the system in time to avoid detection, even with advance warning of a drug test. And *not* flunking the drug test was crucial now.

There would be no more free passes in 2005. MLB now man-dated stiffer penalties—including a 10-day suspension for a first positive. It would have been extremely risky for Alex to inject or ingest anything anabolic, but there were biochemical loopholes for cheaters. By 2004, players were turning to HGH—banned but undetectable—and low dosages of steroids to stay under the radar of the tests. Designer steroids were also a possibility.

There were, in other words, plenty of ways to game the system, but overall, the threat of testing seemed to be working. Many play-ers showed up at spring training as scaled-down versions of their former selves. They seemed to have shrunk during the off-season. That made Alex stand out even more.

As one former steroid user says, "You could look around the league that year and tell guys were losing weight, [because] they were off the stuff. Alex *gained* weight."

Dodd Romero says Alex never took steroids around him, but no one could vouch for what he did in the Dominican Republic during his visits there in the off-season. Alex was still working part-time with the banned trainer Angel Presinal in the D.R. but had ended their regular-season sessions when he was traded to New York.

"Nao was his go-to," says a baseball source, referring to Presi-nal by his nickname. "When all else failed, he went back to Nao."

Alex's extra 15 pounds were rock hard, as was his confidence. "This will be a great year," he told reporters at the start of spring training. His mind, however, was wandering, and wondering. He was shaken early in spring training by the furor over teammate

Jason Giambi's vague apology for using steroids. Giambi had been exposed by his grand jury testimony in the BALCO case, which had been reported in the *San Francisco Chronicle* in December 2004, and spring training was the first chance the beat reporters had to corner him.

In a Clintonesque "What is the meaning of 'is'?" moment, Giambi tiptoed through an opaque confession at a press conference at the opening of spring training. His decision to come forward and address the issue would become the template for other steroid-ensnared players—including Alex—in the years to come. "I was the first," recalls Giambi. "And trust me, first is not always the best. It was tough. It was uncharted water. One side is saying this or that. I'm just glad I did the right thing. I said what I could. I weathered it."

Giambi, noticeably slimmer that season (which gave him the look of an ice sculpture after the party), never mentioned the word "steroid" but said he was sorry just the same. Still, the scene left Steinbrenner fuming. "The Boss really didn't want his players to have anything to do with steroids," says one Yankee source. "He was old-school work ethic and thought of steroids as cheating. Now, the rest of the Yankees brass . . . from them, you'd hear that the steroid issue was nothing more than a media witch hunt."

Yankees President Randy Levine and GM Brian Cashman feigned concern about steroids when they were on camera but scoffed at the congressional circus around the subject in private. In February 2005, Jose Canseco's steroid tell-all, *Juiced*, hit the stores. To Alex's great relief, it did not out him as a user. The book did prompt the House Government Reform Committee to drag in MLB executives, along with Mark McGwire, Rafael Palmeiro, Curt Schilling and Canseco for questioning. McGwire, considerably thinner than when he'd last played—the Incredible Shrinking Slugger—was nearly in tears when responding to a question about his past and the use of performance enhancers. "My lawyers have advised me that I cannot answer these questions without jeopardizing my friends, my family or myself. I intend to follow their advice."

It was a devastating moment for McGwire, but it was all just political theater to the Yankees' front office. Its antidoping message was simple: Don't get caught.

The only Yankee executive a steroid user had to fear was The Boss. A few days after Giambi's press conference, Steinbrenner requested some time with his All-Star third baseman. "The Boss wants you," Alex was told. He tensed up. "Alex kept asking, 'Is this about steroids?'" one Yankee staffer who witnessed the moment says. "It was weird. Why *would* it be about steroids?"

As Alex walked toward Steinbrenner, he huffed and puffed just as he did before a tense at-bat. He couldn't be sure what Steinbrenner knew about his usage, although Alex believed the union and his agent had kept that secret buried deep.

But what about the Boras and Orza camps? Were they leakproof? Alex had no idea as he stared at George Steinbrenner's square jaw. Alex considered The Boss an almost mythical figure, a tough guy who, unlike Hicks, didn't favor Alex over any other Yankee. One longtime friend of Steinbrenner's says, "George had great affection for a lot of his players, but he never mentioned Alex. It's like he didn't feel a connection to him."

This could be bad, Alex thought, but as soon as The Boss started to speak, Alex relaxed. Steinbrenner merely wanted to give him a motivational speech, something on the order of, "Earn your pinstripes." That's it? Alex was visibly relieved, say witnesses.

A few days later, Alex found himself under siege by people far more critical than Steinbrenner. During spring training, Alex took shots from the Red Sox camp, where Curt Schilling, Trot Nixon and David Wells called him "a phony" because of the infamous glove-slapping incident in the play-offs. Nixon also mocked him for being a shameless self-promoter after Alex told a television reporter about his grueling 6 a.m. off-season workouts, which he said lasted six hours. "[Alex] said he's doing all this while six hundred players are still in their bed," Nixon sniped. "I say, 'What's wrong with me taking my kid to school? I'm not a deadbeat dad, you clown. I work out for three hours in the weight room, and I hit for another two or three hours [later in the day]. What makes you so much better?'"

Alex was surprised by Nixon's reaction. "It's the first time I've ever talked about [my workouts]," he said, even though he'd spoken of them many times. "It'll be the last time, too."

It wasn't, of course, but Alex was trying to defuse hostilities with self-deprecation, one of his favorite tactics. When columnists and reporters wrote that Alex had little support from his teammates, pointing out that no one had defended him against the Red Sox jabs, A-Rod jokingly came up with his own tabloid headline: "A-Rod Doesn't Back Up A-Rod."

When the regular season began, the Yankees looked old and complacent and, at 4–8, roused the ire of Steinbrenner. "Enough is enough," he told reporters. "It is unbelievable to me that the highest-paid team in baseball would start the season in such a deep funk. They are not playing like true Yankees."

Alex, though, was looking sharp in pinstripes. He carried the clunky Yankees on his broad back with a sensational spring. His bat was like a Pez dispenser, popping out home runs one after another. A startling highlight came on April 26, in a night game against Angels pitcher Bartolo Colon.

With a slight breeze blowing right to left and the temperature hovering around 56 degrees, Alex ignored the chill and whip-snapped a three-run homer in the first inning, a two-run homer in the third, and a grand slam off a punch-drunk Colon in the fourth. Nine RBIs—and counting. He added a 10th RBI in the sixth inning on a ground ball single.

The negativity around Alex took the night off. As Bill Madden wrote in the New York *Daily News*, "A-Rod gave us a snapshot of the kind of towering player he's supposed to be." A day later, having reveled in the write-ups about his glorious night, Alex shrewdly suppressed his desire to gloat. "Nothing changed," Alex told the *Post*. "My wife made me throw out the garbage [last night]."

It was quintessential A-Rod, a savvy bit of faux humility, conjuring an image of Alex as a sturdy homebody, a doting husband and family man who just happened to have a day job hitting baseballs out of Yankee Stadium. But its real purpose was to throw the listener off the scent. Parse it closely and you'll see that it's a non sequitur. Taking out the garbage has nothing to do with hitting home runs. It was his communications M.O.: misdirection.

Of course, he knew the truth: he was an insatiable hedonist. He was flying girls around the country to keep him warm on road trips. He was parachuting into Vegas on convenient off days and slipping into the VIP rooms at strip clubs. He was sneaking around New York City in the pre-dawn hours. "He's a good guy, but New York offered him a lot of temptation," recalls former Yankee teammate Gary Sheffield. "A bite of the Big Apple is fine. You eat it all, and it's too much."

It seems that even Alex knew he was moving too fast, doing too much, and he sought therapy for his conflicted soul. For most people, this would be a private pursuit, but Alex was a product of the Dr. Phil generation—he went public.

On May 25, he spoke at the Children's Aid Society in Washington Heights—close to the apartment where he had lived during the 1970s. He encouraged the children to reach out for counseling. "I don't think kids need to feel like an oddball," he said. "It's about life in general, managing life. . . . It's not a storybook all the time."

Alex connected with the children by telling them about his childhood, about being abandoned at age ten. By his side was Cynthia, a psychology major who told a reporter at the event that her husband had been in therapy for a year and added, "It's because of therapeutic intervention that he's been able to flourish as a person."

Flourish, indeed. On the field, he was setting records. By the end of May he was leading the league in home runs, with 16, and had a robust .318 average. Then he got hot. The first week of June, he hit two home runs to push his career total to 400, making him the youngest player to reach that elite plateau. He was a few months shy of his 30th birthday. "It's pretty humbling when you see the names of the people you're passing," Alex said. "It's hard to believe. I'm a young man out of Miami who didn't know I could do some of the things I've done." When he turned 30 on July 27, he was well ahead of the home-run pace of Hank Aaron, who had 342 homers at 30, compared to Alex's 409.

Outwardly, Alex seemed to have it all together in 2005, perhaps by the grace of therapy. Yet friends say he didn't know himself at all. He didn't know if he was the Good Alex or the Bad Alex. Was he a giver or taker? Was he a father or a swinger?

He didn't even know if he was Dominican or American. In 1999, he had talked about how important his family heritage was to him in a book, *Gunning for Greatness*, in which he said, "I want to be known as Dominican. That's what I am: 100 percent."

His certitude wavered in July 2005. He hinted to Spanish-speaking reporters that he would love to play for the D.R. in the 2006 World Baseball Classic in a statement sure to please his family, particularly his mother, Lourdes. Alex felt connected to the romance of baseball in the D.R., where he first learned to play the game under the eye of his father. Yet not long after he spoke of his desire to play for the Dominican he did a 180 and hinted that he'd play for the United States. It's where he had grown up; where he did business; where endorsers lined up to shake his hand. It was the choice preferred by his wife.

So many voices were swirling around him that Alex begged Commissioner Bud Selig to make the decision for him.

"I'll do whatever you want me to do," he told Selig.

The debate ended when the WBC agreed to use International Baseball Federation rules, meaning that players played where they had citizenship. Alex was a U.S. resident. "This may sound senti-mental, but when I first reported and saw my uniform with 'Rodri-guez 13' on the back and 'USA' on the front, I got chills," he said upon his arrival to the WBC in March 2006. (His international identity crisis would come up again in December 2008. After a day of playing golf and smoking Cuban cigars at a Dominican resort for a charity event, Alex told local reporters he'd decided to play for the D.R. in the upcoming Classic. "It's a dream come true," he said. WBC rules said a player could elect the country of his ances-tors. The New York *Daily News* reported Alex's allegiance swap with this headline: BENEDICT A-ROD.)

No one could gray up a black-and-white issue like Alex.

Even though Cynthia believed her husband was vanquishing his personal demons through therapy, there was a self-saboteur lurking within Alex. He had pushed the envelope on steroid use—and now his old friends from Texas were getting caught. His former Rangers teammate and onetime mentor from Miami, Rafael Palmeiro, was being crushed for his hypocrisy and lies. In March, at the congres-sional hearings, Palmeiro, now playing for the Orioles, had wagged a finger at Congress and sworn he'd never cheated. "I never used steroids. Period," he'd said. In early August, Palmeiro's name was in headlines reporting that he'd tested positive for a powerful ste-roid, stanozolol, known by the brand name Winstrol.

This made Alex nervous. If Raffy were asked questions, would he give up Alex? Palmeiro had always said that Alex was clean, but friends say he knew that wasn't true. There were plenty of people in Miami who knew Alex was into steroids.

Alex ignored the drama the best he could. And his best was spectacular. In May, he hit .349 with 8 homers and 22 RBIs, despite 22 walks.

He was especially loquacious when he was rolling. The more he talked, though, the more his logic frayed. At one point in 2005—when he was 30 years old and knew he was under contract to play for the Yankees for five more seasons—he told *USA Today*, "I'd be lying if I said I'd play at 40. I'd be lying if I said I'd play at 35."

Was he lying? Or was this more misdirection? Or, as one teammate puts it, "Was he just talking out of his ass?"

It's very likely he had hinted at an early departure because he longed to hear the New York fans plead, "Please don't leave us!" In 2005 he was finally feeling the love. He was Ruthian in August, hitting .324 with 12 home runs. He was even lauded for his flawless return to shortstop for three games when Derek Jeter was injured.

He was now *the* superstar in New York, leading the league for the fourth time in five years with 48 home runs. He pushed the team into the play-offs by hitting .321, with 130 RBIs and 21 stolen bases. He passed DiMaggio's 68-year-old team record for most homers in a season by a right-hander. He won his second MVP award.

Once again—as in 2003—he was hailed as the best player in baseball. And once again, he had reached that pinnacle under suspicion. The muscle gains, the "bitch tits" were warning signs to his teammates, but Alex had produced. No one in the organization wanted to question why.

Unfortunately for Alex, there was no miracle in a syringe that could make him produce in the play-offs. Again, he was dreadful in October. As one baseball source quips, "He was on all this shit, right? And yet it expired at the play-offs." Against the Angels, in an unthinkable first-round play-off exit for the Yankees, Alex went 2 for 15 with no RBI and had a canine-insulting review of his performance: "I played like a dog."

A month later, Alex's mother, Lourdes Navarro, told a Dominican news outlet that her son had floundered against the Angels because he had been grieving for his uncle Augusto Navarro, who had died on September 30.

This depiction of a mourning Alex didn't square with his actions, though. In late September and early October 2005, he was seen frequenting poker parlors into the early hours of the morning. He had become friends with Phil Hellmuth, a poker player of celebrity proportions. He was Alex's card guru.

Alex loved the action. The exotic dancers who worked at Scores men's club in 2005 and 2006—with its Ben Hur decor—say Alex was a VIP guest. In the casinos, workers recall him smoking $800 cigars at the tables, where he sat armed with an aggressive streak and a poker face honed through his years of conning the media. When a Vegas getaway wasn't do-able, Alex, with Hellmuth and some Miami pals on his hip, would pull up to an office building in Manhattan's Flatiron District and spend the night in The Broadway Club, an illegal poker parlor. "I was just trying to be a human being and have a little fun," he'd later explain.

Alex was in a good mood as he walked into The Broadway Club on September 21. The Yankees had just moved into first place in the AL East that night by beating Baltimore 2–1 at the Stadium. He signed autographs and bought more than $5,000 in chips from a cashier. He strolled through a large room that had six tables and several plasma TVs, where card junkies, from cab drivers to Wall Street wonders, were trying to read one another's minds in a game of Texas Hold 'Em.

Alcohol was prohibited at the club. Members were allowed to order food, and, on a lucky night, a handful of cookies was provided by management. Alex drew only a few glances, and took a seat in a glassed-in private room for those with the nerve and the means to compete in high-stakes games.

"It wasn't seedy, like in the movies," says Steven McLoughlin, a poker expert who knows the New York poker world well. "It's not illegal to play in [such a club], but it is illegal to operate one. Alex didn't do anything illegal, but from a PR standpoint . . . no, he shouldn't have been there."

Nothing made Major League Baseball more squeamish than players associating with gamblers, and there is a long, sordid history there that stretches from the Black Sox to Pete Rose. "It was a stunning lack of judgment," one baseball executive says of Alex's taste in off-hours pursuits.

On October 15, four days after Alex had been seen in the Broadway Club, NYPD officers flooded in. Police knew a patron had recently brandished a firearm there. Players were questioned and then released; 13 employees were arrested, and more than $55,000 was seized.

Just a couple of months earlier, cops had raided another A-Rod poker haunt, the PlayStation in Union Square—an austere parlor with a decor reminiscent of a bus station.

Commissioner Bud Selig was furious about the message Alex was sending with his underground gambling. In November, the Yankees warned Alex: Stay out of illegal poker parlors. At first Alex ignored the scolding. "What the hell do I care?" he told a reporter as he walked toward his recently purchased Trump Park Avenue apartment. "All I have to do is hit a baseball. It's not illegal for me to go there. It's illegal for them to operate it."

Alex thought poker was cool. Instead of folding his cards, he doubled down by hosting a charity event: the Dewar's 12 Texas Hold 'Em Charity Poker Tournament in Miami.

On a late January 2006 evening, he lured celebrities to play cards beneath a white tent on the grounds of a waterside estate on the island of Indian Creek Village near Miami Beach. In walked

New England quarterback Tom Brady, a personal favorite of Alex's. (He is so infatuated with Brady that buddies joke about their "bromance.") Also in attendance were Evander Holyfield, Sammy Sosa, Giants tight end Jeremy Shockey, the rapper Jay-Z and Beyoncé. The entertainment was nonstop—a fashion show, Vegas-style showgirls and sexy dancers, which seemed like an odd choice for an event benefiting the Boys & Girls Clubs of Miami.

The evening's main attraction was a Texas Hold 'Em tournament for a 120-player field, with Hellmuth serving as the master of ceremonies. The winner received a 12-month lease on a $50,000 Mercedes C230WZ, courtesy of Alex Rodriguez Mercedes-Benz.

More than $385,000 was reported as income to the AROD Family Foundation from the event, although it was unclear where or even when those funds were distributed. According to tax records, the money was not disbursed. This wasn't an indication of anything unseemly—nobody thinks the foundation misappropriated the funds—but it was yet another example of the mismanagement and misjudgments typical of Alex's life off the field.

As a publicist of Alex once said, "He doesn't listen to us. He listens to his friends." "The Boys" as everyone, including Cynthia, called them, was the traveling pack of pals at Alex's beck and call: Pepe Gomez, Gui Socarras, Yuri Sucart and, later, Ray Corona. They were loyal to Alex—and sycophantic.

"He doesn't have friends who aren't on the payroll," Dodd Romero told a *Sports Illustrated* reporter in the summer of 2008. "He's got errand boys that go for this and go for that and travel with him. They unpack his luggage, pack his luggage, they get his food."

This loyalty extended to Alex's choice of personal role models. To a man, "The Boys" liked Barry Bonds because Alex loved Barry Bonds. The two baseball stars were disparate in public personas— the sweet Alex versus the sour Barry—but they had more in common than any fan imagined. Both were obsessed with fame. Both were enamored of their power. Both were insecure about their place in history. Both would do anything to be known as the best ever. They had friends in common—including Bonds's trainer Greg Anderson, who would be convicted of steroid distribution. "All [three] of them were close," says one relative of Anderson's.

In December 2004, with Bonds's role in the BALCO scandal all over the news, Alex stood by his friend in a joint business venture—The Ultimate Experience—that lowered the bar for cheesy. It was a VIP, meet-and-greet, Christmas spectacular at the Marriott Marquis in Times Square. Alex and Bonds charged fans $10,000 per couple—$7,500 for singles—for the chance to converse with the game's greatest hitters. "The perfect holiday fleece," the *New York Times* said.

The merrily fleeced could ask Bonds and Alex about anything—except steroids. Attendees departed with gift bags and photos and perhaps-priceless conversational memories; Bonds and Alex each left with $750,000 for three hours of "work." Whereas Bonds kept his dough, Eileen Thompson, a publicist for Alex, said her client intended to give the money to two charities: UNICEF and the Boys & Girls Clubs of Miami. UNICEF records indicate that Alex donated $50,000 to early-childhood education programs in 2005. Officials from the Boys & Girls Clubs did not disclose the amount of his donation.

No charitable donation, no matter how large, could alter the fact that this was dirty money. A-Rod and Bonds, the game's most prodigious hitters, were both pulling gawkers into the tent with their inflated numbers and their artificially inflated bodies. It was a circus, and they were the freaks. Alex once wanted to grow up to be just like Barry Bonds. And he had. In the aftermath of BALCO, as Bonds's use of performance enhancers became more obvious based on the work of Mark Fainaru-Wada and Lance Williams in the book *Game of Shadows*, Alex kept repeating the innocent-until-proven-guilty defense.

Prove it, Alex seemed to be saying.

Chapter Ten

THE "FUCK YOU" TOUR

THE 2006 SEASON WAS very likely Alex's cleanest as a Yankee—and his worst.

It was a disappointing year by his standards—a .290 average, with 35 homers and 121 RBIs—topped off by a humiliating playoff series against Detroit. His season was marred by errors, clutch strikeouts and unmerciful boos. "Rip away. Rip away," Alex said in the middle of a June slump. "If I was a writer, I'd probably be writing some nasty things. If I was a fan, I'd be booing me, too."

He was a victim of adulation whiplash. How could Alex have been so lauded for his greatness in 2005 and elicit such venom with his foggy play in 2006? If Alex had used performance enhancers to earn his second MVP, why hadn't he used them in 2006? There was a very obvious reason: players had more to fear in 2006 after MLB pushed the union to toughen penalties for steroid cheats: a

positive test would now draw a 50-game suspension for a first offense, 100 games for a second and a lifetime ban for a third.

There was also another wrinkle: Players competing in the
World Baseball Classic that March in 2006 were subject to the
more rigorous Olympic-style drug testing both before and during
the event.

As his dismal season ground on, the fans and the press got
nastier. One tabloid headline aimed at Alex read DO YOU HATE THIS
MAN? Hitting coach Don Mattingly worked with him on his swing
flaws. His wife counseled him to turn to God. But his circle of
friends kept telling him, "You're still the best."

That's what Alex wanted to hear. He started to rationalize—
the pop fly that landed between third and shortstop with no one
calling for it was *definitely* Jeter's fault. He told himself his sliding
statistics—his batting average was south of .260 for three months
in the summer—were just an aberration.

He read every searing word in the papers about himself but
seemed impervious to the chatter. He walked without a burden, a
man in denial. "He never acted like he had a bad game," ex–Yankee teammate Gary Sheffield says. "He didn't carry an oh-for-four
around like someone else would."

Alex soldiered on with what Yankee teammate Jason Giambi
described in *Sports Illustrated* as "false confidence." In the same article, Giambi recounted a revealing exchange he'd had with Alex.

"We're all rooting for you, and we're behind you 100 percent,"
Giambi had told Alex, "but you've got to get the big hit."

"What do you mean?" Alex responded. "I've had five hits in
Boston."

"You fucking call those hits?" Giambi said. "You had two
fucking dinkers to right field and a ball that bounced over the third
baseman! Look at how many pitches you missed!"

Giambi was right—Alex had lost his confidence, even though
he didn't seem to know it. He was guessing on pitches, whiffing on

fat fastballs and struggling to hit even batting practice pitches over the fence.

Alex's malaise didn't seem to faze him, but it affected his teammates. The tension between Jeter and Rodriguez escalated to the point where the clubhouse—and management—began to take sides. Torre leaned toward Jeter, the player who had been with him from the beginning; GM Brian Cashman supported Alex—after all, acquiring him had been the bold move that had proved Cashman's genius. In the middle was a team that, Sheffield says, "didn't know what to think about the soap opera."

The 2006 drama bubbled over when Torre called Alex into his office inside the visitors' clubhouse in Seattle on August 24. Safeco Field was no paradise for Alex. He had been mocked there since leaving the Mariners in 2001 for Texas. Now, as he battled a sore throat and achiness and endured the steady booing from Seattle fans, his manager challenged him to be accountable for his slump—a word Alex would never use.

"This is all about honesty," Torre told him in a conversation he later recounted for *Sports Illustrated*'s Tom Verducci. "And it's not about anyone else but you. You can't pretend everything is OK when it's not."

That night, Alex came to the plate as a pinch hitter. There were two outs in the ninth; the Yankees were behind 4–2. With fans on his back, two antibiotics coursing through his veins and closer J. J. Putz in front of him, Alex struck out swinging to end the game. He then stunned stadium attendants—many of whom had known Alex as the perfect and proper Mariner in the late 1990s— by throwing a chair across the clubhouse floor. Alex was angry because he was embarrassed.

Where had his confidence gone? Steroids had supplied Alex with an edge in the past. For many players, the "strut" steroids provided was as important as the extra strength they delivered. On steroids, Alex felt invincible; off them, he felt vulnerable.

His worst indignity was still to come. When the lineups for game one of the Yankees first-round play-off series against Detroit were announced, Torre had Alex batting sixth, the lowest spot he'd hit in since his first full season in the majors, 1996. "It crushed him," says a confidant of Alex's. "Nothing after that surprised him. Torre lost him. No question."

He played with zombie eyes for three games. And in game four, Torre dropped him to eighth. The Tigers won the series and Alex had just one hit in four games. "[Alex] was a head case," Charles Zabransky, the longtime Yankee clubhouse guard, recalled. "He wasn't ever settled. He didn't know what he was doing at times."

Alex knew one thing after 2006: Never again would he endure a season like that one. Never again would he be so fragile. So vulnerable.

Alex went into the off-season resolved to change everything—including his look and his attitude—but he also sought out someone familiar: Angel Presinal. The trainer to the stars of the D.R. had been by Alex's side in Texas and had worked with him before the 2005 season.

Alex was determined to reinvent himself for the 2007 season. In front of teammates, he worked out with Romero, who showed up about every fifth day. Behind the scenes, he relied on Presinal, who was still banned by Major League Baseball for his role as Juan Gonzalez's steroid bagman in the incident with Toronto authorities in 2001, but was ubiquitous on Yankee road trips. He didn't sign in on log sheets at stadiums, but he was usually waiting for Alex at the team's hotel.

Alex never tested positive for steroids in 2007, but one baseball source says it's possible Presinal administered a low-dose cycle of steroids with HGH to jump-start his regular season.

In the Dominican Republic, Presinal has a reputation as a

healer who salvages baseball careers from the scrap heap. He had access to the Dominican pharmacies that sold steroids, and baseball sources familiar with his activities in the D.R. say Presinal was a student of performance enhancers, known for rubbing injured players with creams believed to contain steroids. Former Rangers strength and conditioning coach Fernando Montes knew Presinal well from his days working in Cleveland, where Presinal trained Juan Gonzalez in 2001. "He would just take what workouts he saw others do and mimic them," Montes says. "So you have to ask, What does he do that's so special?"

Presinal keeps players' use quiet, or undetectable. One proven trick is to stack testosterone at a low level with HGH. "I absolutely think Alex is using HGH . . . probably a combination of growth and steroids," Canseco says.

Two players close to A-Rod say he has used HGH while with the Yankees based on side effects they've seen and that he likely procured it the same way many major leaguers do—through doctors who have ties to anti-aging clinics. According to one Yankee, players often turn to Dr. Brian Wolstein, a Tampa-area chiropractor who is a self-described anti-aging specialist. A former Mr. Tampa, Wolstein founded Infinite Vitality, which, according to its website, legally prescribes patients HGH. Wolstein says he does not prescribe HGH to pro athletes because it's banned by MLB, but has offered "nutritional advice" to a number of major leaguers, including ex-Yankees Carl Pavano and David Wells. He says Alex is not a client. "I met him in Las Vegas, but he didn't come to me," says Wolstein. "I know he's got his own deals."

Until 2007, Infinite Vitality was less than two miles from the Yankees spring training stadium, George M. Steinbrenner Field. Now based in Clearwater, Infinite Vitality operates out of a one-story brick building that sits among car dealerships and industrial office parks on US-19. It is less than a 30-minute drive from the Yankees' complex.

A former teammate says Alex viewed 2007 as his " 'Fuck You' Tour." He was sick of being the fall guy in New York. He was tired of not being coddled by Torre. And he had an opt-out clause in his contract that would allow him to become a free agent after the season—and let Scott Boras grab him an even richer deal.

He showed up for spring training in Tampa determined to leave every vestige of 2006 behind. He even came clean on the subject that had always left his pin-striped pants on fire: his relationship with Jeter. All the gossip was true, he told reporters—they weren't best friends anymore. They were long past the days of slumber-party pillow talk, dissecting baseball strategy well into the night. They hadn't been close for a while. "Let's make a contract," Rodriguez told the writers. "You don't ask about Derek anymore, and I promise I'll stop lying to you."

"That felt good," Alex said later.

His Jeter cleansing moment actually helped him with teammates. They were happy to hear—for once—what was in Alex's heart instead of the bullshit that was in his script.

Alex seemed more natural now; he wasn't trying so hard to please anymore. He didn't oblige every query from reporters and occasionally snapped off a curt reply to a question he didn't like. He started plugging iPod headphones into his ears when he was in the clubhouse as a built-in buffer to reporters' questions. "Can't hear you," he'd say as he walked by, bobbing his head to his tunes. On opening day, he missed a windblown pop-up—and didn't care. In fact, he poked fun at himself in the dugout. He was totally relaxed at the plate in the eighth when he atoned for his botched catch with a home run.

It was the first of 14 home runs he would hit in April—no player in history had ever hit more homers in the month.

All spring and into summer, he had an edgy attitude, a mean swing and a secret weapon: Presinal, who was always nearby, but in the shadows. Alex had learned his lesson in Texas—he was now discreet when he took Presinal on road trips. The trainer would usually share a room with one of The Boys, Pepe Gomez or Yuri Sucart. Several Yankee players knew Presinal was around constantly and knew he had been banned, but no one said a word. They respected the code about not ratting out a teammate. Besides, Alex was hitting like an MVP.

Alex was feeling so good that he dared try something he would have considered unthinkable just six months before: he hosted a summer barbecue for the team at his suburban home in Rye, New York. "Hell no, never in a million years would I have had people at my house," Alex said. "Again, it's part of the whole thing. People look at [my] numbers—runners in scoring position and fewer errors. But it's the overall comfort level to have a barbecue, to have all my teammates over and enjoy ourselves. I think that's part of being more comfortable in your skin and being more comfortable in New York."

Alex invited everyone but didn't expect a full house. His relationship with some teammates remained strained, and his bond with Torre had been tested through his batting-order demotion in the 2006 playoffs. Alex was buoyed by his season but undeniably fragile. He wanted Torre to show up—he just couldn't be sure if he would.

The party began in the afternoon at Alex's house on the Long Island Sound. In walked a dozen or so teammates, and then, with his daughter by his side, Torre came to the door.

"He made a big to-do about it," Torre recalls. "He couldn't do enough when people got there. He went around and spent time with every group. He made sure I got a cigar and he bent over backwards to make sure everyone was comfortable. To be honest, I was happy that *he* looked so happy."

It didn't matter that Jeter skipped the BBQ—"He didn't want to be a hypocrite," says one person close to the Yankees—Alex enjoyed what he perceived as a breakthrough with Torre.

"Joe was the last guy there," Alex explained. "We almost had to push him out the door. I was really touched by that gesture. He didn't have to spend four hours at my barbecue."

Alex's ebullient reaction to Torre's presence was a reflection of his need to be embraced even as he slipped into more of a rebel's persona. "I didn't realize at the time how much of an impact my being at [his BBQ] had on him," Torre says. "I stayed because I had a good time."

Perhaps Alex finally felt accepted as a Yankee, and yet as a nagging paradox, he seemed to be daring himself to fall.

Feeling suddenly bulletproof, Alex all but dared gossip snoops to catch him merrily debauching from coast to coast. A year earlier, he had met Joslyn Morse—a buxom exotic dancer at the Scores men's club in Las Vegas—on a boy's night out. Other strippers had also caught his eye. Friend says Cynthia knew what her husband was up to, and tried to set boundaries for him, if only to keep his indiscretions from public view.

Alex was getting increasingly careless. That summer, nude pictures of Morse became a popular download after she was photographed on Alex's arm during a team road trip to Toronto. These Morse sightings brought on the first visible fissure in the A-Rod/C-Rod power couple, and the tabloids delighted in exposing Alex's dalliances. Despite this, Cynthia protected and defended Alex. She defiantly took her seat at Yankee Stadium one summer night wearing a T-shirt that read FUCK YOU, her response to the scandalmongers.

The circus didn't distract Alex. In fact, it seemed to sharpen his focus. He liked the cat and mouse with the papers. He liked being all over the tabloids. He liked being talked about, and whispered about. He had his best season ever, hitting .314, with 54 home runs and a career-high 156 RBIs. He took his third MVP award in a rout. And now, he was ready to cash in, and get an even bigger deal. With the Yankees, if possible, but elsewhere, if they wouldn't pay his asking price.

There was an odd push-pull element to his phenomenal season. He wanted to prove he belonged in the Yankee clubhouse and show every New York fan what they would be missing if he left. Casting himself as a flight risk was, however, a ruse. He longed to play out his career in New York, live forever as a Yankee, enter Cooperstown in pinstripes and feed Gotham's bottomless appetite for celebrity. His 2007 season of personal and professional rebellion was an attempt to stay, not escape. "There was no way he was going to leave the Yankees or play for any other team," recalls Romero. "That was the pinnacle of where he could go in baseball."

And, Alex believed, the pinnacle of where he could go outside baseball. He shopped on Madison Avenue because anybody who was somebody shopped there. He ran up $2,000 bills at exclusive Manhattan restaurants such as Daniel, lounged at Jay-Z's 40/40 Club and purchased overpriced art from SoHo galleries. He was bigger than baseball, and he believed New York City was his destiny.

He nearly fumbled his fate, though, with one of the most vilified contract maneuvers in baseball history. On October 28, 2007, in the middle of game four of the World Series, with the Red Sox primed to sweep the Rockies, Jon Heyman on SI.com broke news that threatened to eclipse baseball's fall classic: A-Rod was opting out of the final three years of his Yankees contract. FOX interrupted the game with the bulletin, turning attention from the Red Sox and Colorado Rockies. And newspaper websites began posting headlines about A-Rod above World Series features on the players.

The blowback was immediate. Minutes after Red Sox closer Jonathan Papelbon tossed his glove into the chilly air at Coors Field to celebrate Boston's sweep—its second World Series title in four seasons—Red Sox fans behind the visitors' dugout chanted toward Boston GM Theo Epstein: "Don't sign A-Rod! Don't sign A-Rod!"

Commissioner Bud Selig was livid because Alex's contract ploy had diverted attention away from baseball's biggest event. The leak was blamed on Scott Boras, but friends say Alex pushed to get the news out. Boras took the fall—that was his duty—and no one found it hard to believe he was behind this move. Boras was famous for the pleasure he took in tweaking the baseball establishment—or kicking it in the crotch—when it served his purposes.

The Yankees were as furious as Selig at the move. Yankee GM Brian Cashman refused to negotiate further with Boras. In the run-up to Alex's opt-out, the Yankees had repeatedly called Alex to ask if he could be more reasonable than the $350 million "request" Boras had given them. He never called them back.

Alex was immediately branded a toxic asset. *New York Post* columnist Mike Vaccaro wrote the night the opt-out news was released, "If this is indeed his final dash out the side door—and if we are to take the Yankees at their word, it is absolutely that—then it comes as part of a perfect A-Rod opera, a me-first symphony that would be appalling if it weren't so predictable."

Alex feigned surprise at the leak, even though he knew Boras had e-mailed Cashman's BlackBerry earlier that day to tell him they wanted out. "I can't believe this bullshit," Alex told a friend. "This was not the way it was supposed to go down."

A day later, the Yankees reiterated that they would not try to resign him. "No chance," said Hank Steinbrenner, who, with his brother Hal, was now running their father's storied franchise.

Boras had insisted that deep-pocketed suitors would line up to greet Alex, but no one believed him. "No one was going to come close to $300 million—no one," says a major-league general manager. "There were no other Yankees out there."

That meant Boras and his client had just one potential candidate with the ability to pay Alex the kind of salary he deemed his natural right: the Yankees. And they had slammed the door on him.

Alex had one piece of good timing on his side, though. The Steinbrenner brothers didn't want to look dim-witted twice, and just a month earlier, they, along with team president Randy Levine, had stumbled as they pushed Torre out the door.

Given the city's almost unconditional love for Torre, the firing had been an epic public relations failure. Torre had, with grace and dignity and many cups of green tea, won four championships with the Yankees in 12 years.

Torre was gone by the end of October. This was just fine with Alex. It played into his opt-out strategy. The Yankees couldn't afford another PR quagmire, especially since they were building a new $1.3 billion stadium that would be ready for Opening Day, 2009.

But what could Alex possibly do to make nice with the Yankees? He called the Oracle of Omaha, Warren Buffett. The two had talked at Berkshire Hathaway three years earlier and discussed the responsibilities of wealth. Alex had Warren B. on speed dial. Buffett displayed an autographed jersey of Alex's in his office. When Alex got Buffett on the phone, he told him how badly he had botched his relationship with the Yankees hierarchy. Buffett's advice: Separate yourself from Boras. Call the Yankees yourself. Make your own deal.

On November 7, at around 7 p.m., Levine was weaving through midtown Manhattan foot traffic when his cell phone vibrated. It was Gerald Cardinale, a director at Goldman Sachs, who had a personal message to relay from Alex: He wanted to make amends. He was crawling back to the Yankees.

When Levine told Cashman, the Yankee G.M. said he wasn't

interested. "Cashman was thinking, No way, we're done with Alex," one person close to Cashman says. "He knew it was time to move on. There was an Alex fatigue." The better minds of the Yankees brass agreed. Some also believed that Alex was The Cooler, a tag he'd first picked up in Texas. They pointed out that in his four years in pinstripes, Alex had won two MVP titles and zero rings. Even worse, the Yankees had been eclipsed by the Red Sox, who had captured two World Series titles in that time. "I don't think anyone thought Alex was coming back," says one Yankee source. "He was done. It was over."

And that's how the " 'Fuck You' Tour" evolved into the ' "I Fucked Up' Tour." Alex was going to have to prostrate himself if he hoped to return to the Yankees, but that was fine, because he was prepared to do some major-league groveling.

It was a clear mid-November night like so many others in Tampa. A drought had left the normally lush landscapes in the richest, oldest area of town with patches of brown. Cynthia and Alex Rodriguez looked radiant amongst all those thirsty palms, dressed fashionably but casually as they walked into Hal Steinbrenner's home.

This attempt at a kiss-and-makeup had been Hal's call. His father, George Steinbrenner, was only nominally The Boss these days. Friends whispered that he was struggling with dementia, and his boys were running the team now. He was 77 years old, his skin was chalky and his words were often repetitive. He padded around in slippers, wore a World Series ring and still liked to call up friends to ask if they'd heard any good jokes. On good days, he pored over the Yankee games and box scores with the close attention of a watchmaker. On bad days, he had trouble remembering the names of his players. Almost all signs of his trademark bombast appeared only on paper in the form of press releases from Steinbrenner's longtime PR man, Howard Rubenstein.

Control of the team had quietly been passed on to Hal and his brother, Hank, this season. Hal, 38, was the trim, responsible brother. He had his father's perfect, wind-resistant hair and almost always wore a suit with pressed creases. Hank, 57, was the walking equivalent of a messy teen boy's room in both appearance and demeanor—disheveled and somewhat dark. In private, he battled depression; in public, he made headlines with rants his father might have envied. "Red Sox Nation? What a bunch of bullshit that is," he once said, pissing on the warm-and-fuzzy feelings in Boston after the team's 2007 World Series win.

The Steinbrenner Boys were an odd couple, and they were both at Hal's house this evening, ready to talk to a decidedly more dysfunctional couple, the Rodriguezes. Hank and Hal presumed they would be negotiating from a position of great strength and that Alex was ready to take any deal they offered him. They also figured they could get him at a steep discount and use his return as a way to bury the Torre fiasco. They were about to get played.

For more than an hour, Alex chipped away at the residual hostility in the air. He looked each brother in the eye and apologized for his opt-out ploy in every way imaginable. With the pregnant Cynthia by his side, Alex gave an MVP-worthy performance, oozing sincerity, humility and goodwill as he asked the brothers to give him another chance.

At the end of the evening, Hank and Hal were in love—again. They wanted Alex back. Besides, there were no third basemen available to the Yankees who would even approach what Alex could provide. They certainly couldn't find another marquee player to help open a stadium in 2009 where field-level seats would be topping out at $2,500 per game.

Alex's mea culpa worked. Somehow, some way, he snagged

the $300 million deal he had wanted all along. "It was dumb and dumber," says one American League executive. "Alex played them for fools."

Boras, never far away during the proceedings, quickly worked out the contract language and issued a statement on November 15: "Alex and Cynthia visited with the Steinbrenners and Yankees officials and following the meeting, Alex instructed me to discuss the contract terms with the Yankees."

Alex didn't give up a penny for his transgressions. He agreed to his second career record-breaking deal: 10 years, $275 million, which would balloon to $300 million if and when he became Major League Baseball's new home-run king. Each time he lapped a baseball legend on his journey, he would put another $6 million into his account. With 518 total homers at the end of 2007—after becoming the youngest player ever to 500—Alex Rodriguez would receive a bonus for passing Willie Mays (660), Babe Ruth (714), Hank Aaron (755) and Barry Bonds (762).

"These are not incentive bonuses," Hank explained. "For lack of a better term, they really are historic bonuses. It's a horse of a different color."

With that bamboozle completed, Alex then launched an image makeover. Behind it was yet another handler who'd recently entered his life, Guy Oseary. During a workout in the winter of 2007, Alex surprised his trainer, Dodd Romero, with a question about the world balance of fame: "Who do you think is more popular?" he asked, "Lenny Kravitz or Derek Jeter?"

The question underscored the insecurity Alex still had about Jeter, but it also set up his second question for Romero, who also trained Kravitz: "Who handles Lenny's PR?" Alex wanted to have "people," loads of "people," just as the Hollywood elite did. Alex had Boras, and he'd signed with the William Morris Agency to aid him in his goal of transcending baseball, but he needed more "people" to get to where he knew he should be. "Lenny is cool," he told Romero. "Who is his agent?"

Romero gave him Lenny's number. Soon, Alex had Oseary, the whiz behind Maverick Records, on his team. Oseary was the PR manager for not only Kravitz but also Madonna. It was Oseary who suggested that the quickest way to change Alex's image from greedy opt-out klutz to apologetic prince was to do a prime-time interview.

They settled on *60 Minutes*. To secure the interview, Katie Couric had been in touch with Alex through the final stages of his contract negotiations. He liked her, and wanted her to like him. She later confessed that during one of their talks Alex had asked, "What team do you think I should play for?"

For his Couric interview, Alex wore a dark blazer and white button-down shirt to project a conservative image. Cynthia again was by his side, wearing a black dress and visibly pregnant. Both were asked about the controversial timing of Alex's opt-out of his deal with the Yankees.

"When I realized things were going haywire, at that point I said, 'Wait a minute. I've got to be accountable for my own life,'" Alex told Couric. "This is not the way I wanted it to go. So I got behind the wheel."

Couric asked Cynthia how the opt-out gambit had changed Alex. "He wasn't used to having to take such initiative, such action, especially in this arena," she said. "It's something he wasn't used to doing, and he actually had to pick up the phone, make the calls, make some decisions and stand behind them, be confident and be sure."

Couric then asked about steroids, but Alex was ready for her. He had prepared for this question. He had actually been a bit unlucky with the timing of the *60 Minutes* broadcast. Just a day before his sit-down with Couric, the Mitchell Report had been released,

and it included the names of dozens of players, including Roger
Clemens, who were linked to steroid allegations. Alex wasn't on
the list, but his advisers had coached him on how to talk about the
frenzy surrounding the Mitchell Report.

"For the record," Couric said to Alex on camera, "have you ever
used steroids, human growth hormone or any other performance-
enhancing substance?"

"No," Alex said, his eyes locked on her but with a slight twitch
of his left cheek.

"Have you ever been tempted to use any of those things?"

He looked away for an instant, as if to contemplate the question he'd already been prepped on, then replied, "No."

"You never felt like 'This guy's doing it, maybe I should look
into this too? He's getting better numbers, playing better ball' . . . ?"

"I've never felt overmatched on the baseball field," Alex said
with a steady voice. "I've always been [in] a very strong, dominant
position, and I felt that if I did my work, [which] I've done since
I've been a rookie back in Seattle, I [wouldn't] have a problem competing at any level."

He paused, took a breath and then, with another twitch of his
left cheek, said, "So, no."

It was a lie. Psychologists who study body language and physi-
ological cues say those twitches of his left-cheek gave him away. But
he told the fib well. He answered confidently and without equivo-
cation, just as he'd been trained. He had emphatically declared on
national TV that he was not a drug cheat.

The truth was that Alex's baseball career and almost every
other part of his life consisted of one artifice atop another—a
pileup of deceptions—that was about to come crashing down all
around him.

Chapter Eleven

THE DIMAGGIO WANNABE

THE MATERIAL GIRL BEGAN whispering sweet, pseudo-mystical nothings into Alex's ear in December of 2007, instantly mesmerizing him. They got to know each other through Madonna's close friend, Miami nightclub impresario Ingrid Casares, just after the *60 Minutes* interview.

Alex had always been attracted to older women, powerful people and hard bodies. In Madonna, he hit the trifecta—she was an icon, in great shape and nearing 50. "In his eyes, the higher the influence of the female, the better he scored," says Dodd Romero. "I think that's why he's intrigued with Madonna. In his material mind, he's moving up the ladder."

Alex wanted to impress Madonna, and what better way than to adopt her belief system. He started attending services at the Kabbalah Centre of New York and L. A. where Madonna, Demi Moore,

Ashton Kutcher and Britney Spears worshiped. He told friends this postmodern, self-help version of Kabbalah would change his life—and free his swing in the play-offs. All he had to do was learn to become "an empty vessel."

"That's a well-known Kabbalistic expression," says Rabbi Allan Nadler of Drew University's Jewish Studies Program. "What it means is you have to empty yourself of egotistical, sensual and especially carnal desires. That's the classic view. But The Kabbalah Centre turns that upside down. It says anything getting in the way of your happiness is what you need to empty yourself of, like family obligations. And that's where it's perverse. Somebody gave Alex pseudo-license to leave his family."

Alex hadn't left Cynthia and his kids by the time spring training opened for the 2008 season. In fact, he happily staged an elaborate show of familial bliss in a studio in Miami, where the Yankees television network—YES—was filming a hagiographic feature on Alex for a show called "YESterdays."

The show was to shoot Alex interacting with his family—which included the pregnant Cynthia, Alex's half brother Joe, and half sister Susy—and some of his friends in a "This is Your Life" format.

"Please welcome the man the world knows as A-Rod, the third baseman of the New York Yankees, Alex Rodriguez," the host, Michael Kay, began.

Kay turned to Cynthia, who assured viewers that A-Rod was mortal, sometimes. Yes, he left his socks on the floor—like anyone else.

"You actually experienced him not being so smooth at the birth of Natasha, right?" asked Kay.

"As tough and big as he seems," Cynthia said, "he is really

wimpy around doctors or any type of medical situation. I don't know why I thought the birth of our child would be any different. In the middle of the night, I realized that I needed to go to the hospital. I wake him up. The first thing that comes out of his mouth is 'Can we call your mother?' I stared. 'No, let's wait and make sure that I am in labor. You know, it's the middle of the night.' Finally, a few hours later I said, 'I think you can call my mom now.' And the color came back to his face."

There is laughter on the set.

"Then forget it," Cynthia continues. "I was, like, not even having a baby. *He* was the one. The one nurse had a cold cloth on his head. The other nurse had the blood pressure on his arm. And my mother was, like, rubbing his back."

"Really?"

"No, it was crazy," Cynthia said.

"I was terrible," Alex interjected.

"And he passed out on a couch," Cynthia said. "And I am there, in the middle of labor, and really, I am not being paid much attention to besides the doctor and a couple of nurses. And he is there moaning."

"Get out!" Kay blurted out, laughing.

"She is right," Alex said.

Cynthia said, "In between pushing, I am going, 'Honey, are you okay?' "

YES aired the *A-Rod Family Hour* for only a month before pulling it from their rotation. By then, his home life was no longer suitable for young viewers.

Alex began spring training in 2008 with a new $300 million contract and a carefree air. There was another Joe running the Yankees show now. Joe Girardi had replaced Torre, and the young pitchers

Joba Chamberlain, Ian Kennedy and Phil Hughes were drawing most of the attention from the New York beat writers as the season got underway.

Alex played steady but unspectacular ball for a team that bounced around .500 in the early going. In late April, he injured his quadriceps so he was out of the Yankees lineup when Cynthia gave birth to the couple's second little girl, Ella, on April 21 in Miami. He flew home for three days, then walked into the Yankees clubhouse with pink-wrapped cigars for everyone that read IT'S A GIRL! ELLA ALEXANDER RODRIGUEZ 4-21-08.

One Yankee source says Alex returned from Miami looking tanned and rested, with new blond highlights, as if he'd been to a spa.

A second round of fatherhood didn't ground Alex. He now seemed restless, hitting a tepid .286 in April and .293 in May. His mind was adrift and his marriage was falling apart. Alex told friends he wanted his freedom. "Mentally, he was already single," says a former confidant.

In May, Alex dined at a Hooters restaurant perched on a deck above the paddleboats and dinner cruise yachts bobbing in Baltimore's touristy Inner Harbor. It was about four blocks from Camden Yards, where the Orioles were hosting the Yankees in a three-game series. He had been here before.

He had told the woman at the front desk that he wanted to be seated at a specific table, the one near the restroom, the one with an old photo of Mickey Mantle posing next to a Hooters girl on the wall. He also said he he preferred a Latina waitress. The staff here knew Alex, and greeted him with smiles even though they knew he always left the same tip: 15 percent. "The girls have their issues with him," one manager says. "I don't really want to say he's an asshole. He's definitely, well, rude."

He spoke mostly in Spanish, but several waitresses heard—

and understood—the remarks he made about the women on staff, particularly one he found unattractive. "What is *she* doing working here?" he quipped, "Her father must own Hooters."

"I've been a fan of yours forever," a passing waitress said to him as he sat at his table.

"Can I have blue cheese?" he replied, ignoring her.

"He says he's entitled to whatever he wants," recalls one waitress.

He finished eating and then, as he bolted for the door, he told a waitress, "Nice ass."

This was not the urbane image Cynthia had painstakingly helped her husband project for over a decade. This was his way of lashing out at her, and all she represented. She was the symbol of the Old Alex. He wasn't that man anymore. By the end of May, Dodd Romero had seen enough of the New Alex.

"Brother, I represent good, and what you're doing isn't good," Dodd told him. "I have to step off now."

"What will it take to keep you? Write it down on a piece of paper," Alex replied. "I'll give you whatever you want."

Money was what kept people close to Alex, but Dodd, who had never asked for more than a normal trainer's fee from Alex, picked up a piece of paper and wrote, "Find Jesus."

Alex said nothing as Dodd walked away.

"I have never fought harder for anyone in my life—I sacrificed five years of not making any money at all," Dodd said after dumping Alex as a client. "I always said if he finds Christ, he'll appreciate me. Then, one day, the pennies he has paid me . . . he'll feel ashamed he has done it that way."

Alex didn't have time for Dodd, or his biblical homilies; he was seeking salvation in the arms of Kabbalah, and Madonna.

With Madonna firmly in his life by mid-2008, the ever-malleable Alex had changed his private thoughts and public behavior: Where in March 2007 he donated $6,900 to Republican presidential candidate Rudy Giuliani, in 2008, like Madonna, he was supporting Barack Obama. Where he had been content to live in a Coral Gables estate, Alex, in 2008, rented a mansion on Star Island—Madonna's neighborhood. Where he used to appear regularly on the tabloid sports pages, he was now starting to contrive ways of getting his name into the gossip pages. Where before he was content to hang out with "the Boys" in Vegas strip clubs, he now upgraded to a celebrity circle, taking a helicopter with Madonna to Jerry Seinfeld's $30 million Hampton's estate. Where he had entered the front doors of restaurants he was, in Madonna's company, slipping out the kitchen in a winking avoidance of the paparazzi.

By late June, a daily diet of salacious headlines appeared in the New York and British tabloids: "A-Rod Paying Late-Night Visits to Madge's Love Nest" and "A-Rod Wooed by Madge Cult." The papers claimed that Cynthia had found a love note written by Alex to Madonna that read, "You are my true soul mate."

He listened to Madonna's music. He talked of her constantly—to friends, to players, to casual acquaintances. "Obsessed, pretty much," says one Yankee. "It was like, 'Ok, Alex, you're with Madonna. And I'd give you a big high-five for that—fifteen years ago.' Hey, she looks great, but she's 50. It's like sleeping with your mother."

In a *Daily News* story on July 4, Cynthia was quoted telling friends, "I feel like Madonna is using mind control over [Alex]. I don't recognize the man he's become." She believed Madonna had "brainwashed" her Catholic-raised husband with her celebrity brand of Kabbalah. "It teaches self-fulfillment to the point of becoming God," says Nadler. "So these are gods-in-training."

Alex certainly was acting as though he were invincible. Friends say he fanned his breakup with his wife by giving his friends permission to plant disparaging items about Cynthia in the tabloids attributable to "sources close to A-Rod."

"People say, "Oh, it was for publicity,'" says a friend of Alex's. "Well, real people got hurt."

Madonna was now more important to Alex than his inner-circle. Alex required a staffer on his payroll to deliver the New York *Daily News* and the *New York Post* to him on a tray at breakfast. One day, the employee charged with that task had doodled horns on a photo of Madonna. Alex fired him.

On July 7, 2008, after a 12-year relationship and six years of marriage, Cynthia filed for divorce and moved from New York City to their home in Miami with the couple's two children, Natasha, 3, and Ella, 3 months. On page one, paragraph one of the court documents filed in Miami-Dade Circuit Court, her lawyer claimed: "'Alex' has emotionally abandoned his wife and children and has left her with no choice but to divorce him."

The "abandonment" issue had come full circle for Alex. There was an unsettling symmetry to what he was doing with his life, and what his father had done twenty years earlier. In 1985, his father had left his family in Miami to seek a more exciting life in New York City. "I found out Miami wasn't fast-paced enough for Dad," Alex once said.

Now it was Alex living fast and free in New York. "He'll crash and burn," Romero predicted. "Hopefully, he'll get humbled and become a man."

Alex treated the 2008 All-Star Game at Yankee Stadium as his bachelor party, one that celebrated his liberation from marriage. On July 14, one day before the game, Alex invited Madonna, Beyoncé, Red Sox star David Ortiz and several Yankee teammates to a party he was throwing at Jay-Z's 40/40 Club in Manhattan.

There was a red carpet for guests and ropes marking the area set aside for photographers. Inside, hired dancers shook and shimmied as Madonna classics like "Holiday" blasted from the speakers.

Many A-listers were invited, but few of them showed up. Not even Madonna stopped by, and most of Alex's teammates skipped his bash in favor of the All-Star celebration hosted by Derek Jeter. His party was packed with guests that included Michael Jordan and Billy Crystal. As the gossip pages described it, Alex was last seen sitting in a back booth at the 40/40 Club with his mother and Ingrid Casares.

Friends say Alex was, for the first time, allowing his outside interests to distract him from his job. "Baseball was running a distant third," says one friend. "He'd never acted that way before." Baseball seemed like an annoying chore to Alex at the All-Star Game. In the run-up to the big event, baseball officials had asked him to compete in the Home Run Derby. What a great night it would be, they thought: Last All-Star gala at the old Yankee Stadium. What a treat it would be for fans to see Alex in pinstripes ripping home runs into a night sky with the backdrop of the stadium's famous red, white and blue bunting. MLB officials were desperate for Alex to flex his swing for the cameras, and for the good of the game. Alex declined. "I need my swing to be at its best," he said, not wanting to tweak his mechanics by going all out in a long-ball gimmick. This seemed like an odd excuse to baseball officials—hadn't Alex spent his entire career swinging for the fences?

Alex didn't care whom he angered. He was through trying to please anybody but A-Rod.

The media didn't take the hint; about two-dozen media members—including a camera crew from "Inside Edition"—crowded around Alex during a session with players the day before the game. He was the biggest draw there, and he loved it. His notoriety had finally transcended baseball; he was now in Madonna's orbit. "Look, everybody has distractions and personal things," he told the press, referring to his relationship with Madonna but not mentioning her name. "Mine are on the front pages of the papers—and I'm fine with that."

Alex fielded every question. He spoke earnestly about the hallowed history of Yankee Stadium and the poignancy of this final All-Star Game there. He seemed genuine when talking about what he owed the game's next generation: "I think it's my responsibility to spend a lot of time with these younger guys that are here for the first time."

Alex started at third base, went hitless and was taken out of the game in the fifth inning. He darted to the clubhouse, changed into his nightclub best and left Yankee Stadium before the sixth inning was over. Friends say he went to see Madonna.

The All-Star Game went into extra innings, and didn't end until 1:30 a.m.; writers instantly declared the game a classic. As the AL scored the winning run in the bottom of the 15th inning, Derek Jeter was on the top step of the dugout, pumping his fist. He, like Alex, had been taken out of the game in the fifth inning. Jeter knew what it meant to be part of a team.

The Trump Park Avenue apartment Alex had shared with Cynthia was protected by dutiful doormen who opened golden-barred doors that gave the building's lobby a gilded-cage look. . . and by mid-summer, Alex felt trapped there. He had once aspired to live beside corporate tycoons, but now this luxury building felt old, fussy, way too buttoned-down for a man sleeping with Madonna.

Three years earlier, it had been a perfect reflection of Alex—or, at least, of the image he was creating for himself. It was 2005, when Manhattan was awash in hedge-fund money. There were wait lists for $1 million Ferraris. Private jets were being outfitted with theaters. Back then Alex, with a six-month old baby and his wife, Cynthia, wanted badly to live at a Donald Trump address. Not just any

Trump building—Derek Jeter had bought an apartment at Trump World Plaza in 2001—but the one with the most cachet.

Trump, the pouty-lipped real estate magnate with the dust-bunny coiffure, was a genius at making wretched excess seem glamorous. When he converted the former Hotel Delmonico into high-end condominiums, Alex eagerly bought in. He paid $7.4 million for his apartment. But now the building had the wrong vibe for the new, liberated Alex.

Alex put the place on the market for $14 million and searched for a new dream pad at 15 Central Park West, a building full of A-listers from sports and entertainment—Sting, Denzel Washington and NASCAR superstar Jeff Gordon. A bonus: It was two blocks from Madonna's apartment.

He eventually rented an apartment at 15 Central Park West for $30,000 a month. At the same time he was trying to unload his Trump co-op. It ultimately sold in six months for $9.9 million, $4.1 million less than his asking price.

Alex's broker, the Modlin Group, played around with some catchy phrasing in their sales brochure: "In a League of Its Own!" read the opening sentence, an obvious reference to Madonna's role in the 1992 movie *A League of Their Own*. It seemed as if everyone—including Alex's realtor—was poking fun at the Material Matron/A-Rod affair.

Alex didn't feel like a punchline, however. He felt validated by this affair that, in his mind, conjured up a stunning parallel. Friends say he fancied himself as the embodiment of a legendary Yankee who, like him, had been a multi-talented superstar, the constant obsession of the paparazzi, and like him, romantically-linked to a famous and glamorous woman.

Alex thought of himself as a replica of Joe DiMaggio; Madonna was Marilyn Monroe.

There were obvious differences—DiMaggio was retired when he married Monroe and was a man who militantly guarded his privacy. "DiMaggio practiced being an icon," longtime baseball writer Jack Lang once said, and his aura had legs even after his career ended. Alex liked that. His fascination with Madonna was rivaled only by his attempts to emulate DiMaggio's life. Alex had heard about the Yankee legend as a child, and he identified most strongly with the elegance of DiMaggio, who stroked home runs with an oiled swing and ran the bases with the ease of a pianist running a keyboard. He was beautiful to watch, even stunning.

Alex also admired DiMaggio's consistency—a lifetime batting average of .325, combined with impressive power numbers. He had hit 46 home runs in 1937, his second season, despite the formidable disadvantage of being a right-handed batter in Yankee Stadium, the House That Ruth Built—or, more accurately, the House That Was Built for Lefties. The power alley for a right-handed hitter was left center field, the fence there 457 feet away from home plate, and was reachable for most players only by phone.

Alex also marveled at DiMaggio's life-story. He had been born to immigrants, as had Alex. Like DiMaggio, Alex equated income with stature as a ballplayer. In 1949, DiMaggio had signed a contract with the Yankees for $100,000—unheard-of money in post–World War II America. In 2000, Alex had signed a contract for $252 million—unfathomable numbers for the new millennium. DiMaggio had angered fans when he held out for more. Alex had been excoriated when *he* got more.

Even DiMaggio's pop-culture longevity captivated Alex. Paul Simon's line in a song, "Where have you gone, Joe DiMaggio?" became a catch-phrase of the disillusioned in the '60s. Alex craved such transcendence. But it was all superficial.

When Alex agreed to allow Pulitzer Prize–winning author Richard Ben Cramer—who had written *Joe DiMaggio: The Hero's Life*—to pen his biography, he wasn't aware that Cramer's book had exposed DiMaggio's dark side. He hadn't read it, referring to it as a "thick book." Alex told friends his dream for the book: to be a

New York Times bestseller, to land him on Oprah's couch, to define his fame. As easy as 1, 2, 3.

The mundane part of Alex's life—playing baseball for the New York Yankees—was nearly lost in the hail of newspaper stories about his social life. All summer, he was linked to strippers and fitness contestants. His former teammate, John Rocker, stepped forward to ask the public to look on the bright side of Alex's tawdry romps. "You can't expect him to be a saint," Rocker said. "He has done well. He has no STDs. No illegitimate kids. No multiple wives."

Yankee teammates and executives, however, were dismayed. One official worried about Alex's state of mind and wondered if his handlers had forgotten "that this guy is a baseball player first." This Alex didn't square with the apple-pie image Major League Baseball preferred to project. Its best and richest player was being mentioned too frequently in the *National Enquirer.* This couldn't have pleased the Midwestern sensibilities of Commissioner Bud Selig, who said, "I learned a long time ago that unless a player gets in legal trouble or associates with unsavory characters that threaten the integrity of the game, it is best not to get involved in a player's personal life."

The Yankees, too, refused to meddle, and Alex finally started playing like an All-Star; he hit .337 in July. He was back in the zone.

Dancing to Madonna's choreography, Alex began arranging his public appearances as if he were a shiny bauble in a display case. This was his new MO. A typical snapshot of this occurred on a starry-skied Friday night in Boston on July 27, 2008. Earlier that day at Fenway Park, Alex stepped into the on-deck circle while four young women in the front row greeted him while waving cut-outs of Madonna's face. He had seen and heard worse and, unfazed, went 2 for 4.

Then he went out to be seen, hopefully by a more admiring public, at the team hotel, the Ritz-Carlton. The Yankees' team bus arrived at the hotel around at 11:10 p.m., and Alex walked straight to the city-chic JER-NE Restaurant & Bar next with two pals: Yonder Alonso, a first baseman from the University of Miami who had been chosen in the first round by the Reds, and Pepe Gomez, a childhood friend.

A dimly lit, secluded booth was available in the back, but Alex chose a seat facing the rest of the diners at a table next to a picture window. Only a pane of glass separated him from the busy sidewalk where gawkers turned their heads and pointed at him. He had created his own display case.

Everyone could see Alex, including a group of women in clingy tops and spiked heels who turned all their attention to him. With techno-pop music thumping from the sound system, he exited to take a phone call. He returned a few minutes later, trailed by a hotel security man in a black suit—an impromptu bodyguard—who stood next to Alex's table.

Coach Tony Pena was in the bar; so were Melky Cabrera and a handful of others, such as pitcher Sidney Ponson. In the back of the marble hotel lobby, near an elegant fireplace and out of sight from the groupies, sat Bobby Abreu. He was chatting with family and friends at a quiet lounge table.

The security guard's job was simple: Keep everyone away from Alex while he ate his shrimp cocktail. The women at the bar, who had just refreshed their lip gloss, were undeterred. A few of them—including one in a dress the size and color of a bee's hide—walked back and forth in front of Alex's table, as if auditioning for a part in a movie.

They knew Alex had never been the chaste married man he projected to the public. A year earlier, in this same hotel, he had

had a dalliance with an exotic dancer. "He'll be with these girls who are almost prostitutes," Romero says. "He's so disciplined in one area and not in another."

By 12:15 a.m., Alex tossed a few bills on the table to cover the check and left. This was Ponson's lucky night. The baseball fans in tight skirts who had been flirting with Alex now detoured to his table.

Those unlucky women never had a chance—they didn't know that Alex had promised Madonna he'd remain true to her—at least publicly—while they were a couple.

Alex was having fun with the attention. He was already employing celebrity tricks. Five days later, following a day game at Yankee Stadium, there was an entertainment videographer and an assistant on a stake-out outside Alex's apartment.

They finally spotted Alex's midnight blue Chevy Suburban as it rolled up to the curb in front of the building's doormen. But the only person who stepped out was Gomez. Alex had been dropped off down the street. Gomez and the Suburban were decoys, so Alex could walk into his building unnoticed, but he was still seen. He was still videotaped. "That was for show," the videographer said of Alex's move. For about a half hour, the videographer loitered near the sidewalk planter outside the entrance of Alex's building.

"Who ya waitin' for?" two NYPD officers asked him.

"The usual," he replied.

The cops moved on without pausing.

"Alex had the great stats in July, but they were So-what? numbers," says one instructor who has worked with Alex. "They weren't important to the team. When the Yankees needed him, he wasn't there."

The Yankees were bad in August, and Alex was worse: he had an a 0-for-17 stretch and watched his batting average tumble from

.323 on August 1 to .308 by August 16. And who could he turn to for support, for advice, for consolation? For the first time in his career, he had dropped his motivational guru, Jim Fannin, from his daily ritual. He didn't have Dodd as his trainer and friend anymore. Cynthia was in Miami.

Baseball sources say he reached out to Angel Presinal in August, but even he couldn't pull Alex out of his slump. He was sinking fast and taking the Yankees with him. Steinbrenner's $200 million team was now in danger of missing the postseason for the first time in 14 years. In the *New York Times* on August 27, Tyler Kepner wrote: "It is late August, the Boston Red Sox are in town, and a poor showing by the gurgling Yankees could sink their playoff hopes. This may be the closest the Yankees get to the post-season, and Alex Rodriguez is in October form. Rodriguez went 0 for 5 with two double plays, two strikeouts and a throwing error in the Yankees' 7–3 loss. . . ."

"I pretty much screwed it up every way you can," Alex said after that game.

The Yankees were 11–12 in August at that point, and Alex was hitting .246 with runners in scoring position. "It's terrible," he said. "I have absolutely no excuse."

To friends, he seemed lost. "In a fog," one friend says. He came dangerously close to missing the first pitch of a game on August 30—a cardinal sin in professional baseball. He needed a police escort to get to the stadium in time.

In late September, Alex's divorce was finalized in Miami. Cynthia drove Alex to the Opa-Locka Executive Airport, a private strip with a wood-paneled lobby where the wealthy wait while their private jets are pulled up close to a pair of sliding glass doors. Alex's jet was ready to fly him back to New York, and a couple of his friends, Pudge Rodriguez and Gomez, were already on board.

Alex cried in the car next to his ex-wife, friends say. He was confused. *Why was he doing this? What was wrong with him?* He told Cynthia he loved her, and adored their children. He said that several times, but he still got out of the car, boarded his plane and took off.

Alex and the Yankees had a September to forget—not that anybody would let them—and were eliminated from the play-offs September 23, which meant they played out the last week of the season with no hope. "A wasted season," Derek Jeter told the *New York Post*.

Neither Jeter nor Alex played the final game of the season, the back end of a doubleheader with the Red Sox, who were gleefully moving on to the postseason. Alex ended the 2008 season with decent numbers—.302, 35 homers, and 103 RBIs.

Three days after the season ended, Alex was once again dominating the headlines: "Madge Splits with Ritchie, Turns to A-Rod"; "Madge Wants Child with Baseball Star."

Alex had never had a good post-season, but he was having a very good off-season. In mid-November he was on the red carpet with Kate Hudson and P. Diddy for the reopening of the opulent Fontainebleau Hotel in Miami Beach. Where Sinatra once romped, Mariah Carey now vamped.

Alex's green eyes blazed in the pop of paparazzis' flashbulbs as he ignored the shouts from the ravenous entertainment press asking: "Where's Madonna?" All weekend, celebrity-site bloggers chirped about Alex's escapades inside a curvaceous hotel brimming with celebrities and models. A-Rod was either surrounded by Madonna's gal-pal police, had Gwyneth Paltrow on his arm (to keep him from wandering), or he was being brazenly stolen from Madonna by the flirty Hudson, who was spotted hugging his waist a little *too* tightly.

Alex was now in an Entertainment Tonight world, where he'd always wanted to be.

Romero's gym, where Alex has spilled so much sweat over the years, is just a half hour away from the Fontainebleau. A framed picture of Alex, Romero, Cynthia, Cynthia's brother Constantine Scurtis and a friend, Ray Corona still hangs on the gym's gray walls. All five are leaning forward, arms outstretched behind them, hands clinging to the railing of a concrete bridge, poised to jump into the water about 15 feet below. Alex would later call it the greatest day of his life. He had conquered two fears with one leap: height and water.

The only person in that photo who still stood beside Alex was Corona. Alex had divorced Cynthia, fired Scurtis as the chief of his real estate empire and been "fired" by Romero, his former trainer.

On the morning of Monday, November 17, as news of A-Rod's Fontainebleau dalliances went viral, Romero took a cutout of Alex Rodriguez—a life-sized photo of a focused player in pinstripes, his body coiled for a swing—and threw it into the dusty road that leads to his gym.

For an hour or more, unwitting drivers in cars and trucks ran over the cardboard cut-out. "Someone doesn't like that guy, do they?" said one observer. "A-Rod is getting *trashed*."

There were tire marks all over his image, but Alex was still recognizable. He hadn't fallen apart yet—at least not the cardboard version of him.

Epilogue

As I stood inside the University of Miami weight room on the first Thursday of February 2009 and looked through a window, I could see a group of young athletes in hoodies and sweats trotting around a practice field.

Alex Rodriguez was standing just a few feet from me but he didn't notice them. That's probably because he was intently focused on the question I'd just asked him, and mulling the implications of its unnerving buzzwords: *positive test . . . steroids . . . 2003*. He said nothing for several seconds and then turned toward me. He shrugged and nodded his head at the same time, as if torn between two reactions: *I don't know what you're talking about* and *I know exactly what you're talking about.*

He moved past me, picked up a weight plate the size of a pie tin and placed it on a barbell, then said, "You'll have to talk to the union." I asked if the information could be wrong, if a mistake could have been made, if he'd taken a tainted supplement. He twisted his mouth but said nothing. I could feel him struggling against himself—one part afraid to answer, one part dying to fill the silence. So I tried one more time, asking if there was something more he wanted to explain. "I'm not saying anything," he said as he turned his attention to the barbell.

There was one more question, though. I asked him about being tipped on a 2004 drug test by Gene Orza, the COO of the Players Association. He looked at the trainer standing beside him and said, "Get someone. She's not supposed to be in here."

There was no need. I was ready to leave. I took a business card out of my jacket and offered it to Alex. His buddy Pepe Gomez took it. "Call me if there is something I need to know," I said, "something else you want to say."

"Yeah, okay," he said gripping the barbell as he prepared for a lift.

A half hour later, I saw Gomez walk across the UM parking lot to his Porsche Cayenne. He grabbed gloves and a couple of baseballs from the back and headed toward a field, where Alex awaited.

Later that Thursday, Alex kept an appointment for an interview and cover-photo shoot with *Details* magazine arranged by Guy Oseary. The resulting story was yet another sign of Madonna's influence. Where in a 2001 *Esquire* cover story Alex was shown blowing bubble gum, the *Details* photo spread had him in all his muscle-shirt glory, like Narcissus, kissing his reflection in a mirror. The next day, he jetted on his private plane to the Bahamas, where he was seen in the VIP room at Aura nightclub, drinking Grey Goose and nibbling the ear of a woman lying across his lap. In photos posted on the internet, Alex looked glazed, blissfully out of it. No worries, apparently.

Over those two days, Alex never called me to talk about the fact that he had tested positive for steroids in 2003. Players Association Executive Director Don Fehr did not respond to my detailed messages about that drug test. Alex never even called the Yankees to warn them that the story was about to break.

On Saturday, February 7, a story about Alex's steroid use, written by David Epstein and me, was posted on SI.com at 10:15 a.m. Within a half hour, an alert about the information was stripped across the top of newspaper websites and was a bulletin on CNN; by that evening, it was a lead item on the network newscasts. The *New York Times* placed the story on page one of the Sunday morning edition amid articles on President Obama's stimulus package; and the front-page headline of the New York *Daily News* screamed out A-ROID! with a red box that indicated "11 pages of coverage" inside.

Somewhere beneath this deluge was the now-rattled Alex Rodriguez. "He's a mess," one associate said. "Shocked." But why was he so surprised? Had he really thought the union would protect him yet again?

If so, he was wrong; the union lords abandoned him. For years, they had enabled his use of steroids, advising Alex and others on how to use steroids safely and tipping them about upcoming drug tests—but Fehr and COO Gene Orza said nothing that weekend while their golden goose was getting cooked.

Alex was true to form in this crisis: He turned to his large support group, which included his handlers and his bankrolled pals, "The Boys," as well as the celebrity manager Guy Oseary, his agent, Scott Boras, advisers from the William Morris Agency, the publicist Richard Rubenstein and two lawyers.

By Sunday evening, with the addition of Outside Eyes—an inside-the-Beltway crisis-management operation—Alex's 'Roid Response Team took on the crowded look of a clown car. Outside Eyes' founder, Reed Dickens, played a prominent role in the 2000 Bush-Cheney campaign, and earned a reputation for his scorched-earth style. Outside Eyes boasted of its on-site "war room" and rapid-response instincts. Its point man for Assignment A-Rod was Ben Porritt, whose main qualification seemed to be his camera-ready hair.

The day the news broke on SI.com, executives at ESPN reached out to Boras in an effort to nail down "the get" with Alex, the first interview. Team Alex agreed, but who would do the interview? Boras realized that was the crucial detail for his side, and Alex chose someone he knew: Peter Gammons, a veteran reporter, regarded as a solid interviewer, but not a probing one.

The interview was scheduled to take place Sunday around 8 p.m. at Alex's rental estate on Star Island in Miami. Alex was prepared to blame his positive test result on a doctor who had prescribed medication for a neck injury. But without explanation, the interview was postponed until Monday at 11 a.m. and then pushed back to 1:30 p.m.

The delays bought Alex time. He knew he hadn't been discreet about his steroid use in Texas. He knew his "doctor's excuse" wouldn't fly.

Just before the sit-down with Gammons finally began, Alex stood at the bottom of a stairway with his ex-wife, Cynthia. Both had red eyes from crying. Alex had a red string wrapped around his wrist—the Kabbalist's inoculation from negative energy. And he had Cynthia, who was—as always—a steadying influence amidst the tumult. "God, she rescues him every time," says a friend of the Rodriguez family. "He doesn't know how lucky he is. One day, she won't be there."

As Alex entered the dogleg-shaped living room with cameras set up in one section and monitors in the other, no one on the ESPN crew knew what was about to happen. Boras had only told the producers that Alex would "communicate with sincerity and remorse."

That prediction was proved wrong with Gammons's first question.

GAMMONS: Alex, this weekend *Sports Illustrated* reported that in 2003 you tested positive for testosterone, an anabolic steroid known as Primobolan. What is the truth?

ALEX: When I arrived in Texas in 2001, I felt an enormous amount of pressure. I felt like I had all the weight of the world on top of me, and I needed to perform, and perform at a high level every day. Back then, it was a different culture. It was very loose. I was young. I was stupid. I was naive. And I wanted to prove to everyone that, you know, I was worth being one of the greatest players of all time. And I did take a banned substance. You know, for that I'm very sorry and deeply regretful.

Rangers Owner Tom Hicks was outraged when he heard this. Pressure? That's what made him do it? "I feel absolutely betrayed," says Hicks. "I think he deceived me. We had conversations about the [steroid] subject. He assured me that he wanted to break every record in baseball, and to do that you have to play for 20 years and he had too much respect for his body to do that kind of thing. So I'm almost at a loss for words."

Hicks had given Alex everything. Alex had wanted fawning; he'd gotten fawning. He'd wanted the richest deal; he'd gotten the richest deal. "He damn sure wouldn't have gotten a ten-year contract if we had any reason to suspect he was using performance-enhancing drugs," says Hicks.

In his 42-minute interview with Gammons, Alex also blamed the "loosey-goosey" attitude towards steroids in Texas, and the GNC vitamin and supplement chain for stocking the banned substances he took, whatever those were. He talked vaguely about an epiphany during spring training 2003, when he realized after an injury that he needed "to stop being selfish, stop being stupid and take control of whatever you're ingesting."

It was all an artless fabrication. Alex's one honest emotion surfaced several minutes into the interview, when he talked about the stain on his reputation. "I couldn't feel more regret and feel more sorry because I have so much respect for this game," he said, his voice catching, "And I have millions of fans out there that . . . will never look at me the same."

And then he blamed the messenger for his woes.

I was sitting in my attic office, finishing the article on Alex for *Sports Illustrated*, when I heard him lurch off message and accuse me of three crimes in 30 seconds:

> ALEX: "What makes me upset is that *Sports Illustrated* pays this lady, Selena Roberts, to stalk me. This lady has been thrown out of my apartment in New York City."

REALITY: *SI* reporter David Epstein and I watched Alex maneuver around a member of the paparazzi on the sidewalk in front of his Manhattan apartment in the summer of 2008 as part of a profile I was writing for the magazine on his new life as a celebrity. That was it.

> ALEX: "This lady has five days ago just been thrown out of the University of Miami by police for trespassing."

REALITY: I identified myself wherever I went at UM and never spoke to any police officers there.

> ALEX: "And four days ago she tried to break into my house, where my girls are up there sleeping, and got cited by the Miami Beach police. I have the paper here."

REALITY: I told an employee manning the gate at a guard shack in front of Star Island who I was and that I was heading to Alex's rental home. She told me the neighborhood was private and I couldn't enter. I knew she was wrong and told her the island was a public right-of-way. She didn't budge. I suggested we call the police to end the stalemate. While I waited for Miami's finest, the guard was told by her superior that yes, it was a public road. She then apologized to me—"We have celebrities here. We have to be careful"—and opened the gate. I drove one lap around the neighborhood loop, but didn't stop because Alex's Maybach wasn't in his driveway.

I went back to the guard shack. The guard told me I didn't have to wait for the police, but I wanted to know the rules regarding access to the island in case I had to come back. Officer Juan Rivera arrived a few minutes later and confirmed that Star Island was public and there were no special rules regarding access to it. There was no citation, only an incident log item to note that an officer had responded to a call.

"There's no follow-up," Miami Beach police detective Juan Sanchez told the New York *Daily News* in a story with the headline "A-Rod Strikes Out. Cops: No Record of Trouble with SI Scribe." Sanchez added, "She was not arrested. She was not cited. It doesn't go on her record. It's not even entered into our system."

Alex's fabrications about me were no more credible than the ones he told about his failed drug test, and his suspect semi-confessional on ESPN did not get good reviews. On February 10, the front-page headline of the *New York Post* accompanying a picture of Alex read, "Liar. Cheat." In the New York *Daily News* it was "Body of Lies."

My cell phone rang the afternoon of February 11. It was Ben Porritt, dialing from a number that showed up on my caller ID as Newport Property Ventures. He was at Alex's Coral Gables office.

Porritt told me that Alex wanted to personally apologize. Then he put me on speakerphone.

"Hey, Selena, what's going on?" Alex said.

His apology "for what I thought you committed" unfolded awkwardly and with contradictions. He said his "staff at Star Island" had given him misinformation about the police log, yet he continued to call it a "citation." There were several things he neglected to apologize for, including his misogynistic stalker accusation and the trespassing whopper.

I didn't say much—I had no idea who else was gathered around the speakerphone in that Coral Gables office—but near the end of the conversation I told him, "I get it. I understand."

And I did. Alex couldn't just say, "I'm sorry that I lied." He needed to blame it on his staff. He needed to blame it on his own panic. He needed to be the victim.

"My life will never be the same," he told me.

Alex then embarked on his Forgive Me Tour. He wore the red Kabbalah string on his left wrist, just beneath the black band of his watch, when he spoke to alumni on February 13 at the University of Miami's Dinner on the Diamond, where the décor was an ode to the romance of baseball, with Cracker Jack, baseball cards and miniature bats on the tables. Alex probably would have preferred staying out of sight for a few days, but he was not about to cancel on these people.

"He was nervous," says an associate of Alex's. "But he also thought, 'Hey, I'm loved here,' so I think that helped."

He had come for the official unveiling of Alex Rodriguez Park at Mark Light Field. This was *his* field in many ways, part of a renovation underwritten by his $3.9 million donation. This was *his* crowd as well, many of them boosters who hugged their benefactor that night.

Alex was glib at the podium. "I want to welcome my friends in the back," he said of the many members of the press wedged into the back of the room. "We travel together just like a family—a dysfunctional family." He paused as if waiting for a rim shot, then continued, "As you know, it's been a really quiet week for me, so it's nice to get out on a Friday night."

He maintained his composure throughout his remarks and even managed to look defiant as he gestured with a pointed finger in the air to emphasize his devotion to UM.

Alex had that red string wrapped around his wrist again—this time beneath a silver watch—when he reported to Yankees spring training on Tuesday, February 17. This would be his first press conference since the news had come out. It was to be broadcast live.

A blue tent was set up outside George M. Steinbrenner Field. There were folding chairs for about 150 media members and standing room for 50 more.

At 1:38 p.m., about 18 minutes late, Alex walked into the tent wearing an untucked navy blue button-down shirt and cream-colored pants. He clinched a rolled-up statement in his hand as he took a seat at the dais with Yankees manager Joe Girardi and General Manager Brian Cashman to his right. To Alex's far left stood Porritt, one of Alex's lawyers, and Don Hooton, whose son, Taylor, had died in 2002 as a result of steroid use. To Alex's far right, some of his teammates, including Jorge Posada, Derek Jeter and Andy Pettitte, looked on. Some had come to support Alex. Others seemed to be there out of curiosity. One player was overheard saying to another about the proceedings, ". . . a train-wreck-type thing."

The players, many of them with their arms folded across their chests, watched dispassionately for the next 38 minutes. Jeter sat slumped in his chair, as if numbed by A-Rod's high drama.

Alex was nervous. He sipped from a bottle of water. He looked at his statement, curled from being clinched so tightly, and then began to detail his "recollections." This time, he told a far different steroid tale from the one he'd shoveled to Peter Gammons a week earlier.

"Going back to 2001, my cousin started telling me about a substance that can be purchased over the counter in the [Dominican Republic]," he said. "In the streets it's known as 'boli.' It was his understanding that it would give me a dramatic energy boost and was otherwise harmless. My cousin and I, one more ignorant than the other, decided it was a good idea to start taking it. My cousin would administer it to me, but neither of us knew how to use it properly, providing just how ignorant we both were. It was at this point we decided to take it twice a month for about six months. During the 2001, 2002 and 2003 seasons, we consulted no one and had no good reason to base that decision. It was pretty evident we didn't know what we were doing. We did everything we could to keep it between us, and my cousin did not provide any other players with it. I stopped taking it in 2003 and haven't taken it since."

He ended his lengthy opening remarks with a clumsy bit of stagecraft as he tried to thank his Yankee teammates. He couldn't speak. He pursed his lips, pushed back from the table, sipped water and took a deep breath. It was an awkward 38 seconds of silence.

Rodriguez then answered questions from the media but on his terms, set by Team A-Rod, not the Yankees: He would answer no follow-ups; he would talk for only a half hour. "All these years I never thought I'd done anything wrong," he said. But when *New York Post* columnist Mike Vaccaro asked why, then, he had been so secretive about his use of steroids, Alex replied, "I knew we weren't taking Tic Tacs."

The almost universal response from those under that Yankee Big Top was "Hogwash." They didn't buy that emotional "thank-you" to his teammates, or his latest twist in his steroid tale. First he'd said that the temptation of GNC supplements was the culprit, now the culprit was something his cousin had bought in the D.R., "boli." Whatever that was. Primobolan or Dianabal or Deca-Durabolin?

Not even his oft-repeated defense that he'd been "young and stupid" held up. He kept saying he had been 24 and 25 when he "experimented," but Alex was 26, 27 and 28 from 2001 to 2003, with a wealth of steroid expertise behind him.

The next day, New York *Daily News* columnist Mike Lupica summed up Alex's dubious effort with this: "At this point, you want Alex Rodriguez to find a cousin, any cousin, who will inject him with truth serum." And in the *Bergen Record*, Bob Klapisch asked Alex, "Why are you so afraid of the truth—the unlawyered, bedrock account of your life with steroids?"

Afterward Cashman, perhaps fed up with the A-Rod Opera, was candid when asked if the organization regretted signing Alex to a 10-year, $275 million deal in 2007. "We're not in a position to go backwards on this," he said. "We've got nine years of Alex remaining. . . . And because of that, this is an asset that is going through a crisis. So we'll do everything we can to protect that asset and support that asset and try to salvage that asset.

"This story is going to be with Alex for a long time," Cashman said. "It's going to be with him forever."

Poor Yuri Sucart. Alex hadn't named him in that press conference, but he had fingered a cousin as his "boli" mule, and *ESPN Deportes* discovered that this was Sucart and went knocking on the door of his Miami home less than 48 hours later. Sucart had spent a decade laying out clothes for Alex each day. He had washed the luxury cars, cleaned up the party messes and tipped the strippers—all to be included in Alex's jet-setting world of decadence. And now he stepped forward as the one who would take this bullet for Alex.

"What A-Rod said at the press conference," Sucart's wife, Carmen, told *ESPN Deportes*, "is what happened and that is all."

The explanation was too simple-minded to be plausible. To suggest that Sucart had simply ferried just "boli" to and from the

D.R. was problematic, because steroid users stack their dope—they use, for instance Deca-Durabolin or Winstrol or Primobolan together with testosterone—and take drugs such as Clomid to keep them from morphing into a woman. Alex had called it amateur hour when his cousin injected him, but he was an experienced hand when it came to using steroids.

"He turned out to be an asshole," says Joe Arriola, the respected Miami public servant and longtime friend of the Rodriguez family. "Alex was stupid for what he said and how he said it [in the press conference]. He should've said, 'Yep, I did it,' and not blame anybody else. His cousin, and the D.R. and all that bullshit. You should take your medicine, and that's it. But that's how he was raised. Okay?"

The scorn that greeted Alex's version of his Steroid Wonder Years stunned him. For several days after his press conference, he seemed to be yelling to someone offstage, "Line, please!" as he fumbled for the right words during spring training and the upcoming World Baseball Classic. *What would sound good right now? What lie will cover the last one?*

MLB officials also had some questions about those lies. They met with Alex on Sunday, March 1, for two hours. Alex, coached by his lawyer, was careful not to incriminate himself to the point of setting himself up for punishment by the league. He gave the baseball people nothing new of note.

He exited the meeting relieved and joined the Dominican Republic's World Baseball Classic camp. "He needs to be about baseball, only baseball now," a Yankee official says. "I don't know if he can do that."

Alex certainly would have preferred "being" just about baseball, but he couldn't show up for the WBC workouts as just another member of the D.R. team. He was news. He pulled up to the practice field in Jupiter, Florida, on March 2 in his black Maybach driven by Joe Dunand, his half brother. A handful of fans cheered his arrival, which drew a pumped fist from A-Rod.

Two hours later he stepped onto the field in a red, white and blue Dominican Republic uniform in front of a phalanx of cameras capturing his every move. As Jack Curry wrote in the *New York Times*, "This photo-op took an awkward twist. Rodriguez veered off a walkway and peeked into the windows of a Mercedes sport utility vehicle. After a door opened, Rodriguez plucked out Natasha, his 4-year-old daughter, and kissed her. Cynthia, Rodriguez's former wife, held Ella, their 10-month-old daughter. What could have been a quiet moment in a secluded room turned into another episode of A-Rod's reality show. While Rodriguez snuggled with his older daughter, the cameras were a few feet from their faces. Natasha fidgeted. Rodriguez ignored the attention, even if it was something he helped create."

The transparency of the family-man spin was dismaying: No other D.R. player visited with their children in front of the photographers that day, and Alex knew he would be leaving the field shortly to consult with doctors. Two days earlier, he had an MRI with the Yankees' medical team after complaining about stiffness in his hip. The test had revealed a cyst. By Wednesday, March 4, Alex was on his way to Vail, Colorado, to meet with Dr. Marc Phillipon, a noted hip specialist.

The injury perpetuated the Cirque de Alex in the tabloids. Dr. Phillipon discovered a torn labrum. But what did that mean? The first word, from the Alex camp: he would have surgery and needed 10 weeks to recover. The second word, from the Yankees: he would try to play through the hip injury.

The last word was something in between. On March 9, Phillipon performed arthroscopic surgery on Alex's torn labrum. He stabilized the cartilage in the hope of helping Alex play through the bulk of the season. Alex would remain in Colorado for rehab, with the expectation that he'd return to the Yankees by mid-May. After the season, Phillipon said, Alex would need further surgery. Joel Sherman wrote in the *New York Post*, "Rodriguez will be in Colorado at least three weeks, away from the game and away from the Yankees. He'll have three weeks to ponder where he is and where he might like to go."

This would be the first time Alex Rodriguez has had any downtime during the baseball season in a decade, not since a knee injury in 1999.

Alex used the baseball season to elevate his status and feed his insecurities. The baseball season had given Alex an identity since he was a little boy. Who would he be without it?

The day after his hip surgery, Alex mounted a stationary bike and started his rehab. He couldn't wait to get back—into a Yankee uniform, into the pages of the tabloids, into the spotlight. He didn't want to be gone long. Only one thing scared Alex more than being called a cheater—being ignored.

Acknowledgments

In pulling together the complex details of Alex Rodriguez's life—both for a profile in *Sports Illustrated* that evolved into a news story upon the steroid revelations, and, ultimately, for this book—I couldn't have asked more from my colleague David Epstein. He is one of the finest and most persistent reporters I've known in my 23 years as a journalist. He was by my side through the entire journey, including a few humid afternoons in Georgia, where we killed time answering outdated Trivial Pursuit questions in a Starbucks while waiting for our own Godot.

I'm beholden to the family members, friends, associates and teammates close to Alex for shedding light on his public and private personas with grace under what were, for some, very difficult and emotional circumstances at times. I'm also grateful to the people who, at considerable risk, shared information that was essential in revealing the truth about steroids and Alex. Your efforts and courage never will be forgotten.

Many fine folks at *SI* deserve thanks, as well, especially Terry McDonell, whose guidance, support and faith made pursuing the story possible and finishing the book a reality. I will forever appreciate his patience. Thanks go to Larry Burke and Chris Stone for their determination in seeing the story through, as well as to Craig Neff, Mike Bevans, Chris Hunt and Hank Hersch for their invaluable direction. I'm also indebted to yet another terrific *SI* writer, Melissa Segura, for her insight into the Dominican baseball culture and her tireless reporting.

The sports-writing business is full of incredible people. Enormous gratitude goes to the talented Tom Verducci for being so generous with his time and knowledge, and to my good friend Harvey Araton for indulging every neurotic phone call. The support from colleagues during the aftermath of the steroid piece on Alex was heartening and humbling. I owe many thanks—and lots of drinks—to the friends who had my back.

Over six months of reporting and writing, the book took numerous twists and turns that required the expert handling of HarperCollins executive editor David Hirshey, who stood by me all the way. My editor, Bob Roe, deftly navigated the rapid-fire alterations right to the last minute. I couldn't have made it through a rigorous production schedule and past the finish line without David, Bob, and George Quraishi. The man who remained cool through it all was my agent, Mark Reiter, whose humor became the elixir for many anxious days and nights. Will Reiter (yes, relation) emerged out of nowhere as a key asset, reading over the manuscript with a keen eye.

My family sacrificed the most during this book project while I vanished into my attic office. Apologies to everyone for the cameo Christmas. To my mother, grandmother, Sally, Shawn, Sarah and

Becca—and also to the entire Price clan—I offer a heartfelt thank-you. But no one deserves more gratitude for her unconditional love—and free therapy—than Laura, the best person I've ever known.

Notes on Sources

The information in this book is rooted in my coverage of Alex Rodriguez during my career at the *New York Times* through 2007 and a profile project on the All-Star that I worked on with reporter David Epstein at *Sports Illustrated* during the Yankees' 2008 season. The profile evolved into a breaking news story for SI.com and *Sports Illustrated* in February 2009, when I nailed down evidence about Alex's steroid use as a Texas Ranger in 2003, but a portrait of him remained to be written from the exhaustive interviews David and I gathered both before and after the doping revelations. Here are the people who were interviewed:

Yonder Alonso, Jewel Ames, Fernando Arguelles, Joe Arriola, Brother Herb Baker, David Bar, Steve Butler, Jose Canseco, Brian Cashman, Joey Cora, Tim Crabtree, Jay Crotty, Chad Curtis, Joseph Dion, Susy Dunand, Carl Everett, Amy Fadhli, Jim Fannin, Kevin Fix, Jason Giambi, Burton Goldstein, Alex Gonzalez, Sandra Gonzalez, Bill Haselman, Tom Hicks, Randall Hill, Rich Hofman, Rudy Jaramillo, David Jordan, Andrea Kirby, Mike Lamb, Steve Law, Steve Ludt, Tom McEwen, Steven McLoughlin, Rosa Mendez, Mike Modano, Fernando Montes, Allan Nadler, Steve Phillips, Angel Presinal, Cal Ripken Jr., Juan Rivas, Victor Rodriguez, Victor Rodriguez Jr., Alex Rodriguez-Roig, Dodd Romero, Doreen Ruiz, Bud Selig, Ron Shapiro, Gary Sheffield, Buck Showalter, Stran Smith, Lorna Starr, Steve Swindal, Joe Torre, Dr. Gary Wadler, Jim Warring, A. J. West, Danny Wheat, Steve Winiarski, Dr. Brian Wolstein, Woody Woodward and Charles Zabransky.

Another 19 people spoke on condition of anonymity. Calls to Gene Orza, David Hofman, and Scott Boras were not returned.

Newspaper Sources

Associated Press
Boston Globe
Boston Herald
Chicago Tribune
Daily Mail (London)
Dallas Morning News
Detroit Free-Press
Fort Lauderdale Sun-Sentinel
Fort Worth Star Telegram
Houston Chronicle
Miami Herald
Newark Star-Ledger
New York *Daily News*
New York Post
New York Times
Newsday
Palm Beach Post
Seattle Times
Seattle Post-Intelligencer

St. Petersburg Times
Tampa Tribune
Times, London
USA Today
Wall Street Journal

Magazine/Other Periodical Sources
Baseball Digest
Baseball Weekly
BusinessWeek
ESPN The Magazine
Esquire
Muscle & Fitness
New York Magazine
People
Play
Sports Illustrated
Sporting News
Texas Monthly
The New Yorker
USA Today Sports Weekly
US Weekly

Website Sources
Baseball-Reference.com
Elbohio.com
ESPN.com
Fulgurazosblogspot.com
JoslynMorse.net
MLB.com
Radar.com
Realtor.com
Salon.com

SI.com
SmokingGun.com
TMZ.com

TV Transcripts
60 Minutes (December 14, 2007)
Today (March 2, 2004)
YES Network: *YESterdays*, "Alex Rodriguez" (April 2008)

Books
Jose Canseco, *Juiced: Wild Times, Rampant Roids, Smash Hits, and How Baseball Got Big* (New York: HarperCollins, 2005).

Jose Canseco, *Vindicated: Big Names, Big Liars and the Battle to Save Baseball* (Simon Spotlight Entertainment, 2008).

Matt Christopher, *On the Field with Alex Rodriguez* (New York: Little Brown, 2002).

Richard Ben Cramer, *Joe DiMaggio: The Hero's Life* (New York: Simon and Schuster, 2000).

Jerry Crasnick, *License to Deal: A Season on the Run with a Maverick Baseball Agent* (Emmaus, Pa.: Rodale, 2005).

Dolf de Roos, *Real Estate Riches: How to Become Rich Using Your Banker's Money* (Hoboken, N.J.: Wiley, 2004).

Mark Fainaru-Wada and Lance Williams, *Game of Shadows* (New York: Gotham Books, 2006).

Jim Fannin, *S.C.O.R.E. for Life* (New York: Collins Living, 2006).

Jim Gallagher, *Alex Rodriguez: Latinos in Baseball* (Childs, Md.: Mitchell Lane, 2001).

Alan Klein, *Sugarball: The American Game, the Dominican Dream* (New Haven, Conn.: Yale University Press, 1991).

Buster Olney, *The Last Night of the Yankee Dynasty* (New York: Perennial, 2004).

Alex Rodriguez, *Hit a Grand Slam* (Dallas: Taylor, 1998).

Eric Paul Roorda, *The Dictator Next Door: The Good Neighbor Policy and the Trujillo Regime in the Dominican Republic* (Durham, N.C.: Duke University Press, 1998).

Rob Ruck, *The Tropic of Baseball* (Lincoln, Neb.: University of Nebraska, 1999).

Mike Shalin, *Alex Rodriguez: A+ Shortstop* (Minneapolis, Minn.: Lerner, 1998).

Dan Shaughnessy, *Reversing the Curse* (New York: Houghton Mifflin, 2005).

Wayne Stewart, *Alex Rodriguez: A Biography* (Westport, Conn.: Greenwood Press, 2007).

Joe Torre and Tom Verducci, *The Yankee Years* (New York: Doubleday, 2009).

Mike Vaccaro, *Emperors and Idiots: The Hundred-Year Rivalry Between the Yankess and Red Sox—From the Very Beginning to the End of the Curse* (New York: Doubleday, 2005).

Paula White, *Ten Commandments of Health and Wellness, with Dodd Romero* (Tampa, Fla: Paula White Ministries, 2007).

Documentaries

Joe DiMaggio: The Final Chapter. Directed by Marino Amoruso, 2000.